The Practical Guide
for
Parish Councils

By William J. Rademacher

TWENTY-THIRD PUBLICATIONS
P.O. Box 180   West Mystic, Ct.   06388

Second printing, 1980

Library of Congress Catalog Card Number 79-64211

ISBN 0-89622-111-3

Interior design by Ed Curley and Marie McIntyre

Cover layout by John H. Brett, Jr.

Note:
The logo used in this book was rendered by Geri Guenther and is used with permission of the Parish Council Services Office, Archdiocese of Denver. The logo exemplifies the unity of effort in building up the Kingdom of God. The circles depict the variety of talents of priests, religious and laity working in harmony, sharing responsibility in fulfilling their Baptism/Confirmation commitment and mission. The key symbol of the logo is the dove, indicating the source of the council's unity and love as well as the force of all strategy and action.

Contents

Foreword

Perhaps you've heard the story about the parish council which held its regular meeting while the pastor was sick and hospitalized. Toward the end of the session, a motion was made and seconded to send Father a get-well card. The motion passed 7-5.

You may not have heard however that when the American bishops received directions in 1977 for the preparation of the quinquennial reports due in 1978 on the state of their dioceses, parish councils were included. Not once but in three places, data on parish councils are requested by the Holy See.

The fact that there is already a whole repertoire of parish council stories tells us that the council concept is widely implemented and well into the growing-pains stage. I think our ability to laugh at ourselves in this stage is a good and healthy sign.

The fact that Rome is asking whether parish councils have been established and is concerned about how they are faring tells us that the church is taking the council concept seriously at the highest institutional and pastoral level. I think it is evident that parish councils are not a passing fad but a permanent feature of the renewing church.

It is at this important juncture, when the council concept is experiencing growing pains and the mandate for them is seriously reaffirmed, that I am pleased to recommend to parishioners and pastors, Father William Rademacher's *The Practical Guide for Parish Councils.*

This volume *is* practical, reflecting the experience of thousands of today's Catholics with whom the author has held discussions and explored questions about parish councils.

This volume is a guide, not pretending to be definitive or official, but offering one scholar's considered views on how a parish council can flesh out Vatican II's vision of a coresponsible People of God.

From my own experience as a pastor in the sixties whose parishioners were eager to exercise their coresponsibility and as a bishop in the seventies who finds both clergy and laity sometimes reluctant or disillusioned, I believe two chapters of this book are especially valuable.

Read them all, but dwell on Chapter 6, "The Ministry of the Pastor," and on Chapter 12, "Growing in Holiness."

Several years ago, when I was promoting parish councils in a rural diocese on the Minnesota prairie, a Lutheran pastor who had had difficulties with his church council said to me, "Why don't you leave well enough alone? You Catholics don't know what you're getting into!"

I told him that well enough wasn't sufficient for today's church and that we were going to take our chances. Those chances are considerably enhanced by this practical guide.

Kenneth J Povish
Bishop of Lansing

Preface

It's been 15 years since I started a council at St. James Parish, Mason, Michigan. Since then I've attended numerous council meetings in seven states. I've conducted council workshops in over 25 dioceses. I've responded to numerous questions in a regular column for *Today's Parish.*

It's been a grace and blessing to be close to the parish council movement during these postconciliar years. It's been edifying and exciting to see the change, the growth, the new life in one living cell in the body of the church. In parish halls and over kitchen tables, I've talked with dedicated councilors who shared with me some of their experiences. Often, we discussed some of the problems which relate to the council experience and the postconciliar changes in general. I suspect I learned more from them than they did from me.

During these chats, councilors often admitted they weren't really prepared to serve on the council. Many felt there was a great need for a comprehensive *Guide* or *Handbook* which would furnish background information on both the theory and the practice of parish councils. Some even suggested that I should write it.

So, egged on by council members and by the publisher of Twenty-Third Publications and encouraged by the favorable response to my two earlier books on parish councils, I decided to tackle the job.

When I was first ordained, I used to attend the meetings of the Legion of Mary and the St. Vincent de Paul Society. Both groups referred rather frequently—too frequently I thought— to their *Handbooks.* In those days *Handbooks* were often used in a rather legalistic way as if they had been handed down from Mt. Sinai.

Even though these groups leaned too much on their *Handbooks*, they managed to stay on the right track most of the time. With few exceptions, they did and continue to do, a great job in the apostolate of the church.

I hope the present *Guide* will not become *the* final *Handbook* or *Rule Book* for parish councils. In view of the renewal of Vatican II, I hope the pastoral response of the church does not again become hardened into one rigid form canonized by a *Guide*. The form of the church's pastoral ministry, including its structures, has to be an ongoing response to the signs of the times and the new calls of the Spirit.

On the other hand, many of us have had 10-15 years experience with parish councils. Maybe it's time to reflect on our common experience and share what we've learned. And that's one of the main purposes of this *Guide*--to share at least part of the pastoral experience of the church regarding parish councils. I hope this kind of sharing will help councils fulfill their responsibilities in the apostolate of today's church.

This book, therefore, is an invitation to dialogue. It's a first draft. It assumes that the parish experience has something to say to theology and that theology has something to say to the parish experience. It assumes that a lively interaction between these two aspects of the church is important to the life of both.

Many readers may feel that the council movement is still too young, that it's too early to catch the movement between the covers of a book. They may be right. On the other hand, it may not be too soon to begin a dialogue. This *Guide* is just one voice in the conversation over the kitchen table. It's not an answer, but a question. It's one pilgrim's contribution to our common search. Other councilors, reflecting on their experience and responding to the Spirit, will be making their own contributions. That's what this discussion is all about.

For this reason, I've attached a *Reaction Sheet* at the end of this book, inviting the readers' comments, reactions, criticisms. No doubt if this *Guide* is to be useful to councils it will have to be revised. It will have to keep pace with the council experience. Through the *Reaction Sheet*, I would like to invite the reader to contribute to the next revision. I hope this *Guide*, like the new *Catechetical Directory*, will develop "from below" as well as "from above."

In the hope of generating a lively debate, I have often taken a very specific position. Although the risk of error is greater that way, I assume readers will find it easier to react to specifics than to vague generalities.

Also in the hope of stimulating discussion, I have, in a kind of prophetic ministry, been bold enough to discuss not only where councils are at this stage of growth, but more especially, where they might go. Councilors may feel that there's a great gap between the ideal expressed in this *Guide* and their actual experience on *their* council. For this I make no apology. If a *Guide* is going to guide, it has to hold up a high ideal. It needs to suggest a goal which councils are invited to accept as their own.

As this book finally goes to the publisher, I'm deeply grateful to many co-workers who ministered to me in bringing it to completion. I want to thank Clyde Pidgeon, William Siebert and Kenneth Schmidt for helping me with the bibliography and the resource lists for the council committees.

Thanks to Mrs. Marylyn Schoof, Ms. Kay Grismer and Mrs. Kathleen Prantner for their painstaking care in typing the manuscript and for gently correcting my occasional lapses into male chauvinism.

Thanks to Sr. Claudia Carlen for copy editing the entire manuscript. And thanks to my bishop, Kenneth Povish, for writing the Foreword.

Special thanks go to the archdioceses of Baltimore, Denver, Newark and Milwaukee for generously giving me free rein to use so much of their excellent materials. Their gracious Christian spirit in sharing the fruits of their council experience with the rest of the church augers well for that continuous sharing envisioned by this *Guide*.

Finally, for reading the manuscript and offering extremely helpful critique and comments, my thanks to the following: Mr. James De Boy, Baltimore; Rev. Dale Melczek, Detroit; Rev. Frank Murray, Lansing; Rev. Ralph Starus, Chicago; and Ms. Cyndi Thero, Denver. Their support and encouraging words were no small factor in gathering strength for that last push to the finish line.

All scripture references are from the Revised Standard Version/Catholic Edition. References to Vatican II documents are from *Vatican Council II*, edited by Austin Flannery O.P., and published by Costello Publishing Co., Northport, N.Y.

As everyone knows, the English language is in process of responding to the feminist movement. After seeking advice from women writers, I have adopted the general practice of using the double masculine/feminine pronoun (he/she) at the beginning of each new section and then returning to the use of the single masculine pronoun (he) for the rest of the section. I hope this system will help both male and female readers to understand the single masculine pronoun in a generic sense. I'm assuming that the use of a single pronoun makes for less cumbersome reading than the constant repetition of the double he/she.

I hope this *Guide* will be a helpful service to the many councilors on our continent and elsewhere. I pray that the Holy Spirit will use it as one means to usher in an era of shared ministry at the parish level. I hope, too, that it will play some small role in the renewal and upbuilding of the church and so serve as one "seed and beginning" of the kingdom of God on earth.

                                             William J. Rademacher
All Saints   *St. John's Provincial Seminary*
November 1, 1978   *Plymouth, Michigan 48170*

Chapter 1

Congratulations!

The votes are in. You've been elected to the parish council. You have mixed feelings. On the one hand, you are excited about the prospect of sharing your talents and experience with the parish council. On the other hand, you wonder what it's all about. "Will it be worth it? What's the next step?"

First, congratulations on your call to serve on the council! Maybe you got on the council because "no one else wanted the job." Maybe a friend or the pastor "dragged" you into it. No matter! You are now on the council. And that's what counts. You now have a unique opportunity to help build up your council, your parish, your church.

Serving on the council can actually be a challenging experience. It's a time for giving. A time for receiving. A time for growing. It's a time to be a pioneer in creating a more responsive and more responsible church. It all begins with *you* in *your* parish. Your council, just like the parish, is a living organism. It's a unique and often mysterious meeting of the human and the divine. Your very presence affects the human chemistry of the council. Your timely humor reduces tension. Your optimism kindles hope. Your questions open new doors. Your faith strengthens the weak. Your cheerful acceptance of committee work lights a spark in the passive and apathetic. Your attentive listening is healing and compassion for the pain of rejection and loneliness within the Christian community.

Besides, the risen Lord, in his own mysterious ways, builds up his church through you. He uses humble elements like water and oil in baptism. He uses simple bread and wine in the eucharist. He uses you in the council. "For where two or three are gathered in my name, there am I in the midst of them" (Matt. 18,20). At times you may not feel up to the task. That's understandable. However, Paul has a word for you: "But thanks be to God, who in Christ always leads us in triumph and through us spreads the fragrance of knowledge of him everywhere. For we are the aroma of Christ . . ." (1 Cor. 14-15). "My grace is sufficient for you, for my power is made perfect in weakness" (2 Cor. 12,9).

The council is a microcosm of the Christian community. It brings together one living cell of the body that is the church. It's a meeting of the mystery of holiness and the mystery of evil. It's a "get-together" of Christian believers who come with different visions, different perspectives and even different expressions of the faith. They are all graced by the Lord's holiness and, at the same time, flawed by the effects of original sin. The charismatic will smile: "Jesus is Lord." The school people will plead: "More money for our school." The director of religious education will beg: "More money for our religious education programs."

Dreamers, Doers, Criticizers

The council also brings together the *Dreamers,* the *Doers,* and the *Criticizers.* The *dreamer* at heart is a poet, an artist or a mystic. Responding to intuition, he/she is full of great ideas. Rich in imagination, he soars high above the nitty-gritty of the organizational details. He has the grand, and sometimes, grandiose vision. But he doesn't know how to put it into practice. He can't come up with any concrete plan of action. For that, he needs someone else. The *doer* is the practical one. He/she wants to get moving. He gets impatient with all the talk about goals, vision and pastoral priorities. "Let's cut the discussion! Let's get on with the building campaign." The *criticizer* is skeptical. He/she questions everything. He tests and challenges: "It won't work. We tried that before." He's super-cautious. He has no patience for the dreamer and is skeptical of the doer.

Now a good council needs them all--the *dreamer,* the *doer* and the *criticizer.* It's from the fruitful interaction of all three types that the best parish policies will emerge. Needless to say, your parish council is not perfect. Like the church itself, it's

constantly in need of renewal and reform. It hasn't arrived at
the kingdom of heaven yet. It's still "on the way." It's still
searching. It's very much a part of the church's earthly pilgrimage. That means there's lots of room for human folks like yourself.

So, once again, *welcome aboard!* I hope serving on the council will be a pleasant and challenging experience. I hope this
book will become your friend and guide as you offer your gifts
and talents to the upbuilding of the church.

Chapter 2

What Do Councils Do?

Most parish councils were organized after the Second Vatican Council. In general, they are part of the postconciliar movement toward shared responsibility and shared ministry. They are so many little models of the church as a communion of the People of God. They witness to the basic equality of all the baptized. But even if Vatican II had not recommended the formation of councils, there are many reasons why they make a lot of sense. Basically, *the parish council is an idea whose time has come.*

In the *first* place, parish councils help to discern the needs of the parish and the community. Since councilors ideally represent all the parishioners, they have their finger on the pulse of the parish. They can report what they feel. They can sense the gap between the demands of the Gospel proclaimed in the pulpit and the actual Christian life in the world. Parish councils often conduct open forums to learn more about the needs and concerns of people in the local community. They hold weekend workshops where they have brainstorm sessions concerning the needs of the parish.

For example, one council, while brainstorming for parish needs, discovered that it had no programs for its senior citizens and no committee to welcome new parishioners. In another parish, the council's worship committee discovered that the lectors were poorly prepared to read the scriptures on Sunday. There were no criteria for selecting lectors. There was no training program. In another parish, the extraordinary ministers of the eucharist were all white and male even though many women and Mexicans were active in the parish. The Christian service committee learned that no one was visiting the sick at a local convalescent home. Also, no one was doing anything about a serious drug problem at a nearby high school.

Second, parish councils help to set goals and priorities to respond to the needs of the parish and the community. For instance, one council decided to make adult education its top priority. Then it passed a resolution to hire a full-time adult education coordinator. Another council decided to make the religious education program its top priority. It passed a resolution to hire a full-time director of religious education and to set up an advisory religious education committee composed of four parents and four teenagers.

Third, councils discover all kinds of new talents in the parish. They go through the parish census and compile a list of all the skills and talents in the parish. Then they invite the educator to serve on the education committee, the accountant to serve on the finance committee, the writer to serve on the communications committee, etc. They recruit lectors, teachers, ministers of music and of the eucharist. Often, they find out that they have more than enough gifts and resources to respond to the parish's needs.

Fourth, councils are effective organs for dialogue within the Christian community. At council meetings, the teacher talks to the pastor; the director of religious education talks to the principal of the school; the teenager talks to the senior citizen. Besides, most council meetings are open to all parishioners who want to express their opinions. And, many councils conduct an open forum twice a year so everyone in the parish can come and "speak his piece."

Fifth, the councils are a living sign of the partnership every Christian community is called to be. They are a sign of the basic equality of all the baptized in Christ. By getting many diverse people to work together, councils bring about a greater unity. Thus they eliminate overlapping and competitive activities. The parish societies see themselves as partners in the larger parish plan. So they don't waste a lot of time defending their own turf against someone else.

Sixth, councils bring together a variety of ministers--priests, deacons, sisters, brothers, laymen and laywomen. Every coun-

cil meeting is a reminder that *everybody,* no matter what his/
her talent, belongs to one and the same church.

Seventh, councils are called to make the Gospel known.
Vatican II tells us that the purpose of councils is: "to assist the
Church's apostolic work, whether in the field of evangelization
and sanctification or in the fields of charity, social relations
and the rest."[1] They are called to witness to the biblical mandate: "But seek first his kingdom and his righteousness and all
these things shall be yours as well" (Matt. 6:33). Councils are
formed to make sure the parish gives top priority to the apostolic, missionary and spiritual needs of the parish.

Eighth, councils, while they are definitely not *lay* boards,
are, nevertheless, one good way of implementing Vatican II's
teaching on the role of the laity in the church. "According to
their abilities the laity ought to cooperate in all the apostolic
and missionary enterprises of their ecclesial family."[2] "The
apostolate of the laity is a sharing in the salvific mission of the
Church. Through Baptism and Confirmation all are appointed
to this apostolate by the Lord himself."[3]

Ninth, councils are the natural vehicle for renewing the
parish. Every parish, like the church itself, is constantly in need
of renewal. And parish councils are rightly concerned about
fostering that ongoing process of parish renewal. But such renewal begins with the individual councilor himself when he/
she commits himself to a life of service to Christ. Councils are
not an end unto themselves. They serve the Spirit who comes
to renew the face of the earth and the church.

Tenth, councils are a precious opportunity for adult education in the faith. They become a learning experience when they
tackle specific pastoral problems. As the councilors wrestle
with each new problem, they tap the riches of their faith in a
wide variety of ways. They call on resource persons who are
well versed in liturgy, theology, religious education, etc. They
read up on their faith and so fill in the gaps between their catechism days and their present adult life.

Eleventh, council meetings provide an excellent opportunity for shared prayer and for growth in the spiritual life. Often
councils read the scriptures together and then share their re-

flections on its meaning for their lives. The council is small enough to provide all its members a rich experience in a common sharing in the faith and prayer life of one another.

Twelfth, councils foster a climate of mutual support and accountability. Everyone who ministers in a parish (laypersons, sisters, brothers, deacons, priests) is accountable to God, to the Gospel and to Christian community. Councils generate many questions: *What is the best way to spend the parish money, in view of the Gospel? What priorities determine the parish budget? Who was supposed to talk to the public school board about renting its classrooms? Who was going to call the diocesan office of education?* The council meeting is a public forum where the Lord's servants render an account of their stewardship to one another and, at the same time, receive one another's support for their ministries.

Thirteenth, councils broaden the members' vision. When they discuss the annual budget, councilors have to reflect on the broad vision of the church. During the course of the year they also learn to work with neighboring parishes, both Catholic and Protestant. Then too, diocesan offices frequently invite councils to offer suggestions regarding the pastoral policies of the diocese. Thus, councils learn to work with diocesan offices and departments. In this way, councilors gain a deeper understanding of the relationship between the parish and the diocesan church.

Fourteenth, councils are also training schools for new and diverse lay ministries. As the number of sisters and priest continues to decrease in the years ahead, the church will rely more and more on lay ministers. Sometimes they will be paid; other times they will be volunteers. Lay persons will be appointed administrators of parishes, institutions and missions. They will assume more responsible roles in preparing the people for baptism and marriage and in the pastoral care of the sick. The parish councils, with their growing emphasis on spiritual development, will produce a pool of highly motivated and knowledgeable lay ministers who will be ready and willing to serve when the time comes. The so-called vocation shortage may be God's way of reminding the church of the biblical truth that all the baptized have a vocation to minister.

Finally, councils provide their members an opportunity to share in participative decision-making in a Christian context. Members are encouraged to share in discussions and so to make some contribution to the final decision. Since North American Catholics have been conditioned by the democratic process, they are very much at home in a parish council.

Of course the parish council is not a democracy. Nor is it a legislative assembly or corporation board. It's primarily a faith community, a communion of disciples, gathered together to discern the will of God for a specific parish. It's a brother-sisterhood listening to God's word and then responding in faith and obedience to that word. The parish council is a unique form of collegiality which brings the parishioners into the decision-reaching process of the church at an adult, responsible level. It is one of the fruits of Pope John XXIII's New Pentecost. *It is an idea whose time has come.*

Footnotes

1. "Decree on the Apostolate of Lay People" in *Vatican Council II,* Austin Flannery, O.P. ed. (Northport, N.Y.: Costello Publishing Co., 1975), p. 791. (Henceforth all reference to Vatican II documents will be to the Flannery edition.)

2. Ibid., p. 778.

3. "Dogmatic Constitution on the Church," in *Vatican Council II,* p. 390.

Chapter 3

Councils and the People of God

Vatican II doesn't give us a blueprint about either the theory or the practice of parish councils. Vatican II does however, provide us with the broad themes which rightly lead to the formation of parish councils. One such theme is the image or model of the church as the People of God. This model is described at length in the second chapter of *The Constitution on the Church,* entitled, "The People of God." Fr. Avery Dulles, S.J., in his book, *Models of the Church,* explains the historical development of this model in his chapter, "The Church as Mystical Communion."

The bishops of Vatican II chose the title "People of God" first, because they wanted the church to be seen in its totality according to what is common to *all the faithful* and second, because the pastors and the faithful *collaborate in* the diffusion and sanctification of the whole church.

The themes which have a special application to parish councils can be quickly summarized: *First,* the church is seen as a new People of God coming into existence because Christ instituted a new covenant in his blood.[1] *Second,* this people is established as a communion of life, love and truth. *Third,* this people is used by Christ as the instrument of salvation for all. *Fourth,* the state of this people is that of the dignity and freedom of the sons (and daughters) of God. *Fifth,* in virtue of baptism, this people is "consecrated . . . to be a holy priesthood" and "shares in the one priesthood of Christ." *Sixth,* it shares in the prophetic office of Christ. *Seventh,* it is filled with the Holy Spirit who allots his gifts according as he wills, distributing special graces among the faithful of every rank, making them fit and ready to undertake various tasks and offices for the renewal and building up of the church.[2] *Eighth,* this people is a communion of disciples who have the obligation of spreading the faith to the best of their ability.[3]

Now let's discuss these eight themes in order. The *first* point to note in the formation of the People of God is that it is *God* who chooses his people. Christians do not become God's people by lifting themselves up by their own bootstraps. It's not by their own efforts, however pious, that they acquire a claim on God to be called his people. God of his own free and gracious will decides to choose them. They become God's people when they respond in *faith* to God's choice, i.e., when, by saying "Yes," they let God make them his people.

We don't belong to the People of God because we are Mexican, Canadian, German, Polish, Irish or American, or because we all went to a Catholic school together, or because we were all "brought up Catholic", or because we all worked so hard together building our parish. We don't belong to the People of God because we pray the rosary and obey the pope, or because we belong to the Knights of Columbus, or even because we go to church on Sunday.

We belong to the People of God because God freely chooses us, because in faith we say "Yes," and finally, because in baptism we become part of that new covenant instituted by the blood of Christ. The People of God comes into existence not through church law, custom, or tradition but through God's free choice.

Second, this people is called *to be a community.* The People of God become *one* people, not because the laws are the same in every diocese, but because they all respond to one call. They become a communion in "one body, one Spirit . . . one Lord, one faith, one baptism, one God and Father of us all, who is above all, through all and in all" (Eph. 4:4-6). Because of God's call (vocation) and the people's "Yes," there comes into existence "a communion of life, love and truth."

The People of God's unity or communion of life, love and truth consists in the following: 1) oneness in mission, 2) oneness in witness, 3) oneness in prayer and praise, 4) mutual dependence and interdependence conferred by common faith, 5) the bonds of faith being more powerful and more demanding than a table of laws, 6) the brother-sisterhood of faith fashioning or constituting all the structures (such as diocesan and parish councils) within the People of God.

Third, this community is called to be a community of salvation. When God chooses us to be his people, he does so for a purpose. He doesn't choose us so "we can save our souls," or so "we'll get to heaven." He chooses us so we can be instruments of salvation *for all.* He chooses us not for privilege, but for responsibility, not for security, but for service. His call is not a once-for-all happening at a particular hour on the clock. Like the jealous lover he is, God calls us constantly. He calls us to *new* responsibility and to *new* service. That is why we need constantly to come together in meetings (even council meetings) to discern the Father's will, to hear and respond to his call *anew.*

Fourth, this people is "graced" with Christian dignity and freedom. Since this people belongs to God, it is a *free* people. It cannot again become enslaved to mere human laws. By Christ's death and resurrection, it has been freed from demonic power, from the stranglehold of evil. It has also been freed from slavery to the law. It cannot be forced to march like an army. Its freedom and dignity must be respected. No one can legislate or pre-program the form of the people's response to God's call to service. It must be the free, internal response of a lover.

It must also be the response of mature, adult, *responsible* men and women. Paternalism and authoritarianism can have no place within this new people. No one may assault its freedom and dignity and reduce the citizens of the kingdom of God to the status of children even though some people would perfer that. ("Let Father do it. I'm not interested in responsibility.") Laity who passively accept token or "paper" councils demean their own dignity and status as a People of God.

Fifth, this new people, in virtue of one baptism, shares in the one priesthood of Christ. This means that the risen Lord's present saving activity is at work, in some way, through *all* the baptized, without regard to sex or ecclesiastical ranking systems. The risen Lord does not have to ask for Father's blessing or permission before he uses a baptized person "as instrument of salvation for all."

As the risen Lord uses water, oil, bread and wine as instruments of his saving grace, so he can and does use all the baptized as his anointed instruments and ministers of his own holiness. This means that the baptized participate in the mission of Christ, not the mission of Fr. Joe Smith. It means, further, that the baptized are not *"Father's* helpers," but like Prisca and Aquila, "fellow workers in Christ Jesus" (Rom. 16,3). "So neither he who plants nor he who waters is anything but only God who gives the growth" (1 Cor. 3,7).

Sixth, all the People of God also share in Christ's prophetic office. The Jesus in the New Testament is more prophet than priest. This does not mean that in the New Testament Jesus spends all his time predicting the future. It means he confronts the value systems of both the *religious* and secular establishment. When the Jewish religious leaders say: "Stone the woman," Jesus says: "Accept her." When the religious and civil law says: "Do not associate with women, sinners or Samaritans," Jesus "eats and drinks with them." When society says: "Pay special attention to what you shall eat, drink and wear," Jesus says: "Do not be anxious saying, 'What shall we eat?' or 'What shall we drink?' or 'What shall we wear?'"

In their prophetic ministry, the baptized people of today share in that same mission whereby the risen Lord still confronts the value systems of today's society. When society says: "First seek your own human fulfillment," the People of God say: "Deny yourself." When society says: "Look first to your own security in stocks, housing and insurance," the People of God say: "Seek first the kingdom of God." When society practices racial and sexual discrimination, the People of God say: "In the kingdom of God there is neither Jew nor Greek, there is neither slave nor free, there is neither male nor female" (Gal. 3,28).

Seventh, the Spirit himself equips the People of God for the work of the ministry (Eph. 4,12). He allots his gifts according as he wills, according to the measure of *faith*. He makes his people fit and ready to undertake various tasks and offices for the renewal and upbuilding of the church. This means that the Spirit is constantly active in every believing Christian. He acts on *his* terms, not theirs.

This mysterious activity of the Spirit means that Christians don't have to be ordained before they begin to minister in the building up of the church. It also means that most parishes probably have more gifts and talents than they need. These gifts may still need to be discovered, trained and then supported by the People of God. These gifts also need to be submitted to a process of prayerful discernment to determine if they are truly of the Spirit. For the mystery of evil is also at work within the People of God. Not every movement, inspiration or religious outburst is of the Spirit.

Eighth, the People of God are all called to be a communion of disciples in the Lord. They are called to follow him in laying down their lives for others. To follow the Lord as a disciple is to become totally identified with his mission in today's world. The word "disciple" is used 250 times in the New Testament. Discipleship is one of the most pervasive themes in the early church. All councilors, therefore, when they gather around the table for their monthly meeting, are first called to be faithful disciples of the Lord.

Since the sister-brotherhood of faith is the first and foremost reality of the People of God, a parish council needs to grow out of, and witness to, that reality. It needs to be a sign of the *basic equality* of all the members rather than a sign of social or religious castes. It needs to witness to unity as a unique and precious value within the Christian community.

While there's always room for healthy conflict, the council is no place for cliques, factionalism or political partisanship. The council can't be a lay group organized against the rectory or the clergy. The priests, deacons and religious, in spite of their unique ministries, are all members of the council. Like the rest of the councilors, they are first baptized Christians and disciples of the Lord.

Now, the theology of the People of God, just explained, has some practical application for the operation of parish councils.

It means that the council is called to rely more on faith, prayer and the Spirit than on its bylaws and constitution. *Robert's Rules of Order* may be helpful but faith in the Lord and in fellow Christians is primary. Every meeting is meant to be an experience in faith and in community. Since councilors are citizens of the kingdom, they enjoy the freedom and dignity of the sons and daughters of God. They may not be used as rubber stamps. They may not be manipulated by agenda control or by invoking the mystery of secret knowledge, i.e., canon law, theology, the "mind" of the bishop, etc.

Even though a pastor could easily take advantage of some passive and ignorant lay persons, he needs to challenge them to assume their full responsibility in serious, and often unpopular, decisions. He may have to pitch some "hot potatoes" into the lap of the council. It may take more time to reach a decision that way, but a lot of people will become more mature and more responsible in the process. Since the baptized laypersons share in the priestly and prophetic mission of Christ, and not of the pastor, their service on the council can hardly be reduced to advice-giving. When Paul tells us in Eph. 4,11 that Christ equips the saints (i.e., the baptized) for the work of the ministry, he speaks of prophets, evangelists and teachers. It is evident that the Spirit doesn't limit the baptized to one gift, viz., advice-giving. (More about this in Chapter 6.)

Just as the prophets Amos and Micah rebuked the old People of God for their sins against justice, so councilors today may be called, in view of their prophetic ministry, to confront the new People of God for their sins against justice. The Detroit *Call to Action Conference,* held in October 1976, is a good example of laypersons performing a prophetic ministry. They called their own church to task for neglecting the poor and for practicing racial and sexual discrimination.

Since the Spirit is in all the baptized according to *the measure of faith,* councils must have respect and even reverence for the opinions of the most uneducated member of the council. The Spirit's activity is not limited to Ph.D.s. On the other hand, Paul tells us the Spirit gives many "natural" gifts. He mentions teaching, helping, administering, serving and exhorting. Thus, the Spirit can and does act through professional experts who have their "measure of faith" and who give the gift of their specialized training to the upbuilding of the church. The council needs the gifts of the trained teacher, the accountant, the writer, the communications expert. It needs to keep a balance between the grassroots people and the trained experts. The Spirit has made no covenant to work more through one than through the other.

A meeting of the council, therefore, isn't just another meeting. It's an experience in the mystery of being church according to the model of the People of God. Since the People of God is a sharing community, it is called especially to share the Lord's gifts. The next chapter will explore how this sharing of gifts can be carried out.

Footnotes

1. "Dogmatic Constitution on the Church," in *Vatican Council II*, p. 359.

2. Ibid., p. 363.

3. Ibid., p. 369.

Chapter 4

Sharing Our Diverse Ministries

"Having gifts that differ . . . let us use them" (Rom. 12,6).

When Neil Armstrong returned from the moon, he was quick to give credit to the hard work of the ground team. Without the team work of a wide variety of skilled technicians, the moon trip would have been impossible. We live in a world of team work. Every ship heading out to sea needs a radio operator, an engineer, a mechanic, a navigator, a cook, a captain, etc. Every jet winging into the sky needs a pilot, a co-pilot, flight attendants, an air traffic controller, etc.

The parish, too, needs the help of diverse skills, talents and services. In the church we call these services ministries. Some Catholics feel the word ministry is "Protestant." Others feel that it has something to do with ordination and therefore applies mostly to what goes on in the sanctuary.

Ministry is not a Protestant word. Nor is it restricted to ordination or to "churchy" activity. In the New Testament, *ministry is any service offered in genuine love for the common good in the name of the Lord.* In the early church, any significant activity which is done for the upbuilding of the church is considered ministry. Thus, in Acts 6:3, serving at table is ministry. It's at least possible that this ministry includes managing the money table (like operating the cash register) for the daily distribution to the poor. In 2 Cor. 9,12 the collection for "the saints" in Jerusalem is called a ministry. In 1 Cor. 16:15 Stephanas is overseeing a house church. His service is called a "ministry to the saints."

Whether it is preaching the word (Acts 6:4), or washing the feet of the disciples (John 13:15), it's called ministry. In the early church, ministry, in the humble sense of the servant who waits at table, is the word for all loving care for others. The crucial point is not the kind of work being done, but the quality of love which inspires that work.

That ministry is not restricted to ordination is also plain from Pope Paul VI's exhortation, "On Evangelization in the Modern World." He writes:

> The laity can also feel themselves called, or be called, to work with their pastors in the service of the ecclesial community, for its growth and life, by exercising a great variety of ministries according to the grace and charisms which the Lord is pleased to give them. It is certain that, side by side with the ordained ministries . . . the church recognizes the place of nonordained ministries which are able to offer a particular service to the church.[1]

The spirit gives gifts to all the baptized according to the measure of faith (Rom. 12:3). "Having gifts that differ according to the grace given to us, let us use them. . . . if service, in our serving; he who teaches, in his teaching; he who exhorts, in his exhortation . . . he who does acts of mercy, with cheerfulness" (Rom. 12:6-8). In 1 Cor. 12:28 Paul lists the ministries of healing, helping and administering along with the ministry of the apostles and prophets. He doesn't require ordination as a prerequisite to ministry. No doubt, if Paul were writing today, he would list service on the parish council as a ministry.

In spite of the bible's broad use of the word ministry, however, not every good deed is ministry. First, it has to be done in the *name of Jesus/Lord* (Col. 3,17). Your agnostic humanist who feeds the hungry and gives drink to the thirsty is not doing ministry. He's not doing it in the name of the Lord. It's still a good deed but it's not ministry.

Second, ministry needs to be done for the upbuilding of the church, i.e., the People of God. That means that whatever is done can't wreck or tear down the church, like preaching heresy, profaning the sacraments, etc. It needs to witness to the *saving* activity of the risen Lord in and through his people.

Third, all ministry has a *public* dimension to it. The church, as a recognizable group of people, is by its very nature public. So ministry needs to be for the common good and recognizable as such. Strictly private and personal services or love which does not issue into action are not ministry.

Fourth, ministry is not really reducible to a single external act. It needs to flow from an inner, more or less permanent, *commitment* to the Lord. And it can't be separated from that inner commitment. It has to be done out of genuine love.

Fifth, all ministry is *accountable* to the church, i.e., the People of God, especially to its leaders. Paul told the speakers in tongues, (one of the ministries listed in 1 Cor. 12,10) to be silent (1 Cor. 14,28). The reason was that, without an interpreter, their ministry wasn't building up the church. Paul, in virtue of his apostolic authority, made a judgment about their ministry and found it wanting in its upbuilding dimension.

Finally, ministry needs to be done in a context of ordered relationships. Paul's two images of the *body* (1 Cor. 12:12-26) and the *building* of God (1 Cor. 3,9) help us here. If the teeth start biting the fingernails and then the fingers, the brain has to tell the teeth to stop. The teeth are "ministering" out of order. They are "ministering" in the wrong place.

In the same way, in Paul's image of the building of God, if a carpenter, on some early Monday morning, is found nailing in a 2 x 4 in the middle of the living room, someone has to say: "Hey, you're nailing that 2 x 4 in the wrong place." It may be a fellow carpenter (fraternal correction) or the supervisor (bishop), but someone has to do it. So, too, in the church, a ministering person can't just go around doing his/her own thing. He has to do it in an order of relationships with the other ministries and with the total mission of the church. Otherwise, he may indeed be working hard, but nailing his 2 x 4 in the wrong place.

Ministry and the Council

Now how does this explanation of ministry apply to councils? In the first place, it should have some effect on the *attitude* of the councilor. What motives inspire the ministry of the man or woman who is elected to serve on the council? Writing in *The Michigan Catholic,* Fr. Kenneth Untener speaks to this question: "If parish council service were considered a ministry, the whole process (of elections) would be cast in a new light. A ministry is a gift from God, and candidates for ministry respond because they sense a call from God to use that gift-- even when it is not something they particularly feel like doing. (Moses, for example, did not jump at the chance to lead the Israelites . . . but he was called by God to do so.) That should be the spirit of parish council nominations."[2]

Ministry accents *serving* more than *representing*. The councilor sits on the council because God has "gifted" him and called him to serve the whole parish. "When parish council members see their role as a ministry to the entire parish, they try to build a community rather than a constituency. They are called, as every minister is called, to join in searching out the will of the Father rather than simply representing special interests."[3]

Second, ministry means that he/she who serves on the council is expected to be *accountable*. He is accountable in the first instance to the council itself. But more especially, he is accountable to the Lord, to the diocesan church and to the *whole parish community*. Ministry in the New Testament is not for the minister, but for the upbuilding of the church. For this reason, the church and the parish community can set down certain standards or qualifications for ministry on the council. They can insist that councilors be exemplary Christians, that they have sufficient knowledge, that they truly wish to prepare themselves to serve the *whole* parish, etc. (More about this in Chapter 9.)

Finally, serving on the council is a *public* ministry. This means, among other things, that some kind of public installation ceremony is entirely appropriate. This ceremony first praises God for the gift he has given to the *church* in the person of the councilor. Then it establishes a relationship of support and accountability between the serving councilor and the whole parish community which, by its applause, expresses its support of the councilor's ministry.

Shared Ministries

Now that we know that serving on the council is true ministry, we can proceed to the shared aspect of *all* ministry.

In the church, there is no "Lone Ranger" ministry. The shared aspect of ministry flows from the fact that the Christian community as such is a *sharing* community. It shares in the breaking of the bread and in the drinking of the cup. It shares in a *"partnership* in the gospel" (Phil. 1:5). Apples should look like, and taste like, apples. Married couples should look like, and act like, married couples. So a Christian community should look like, and act like, a *sharing* community.

Paul calls the Christian community a *koinonia* (1 Cor. 1:9). The literal meaning of this Greek word is *partnership*. It means "a sharing in." It can also mean "fellowship." In secular Greek, *koinonia* refers to the intimate partnership of the marriage relationship. It indicates the mutual, reciprocal giving and receiving which is the very life of any true partnership. As apples come from an apple tree, so shared ministry comes from a sharing community. If ministry is going to be truly Christian, it needs to be true to the shared aspect of a sharing Christian community. The meeting of a parish council is a time for that mutual giving and receiving which is a mark of a sharing Christian community.

In the church, therefore, all ministry is to some extent incomplete. In Phil. 2:25 Paul does not hesitate to acknowledge that Epaphroditus ministers to his need. Paul commends Epaphroditus "for . . . risking his life to complete your service to me" (Phil. 2:30). Paul often refers to Timothy, Titus, Stephanas and Apollos as his *fellow* workers. In Phil 4:2 Paul writes: "And I ask you also, true yokefellow, help these women for they have labored side by side with me in the gospel . . ." In Rom. 16:3 we read: "Greet Prisca and Aquila, my fellow workers in Christ Jesus."

It's okay, therefore, to admit the incompleteness of our ministry. We can say that we can't do everything. The pastor needs the ministry of the accountant. The teacher needs the ministry of the printer. The marriage councilor needs the reconciling ministry of the priest. And the priest who by listening, ministers healing to his people, is himself in need of being healed.

Fortunately, we don't need to do everything. We don't need to be omni-competent. Millions of baptized Christians are both able and willing to complete the incompleteness of our ministry. The process whereby one ministry is completed by another is easily understood from the two Pauline images: the body of Christ and the building of God. In Rom. 12:4-6 Paul writes: "for as in one body we have many members, and all the members do not have the same function, so we, though many, are one body in Christ, and individual members of one another."

The human body is an interlinkage of many services: the service of the hands, helping the feet; the service of the tongue, helping the teeth; the service of the ears, helping the eyes; the service of the heart, helping the brain, etc. The service of one member is, to some extent, incomplete without the service of another. The Pauline body image is a sign that the pluriformity and the interdependence of various ministries is an essential part of the life of the church.

We don't need to be housebuilders to understand Paul's second image, the building of God (1 Cor. 3,9). For Paul, the church is always in process of being built up by God through all its members. The church gets built up because it members, responding to the Lord's grace, are all offering their different skills as ministries in the church.

Building a house requires a variety of builders: a carpenter, a painter, a plumber, a plasterer, an electrician, a sweeper, etc. Paul's idea is that every Christian has been gifted with some talent to serve the total upbuilding process. This skill or talent can rightly be called a ministry. In Paul's upbuilding process, there's no passive audience. There aren't any bleachers. Everybody is in the building process, doing his/her part. An electrician can't build the house alone. He needs the help of a variety of skills. At the same time, he needs to check the blueprints and coordinate his skill with all the other builders. Sometimes he needs to meet with them to relate his incomplete skill to the other builders.

So also in the parish. Each parish community needs a variety of ministers: lectors, teachers, religious education coordinators, ministers of eucharist and of music, ministers to the poor and to the sick, ministers for communications, for health care, helpers, administrators, accountants, preachers of the Word and councilors. None of these ministers can build up the church alone. All need to relate their ministries to one another so they will truly be partners in the total upbuilding process. They need to coordinate their ministries by working from one common blueprint.

In this upbuilding process, parish councils have a threefold function: first, they take an inventory of the needs of the parish and the civic community; second, they discern who in the parish and civic community has what gift, skill or ministry; third, they serve as the overall coordinating body in relating the ministries to the needs and the ministries to one another. Thus, the social worker becomes the youth minister; the accountant becomes the financial administrator; the public school teacher becomes the C.C.D. teacher; the radio announcer becomes the lector, etc.

Since in each parish there's a wide variety of needs, it's plain that each parish needs a diversity of skills or ministries. At the same time, if the parish is going to be true to its call to be a sharing community, all these ministries need constantly to be in a sharing relationship with one another. They need to support one another in a concrete, positive way. As a husband is supportive of his wife and vice-versa, so each minister is supportive of the other ministries. That's how the church gets built up.

It hardly needs saying that Paul doesn't view the church as a coming together of distinct classes of people, i.e., priests, deacons, laity, brothers, sisters, etc. He doesn't believe in a caste system. His church gets built up on the basis of different *functions:* i.e., evangelists, pastors, teachers, healers, helpers, prophets, administrators, etc.

Parish councils, therefore, are not *primarily* bodies which represent various classes of people: i.e., youth, senior citizens, clergy, laity, religious, minority groups, etc. A councilor doesn't come to a meeting primarily to represent, or lobby for, his class or his faction in the parish. He/she comes because he has a function, a ministry, to offer for the whole parish. He may be a youth or a senior citizen, a black or a white but his function, his ministry, is more important than either his age or the color of his skin. For neither his age nor his skin *by itself* builds up the church.

Finally, Paul doesn't measure the value of a ministry by any kind of ecclesiastical ranking system. Whatever ministry builds up the church most, that's the most valuable. Thus, many lay ministries may be more valuable than priestly ministries because they build up the church more. On Paul's scale, the ministry of Mother Teresa of Calcutta is probably more valuable than that of many priests and bishops. In the final analysis only God knows whose ministry is the more valuable.

The council is, of course, not concerned about ranking any ministries. It is more concerned about serving as midwife to an ongoing process which activates all the people of the parish to share and develop their diverse ministries. They serve as enablers for all the ministries in the whole parish.

Councilors, therefore, have to resist the temptation to do everything themselves. Before Vatican II the priest did everything. Now, in some parishes, the council does everything. That means the number of ministers has increased from one to about 15. That's not much progress. It means that the council hasn't understood that its first ministry is to enable and facilitate the diverse ministries in the rest of the parish. Councilors should not give the impression that the Spirit has favored them with his gifts, but bypassed everybody else. They need to help the people in initiating the development of their untapped gifts.

The council will be a leaven for all the gifts of the parish if it takes to heart the advice of St. Ignatius of Antioch (c. 107) writing to the Church of the Smyrnaeans: "Labour with one another, struggle together, run together, suffer together, rest together, rise up together as God's stewards and assessors and servants."[4] The meetings of the council may be a time to get some business done. But more importantly, they are a time to share, support, complete, coordinate and evaluate the various ministries which build up the parish.

Now we need to figure out how these ministries relate to the parish council and its functions. That will be the task of the next chapter.

Footnotes

1.   New York: Daughters of St. Paul Press, 1976, p. 48.

2.   Kenneth Untener, *The Michigan Catholic* (Editorial), March 18, 1977.

3.   Ibid.

4.   *The Apostolic Fathers*, Kirsopp Lake, Trans. (Cambridge: Harvard University Press, 1970), p. 275.

Chapter 5

The Parish Council and its Functions

We've talked about the broad foundations for parish councils. Now it's time to get down to business and explain what a council is, what it does, and finally, how to start one.

A parish council is a body or organism of shared ministry which plans and coordinates the overall policy of the parish in order to carry out the mission of Christ in the church. It is a decision-making body within the boundaries of the doctrine, liturgy and laws of the church. It's a model of what the parish community is. But insofar as it's a body of leaders, it's also a model of what the parish community might become.

The Archdiocese of Newark, N.J. offers the following definition:

> The parish council is a leadership community comprised of the pastor, parish priest, deacons, religious and lay persons. The main purpose of the parish council is to provide direction for the parish based on the presence of the Holy Spirit dwelling in the community. The main task of the council is formulating and implementing parish policies and plans, as well as coordinating all parish activities. It is to be remembered, of course, that the parish council is accountable to the parish, which it serves and to the larger church of which it is a part.[1]

The Archdiocese of St. Paul-Minneapolis defines the council this way:

> The parish council must be conceived of as the coordinating and unifying structure of the local Christian community. It should be the means of achieving full participation of the whole parish in extending Christ's mission by giving all of the parish a voice in encouraging, guiding and directing the various aspects of parish life. The people of the parish are seen as co-workers in the mission of the church, but clearly co-workers under the direction of the pastor who represents the bishop.[2]

Now that we know what a parish council is, what is it supposed to do? Again, St. Paul-Minneapolis says it well:

> The council must see as its purpose the coordinating, encouraging and promotion of every apostolic activity through which the parish community discharges its common responsibility in making the gospel known and in aiding men and women to live holy lives. This includes liturgical, charitable, ecumenical, social, educational and administrative activities, as well as those other aspects of parish life which contribute to a full living of the gospel by the Christian community.[3]

The Archdiocese of Newark says their councils have a threefold purpose:

> "1) To provide direction for the parish based on the mission of Christ and the will of the Holy Spirit as He speaks and moves through all His people.
>
> 2) To serve as an instrument for sharing the mission of Jesus, proclaiming His Word, building His community, celebrating His liturgy and serving His people.
>
> 3) To set an example of unity and cooperation as the People of God to both the parish and the larger community."[4]

A listing of what the council is supposed to do shapes up this way:

1) To pray together, to nurture faith and to reflect on the gospel.

2) To be a sign of a truly Christian community before the church and the world.

3) To work in union with the diocese and its priorities.

4) To assure through its committees a continuous and integrated survey of both spiritual and temporal needs of the parish, community and diocese and, after setting priorities, to develop and implement programs aimed at meeting these needs.

5) To serve as a permanent structure for constructive dialogue among priests, religious, and laity of the parish and with the bishop and his representatives, so that they can work in close cooperation, as a truly Christian community, in fulfilling Christ's saving mission.

6) To provide leadership, direction, education, resources and encouragement in accordance with the constant and continuing goals of the parish and current and stated priorities and programs.

7) To coordinate parish activities with the area or deanery councils and with the diocesan pastoral council.

8) To identify, support and maximize the gifts and talents of all the members of the parish.

9) To develop a parish mission statement in accordance with the mission of the church.

10) To develop and train lay ministers with diverse skills.

11) To hold orientation meetings for all prospective council members.[5]

Now that we know what a parish council is and what it does, how do you go about starting one? How do you get the show on the road?

Careful Foundation

In starting a parish council it's best to make haste slowly. It may take a good year to do the job well. It just doesn't pay to skip any essential steps. The step by step procedure goes something like this:

First, the pastor appoints a *steering committee.* He's careful to select members who represent a variety of viewpoints and experiences. He includes old and young, joiners and non-joiners, new and old-timers, men and women. In this way, the steering committee will already be a preview of what the council should be.

Second, the steering committee begins to *pray together* and asks the parish to join them, for the success of their efforts. The pastor explains the process of consensus decision-making and then the committee begins to practice it. In this way, the steering committee gets initiated into a process which may become the normal procedure once the council gets going.

Third, the steering committee launches a program of self-education. The members read at least two documents of Vatican II, viz., *The Dogmatic Constitution on the Church* and *The Decree on the Laity.* Then they form discussion groups. They study the nature of the church, the diocese and the parish. The priests and sisters teach and learn with the rest of the committee.

Fourth, the committee launches an educational program for the whole parish. To do this they gather up a good supply of materials. Books, articles, magazines, etc. are available through Twenty-Third Publications, Box 180, West Mystic, Conn. 06388.

The educational program may include the following:

a) series of sermons
b) bulletin inserts
c) showing a filmstrip on parish councils during all the Sunday Masses
d) attendance at open parish forums conducted by the steering committee
e) open discussion during meetings of all existing parish organizations
f) neighborhood discussions in various sections of the parish conducted by the steering committee
g) outside speakers, including priests and laity from other councils, as well as experts on group dynamics
h) parish survey of special talents, ministries, areas of interest.

Fifth, the steering committee develops a set of *interim guidelines* for the future parish council. Usually the committee collects copies of other council guidelines, perhaps from a diocesan office or from neighboring parishes. At this stage guidelines are broad, flexible and temporary—just enough to give the parishioners an idea about what the parish council will be like. They may eventually become a part of a constitution, but that step is a long way down the road. The committee, however, does have to decide how many will serve on the council.

At this stage, the committee will have to figure out how the parish organizations will fit into the picture. The committee may survey the parish to find out how many parishioners are still active in each organization. Then it consults the various organizations to get their ideas on how they might best fit into the council structure. After dialoguing with the officers, the committee decides how its parish organizations will relate to the council.

Finally, the steering committee sets up the procedures for the first elections. It will determine eligibility to vote, qualifications of candidates, list of nominees and, finally, the form of the ballot. The committee will also decide whether elections take place by mail, by special meeting or during Sunday Liturgy.

Some steering committees print a special bulletin insert with pictures and biographical data of each candidate. Sometimes the pastor or the chairperson on the steering committee introduces each candidate to the people before the Sunday Masses. Coffee and donuts after the Masses provide another opportunity to meet the candidates. (More about this in Chapter 9.) In some parishes, the steering committee prepares a special liturgy for election Sunday. The scripture readings, homily and prayer of the faithful concentrate on the "diverse ministries given by the Spirit for the upbuilding of the church."

Of course, the key factor in starting a council is communication at all levels. Open and honest dialogue with everybody is crucial. It takes time, but it's worth it. It can be the difference between success or failure.

Now that we know what a parish council is, what it does and how it gets started, we can move on to identify more clearly the various ministries and committees. We'll start with the ministry of the pastor.

Footnotes

1. *Parish Council Guidelines* (Newark, N.J.: Archdiocese of Newark, n.d.), p. 2.

2. *Origins*, 5 (April 1, 1976) p. 647.

3. Ibid.

4. *Parish Council Guidelines*, p. 12.

5. See Appendix to this chapter.

Appendix I

An Orientation Program for Parish Councilors
Archdiocese of Milwaukee
Milwaukee, Wisconsin

Many parish councils are ineffective because they do not understand the meaning and goals of leadership in the contemporary church. This orientation program explores the meaning of lay leadership as given both in the Old and New Testaments, as well as the history of lay leadership within organized Catholicism up to the Second Vatican Council. There is an examination of the practical problems which most parish councils face. Finally, a group process is modelled in which the participating members actually cope with the dynamics of a parish council meeting.

Participation in this program is suggested as a prerequisite for membership on a parish council. Present councilors and other interested parishioners will also benefit.

The orientation program consists of three sessions (ideally held in three successive weeks):

Session I:
1. Is lay leadership in the Church really new? An historical overview of the role of the laity from the Old Testament to the present.
2. The priestly, prophetic and kingly mission of Jesus: how do we share in that mission today as the People of God, the Church?
   Priestly - pray - liturgy, worship
   Prophetic - teach - education
   Kingly - serve - social concerns

Session II:

1. Clarifying roles, power and identity: who are we as a parish council? Are we consultative or policy making? Or both?
2. Establishing realistic goals—is our role merely representative or also prophetic? Helping parish council members to individually accept the goals and work responsibly toward achieving them.
3. Review the relationship between the council and its committees. Do some committees overlap? Are others needed?
4. Discuss time commitments and fostering involvement of all parishioners.
5. Explain the council's plans for its own spiritual renewal.

Session III:
Knowing Our Parish Council Identity

This session should be handled by a facilitator who is knowledgeable about council work in general and the work and past history of a council in a particular parish (perhaps a past officer). This is a suggested agenda:

1. *Welcome and Introduction of New Councilors* (or nominees).
2. *History of the Parish Council in our Parish:* Some of the issues handled in the past; how our past experience affects the manner in which our councils function.
3. *Constitution:* Review and explain (do not simply read it). Have copies available for all nominees.
4. *The Role of Parish Council Committees:* Review the relationship between the parish council and the committees. Each committee chairperson can briefly outline the work his/her committee does. Encourage new members to be part of one of the committees.
5. *Time Commitments:* Communication with the parish at large; the importance of building a unified community in which each person is truly "listened to."
6. *Goals of the Parish Council in Our Parish:* Informing new councilors about the goals the parish has set for itself in the next few years so as to help them make these goals their

own. Review of the *covenant statement*, if your parish has developed one.

7. *Prayer Service:* Stressing unity and commitment (below is a suggested service, but parishes are encouraged to develop their own to suit their particular needs).

8. *Social "Get Acquainted" Time:* Present committee members, as well as parish councilors could be invited to participate in the evening, and especially the social.

Prayer Service — Orientation Program "Our Common Discipleship"
Archdiocese of Milwaukee
Milwaukee, Wisconsin

Leader: And now, my friends, I want to invite you to pray and reflect with me on the challenge which Our Lord Jesus has offered to us: "Come and follow me." The call to discipleship is a personal one. How will we respond?

First Reading: John 15: 5-10

Response: Lord, you have called us to be hearers of the Word—open our minds to what you have to say to us.

Second Reading: from *The Gospel Without Compromise* by Catherine deHueck Doherty

"The role of Christians especially will be to establish communities of love and to show to others the mutual love of the members, one for another. In this way they will present the face of the living God, the the resurrected Christ. He will so powerfully dwell in such communities that, far from being dead, he will be touched and seen in those who call themselves his followers. . . This is the witnessing that we, the people of God, must do today. We can only do it by praying for an increase in faith, in courage and love."

Response: Lord, you have called us to be doers of the Word—open our hearts to the needs around us.
(Period of silent meditation or shared reflections:)

Leader: *Prayers of Petition:*
That through our union with Christ in baptism and our growth in confirmation, we may attain a full maturity in a spirit of charity and responsibility. LORD, WE PRAY.

That we may share our talents and resoures for the building up of the districts and the archdiocese. LORD, WE PRAY.

That we may exercise our common discipleship with faith, courage and love. LORD, WE PRAY.

Closing Prayer: (All) We thank you, Lord, for the gift of your holy Spirit. Help us to use the Spirit's gifts in love for one another and to encourage the people of our parishes to offer their talents gladly to build up the Body of Christ, which is the Church. Grant zeal, courage and caring to all our councils and committees. May your name be blessed now and forever. Amen!

Chapter 6

The Ministry of the Pastor

"Tend the flock of God . . . not as domineering over those in your charge, but being examples of the flock" (1 Peter 5:2-3).

When parish councils first started, many pastors had an identity crisis. They didn't know how to relate to this new, shared decision-making body. They went in different directions, trying to figure out what their new role should be. They got all kinds of advice. Some sisters said: "We're all equal." And some laity concluded: "We're the corporation board. We run the parish. The pastor is our hired man."

In the confusion some pastors beat a hasty retreat: "This is the age of the laity. Let'em run the parish." Or again: "I don't go to council meetings. That way the laity will feel more at ease. I can veto everything anyway." Others abdicated responsibility. They threw the ball at the laity and were disappointed that the laity didn't want to run with it. Some pastors, in a magnanimous gesture, gave up the veto power: "We've agreed to settle everything by majority vote. I told the council I wouldn't veto anything, no matter what." Not a few pastors, threatened by vocal and articulate laity, got on their high horse to defend their post: "I'm the pastor here. I have full authority from the bishop."

This confusion of roles had its effect in shaping the councils. Since most pastors felt secure in their cultic and sacramental roles, they clung to "the spiritual" and gave finances and administration to the laity. As a result, many councils felt they were supposed to deal only with the nuts and bolts of maintenance. In more than one parish, pastors identified their role with the veto power. They didn't see themselves as members of the council. They gave up their vote. As one pastor put it: "I didn't feel I should vote on the advice I gave myself."

As a result, some councils looked and acted like bodies organized against the pastor. Before Vatican II the church had been divided into clergy and laity. Now it was divided into decision-makers and advice-givers. It hardly needs saying that most pastors received no preparation in the seminary, either in the theory or in the practice of parish councils. The confusion was predictable and understandable.

The Pastor of the Parish

To get a clearer understanding of the pastor's role on the council, we have to look first at his role as pastor of the parish. Then we'll see how he relates to the parish council. The pastor who is appointed to a parish gets his role and his job description from three different sources: 1) the pastor's office, 2) ordination, and 3) personal skills.

The Pastor's Office

It may be helpful to distinguish the pastor's office as such from the particular priest who happens to occupy that office. Already in the New Testament church, we see that a distinct office exists as something to which a person can aspire: "If anyone aspires to the office of bishop . . ." (1 Tim. 3,1).

Since the Spirit is in the church, it's at least possible that the development of the pastor's office is one of the fruits of the Spirit's activity, his gift (charism) to the church. One can hardly say, as some Protestant theologians do, that the evolution of office is a corruption of the ideal, free-spirit church.

Of course, a particular pastor can exploit office for selfish purposes. He can use it as an authority crutch against the council. He can take refuge in it and so sidestep personal accountability. He can endow it with an aura of infallibility. He can make it appear so holy and sacred that any questions about it will seem irreverent or sacrilegious. He can act as if it is a "thing," awarded to him as his personal possession. He can use it as power, rather than service. In short, he can forget that office is in the service of the church, not of the pastor. The pastor's office, like the president's office, can be abused.

On the other hand, office as such can be a positive good in the church. It can, to some extent, deliver the parish and the council from the pastor's personal whims. It can deliver the people from the cult of personality condemned in 1 Cor. 3:4-9. It can arrest the privatizing tendencies in religion. It can protect the people from doctrinal error. It can serve as a more or less objective standard for holding the pastor accountable. Finally, it can provide some continuity with tradition.

The pastor's office is, of course, not an absolute. It is the product of a long historical development. And, like the church itself, it is always in need of renewal and reform. Recent experiments with team ministry are even now in process of reforming it. No doubt, with the growing shortage of priests, lay men and women will soon be appointed to the pastor's office. (This is already happening in Chile.) That will usher in a new phase of renewal and reform. Nevertheless, someone will always remain responsible for the duties attached to the pastor's office. It's possible to distinguish four factors which have shaped the pastor's office: 1) *the shepherd image,* 2) *the presiding chair,* 3) *canon law,* and 4) *Vatican II.*

The Shepherd Image

In Ephesians 4:11 we read: "And his gifts were that some should be apostles, some prophets, some evangelists, some pastors . . ." In the New Testament period "pastor" evokes the image of the shepherd leading his sheep to green pastures. In our urban, industrialized society the shepherd/sheep image can hardly be applied literally to the pastor and "the faithful." Sheep are dumb, passive and easily led. Today's Catholics, on the other hand, are often as well educated as the pastor. And, thanks be to God, they aren't easily led.

The *first* point of the shepherd image is that, like Jesus, "the good shepherd lays down his life for the sheep" (John 10:11). The pastor, therefore, is called to lay down his life for his people. *Second,* as the shepherd knows his sheep by name (John 10:3), so the pastor is called to know his people by name. *Third,* the shepherd goes out looking for the lost sheep (Matt. 18,12). In so doing, he proclaims God's mercy for the sinner. So the pastor, in virtue of his office, is called to search for and accept those who have gone astray. *Fourth,* the shepherd leads the sheep to green pastures. He cares for them. He protects them from the teeth of wild animals. So too, the pastor, in virtue of his office, is called to have pastoral care for his people, to be concerned about their physical and spiritual welfare.

Of course the council members are joined in a partnership with their pastor. In virtue of their baptism they share in these four responsibilities of the pastor's office. The shepherd image is a *Christ* image. This means that all who are baptized in Christ are called to be his witnesses in laying down their lives for others, in showing mercy to the sinner, in caring, like a shepherd, for the physical and spiritual needs of the *Lord's* flock. The shepherd image is not the property of clerics or officeholders in the church. At the present time in the Catholic church, however, the pastor bears the burden of *ultimate* responsibility at the parish level. Council members, therefore, cannot "take over" ultimate pastoral responsibility without taking over the pastor's office itself.

The Presiding Chair

In 1969, St. John's University, Collegeville, Minn. established the chair of Jewish Studies. The first occupant of that chair was Rabbi Schulmann. It was endowed by a Minneapolis foundation. The occupant of that chair may change through the years, but the chair with its teaching responsibilities will remain.

After Vatican II many pastors, responding to the liturgical reform, renovated the sanctuary. They carried the statues into the church basement. They dismantled communion railings and stored the wood in the janitor's workshop. When the storm was over, three pieces of furniture remained: the altar, the pulpit and the *presiding chair.*

Instead of "saying Mass" the pastor now "presides at the liturgy." While the word "preside" seems new to us, it actually conveys an old idea. St. Justin (c. 150), describing the liturgy of his time, refers to the presiding priest as the *president:* "Then is brought to the president of the brethren bread and a cup of water and wine . . . When the president has given thanks and all the people have assented. . . ."[1]

"Preside" comes from the latin *praesedere,* meaning "to sit before, or in front of." It can also mean "to have the care or management of." The Greek word which expresses the same idea is *prohistemi,* "to be at the head of." This word is used in 1 Tim. 5:17: "Let the elders who rule well be considered worthy of double honor . . ."

As early as the second century, the bishop *presided* over the liturgy from the presiding chair. As a liturgical symbol the chair acquired a twofold meaning: "In the first place, sitting was associated with teaching. This is so in the gospels, particularly as applied to Jesus, but also to the rabbis. In the second place, sitting was associated with government and most importantly in eschatological contexts. These two lines of thought converged upon the bishop's chair. For the bishop sat in his chair to teach true doctrine. And the bishop sat in his chair to preside over the corporate life of the believing community."[2]

The presiding chair came to have highly symbolic meaning in the installation of new ministries: ". . . before there were any other rites for the inauguration of ministries in the Christian congregation, one primitive rite obtained everywhere, namely the leading of the new minister to take his place in the seat appropriate to his office. For when, at the end of the second century, the notion of continuous succession from the apostles came to expression, it did not do so in the form of a consecrated from consecrators, but altogether as a continuity in the occupation of a certain chair."[3]

The chair of Jewish Studies at St. John's University remains even after the occupant dies or moves. So too, the presiding chair in the sanctuary remains even after the pastor dies or moves. The chair remains as a sign of the pastor's office. It will "hand on" its list of responsibilities to the new pastor when he arrives.

Of course the pastor's chair doesn't exist by itself. It gets its meaning, its list of responsibilities, in continuity with the teaching and governing mission of the larger church. For this reason, the presiding chair is best understood as a replica of the bishop's chair in the cathedral which in Greek *(Cathedra)* means "a chair." The pastor who occupies the presiding chair is therefore a delegate of the bishop's presiding chair in the cathedral. His duty to represent the diocese continues even if the bishop's chair is vacant. That's part of his responsibility as occupant of the pastor's office.

The presiding chair with its present list of responsibilities is not an absolute. It's not of divine law. It's not necessary, for instance, that he who presides over the liturgical celebrations also preside over the administration of the parish. It's quite possible that in the future an ordained minister will preside over the eucharist and a non-ordained minister will preside over administration. Since presiding and administering are two distinct ministries, they could, in Paul's view of church, easily be separated. The presiding chair may be a helpful symbol. It should not become a justification for one ministry to absorb all the others.

Canon Law

A rather long section of the code of canon law is devoted to the duties of pastors (canons 451-486). It's impossible to review all these canons. Here is a partial listing of some of the duties which automatically fall on the man who sits in the presiding chair:

a)   to confer baptism solemnly
b)   to assist at marriages and impart the nuptial blessing
c)   to perform funeral services
d)   to bless the baptismal font
e)   to celebrate divine services
f)   to administer the sacraments to the faithful as often as they lawfully ask for them
g)   to know his parishioners

h)   prudently to correct those who go astray

i)   to embrace in his paternal charity the poor and the distressed

j)   to employ the greatest care in the Catholic education of children.

Canon law is, of course, in process of reform. Hopefully, the revised law will reflect the pastoral experience of the church since Vatican II. Large numbers of sisters, brothers and lay men and women are now active in full-time pastoral ministry. The new canon law will need to redefine the pastor's office in view of the present and future shared ministries. Parish councils, therefore, have an important role in shaping the canon law of the future.

Vatican II

Some other duties which come with the chair of the pastor's office can be drawn from Vatican II's "Decree on the Ministry and Life of Priests":

a)   to serve as the chief proclaimer of the Word and presider over the eucharistic celebration

b)   to be the *public* reconciler of the members of the community

c)   to serve as the *public* witness of the diocesan church to the local community and vice versa

d)   to be the chief minister of unity in the community

e)   to be the *public* leader of community prayer

f)   to be a leader of the general spiritual formation and growth of the community

g)   to nurture, support and unify the various charisms within the community

h)   to witness to the faith of the community

i)   to witness to the church's universal call to holiness

j)   to oversee the teaching mission of the church in his parish.

In actual practice, the pastor often delegates some of the above responsibilities. He just can't wear that many hats. But it may be an eye-opener for new councilors to see what the pastor's "boss" (canon law, Vatican II) expects him to do.

Ordination

On this continent, the pastor is usually an ordained priest. Ordination is a time when the People of God accept the priest as their leader. They affirm that he is fit and suitable, and then they support him by their applause. It's also a time when the bishop imposes hands and gives the priest "his marching orders." And, let's face it--in the Roman Catholic system those orders aren't subject to review by the parish council.

In the rite of ordination, we see that the priest is ordained to "preach the gospel, sustain the people of God, and celebrate sacred rites especially the Lord's sacrifice." In his instruction, the ordaining bishop lists some of the priest's duties: "In baptizing men you will bring them into the people of God; in the sacrament of penance you will forgive sins in the name of Christ and the church; with holy oil you will relieve and console the sick. You will celebrate the liturgy, offer thanks and praise to God through every hour of the day, praying for the people of God and the world as well. As you do this, always keep in mind that you are a man chosen from among men and appointed to act for men in their relations with God. Do your part in the work of Christ the Priest with the unfailing gladness of genuine charity, and look after the concerns of Christ, not your own."

In virtue of his sacramental anointing, the priest shares in a more intense way in the priestly, prophetic and kingly mission of Christ. He already shares in that mission in virtue of his baptism. But, because he's an ordained priest, his responsibilities in that mission are more serious. Vatican II teaches that there is an *essential* difference between the common priesthood of all the baptized and the priesthood of the ordained ministers.

Ordination means that the priest is accountable to the diocesan church, to its bishop and to its diocesan offices, e.g., education, liturgy, tribunal, etc. The priest ministers within a context of defined relationships with the diocesan church. If he steps too far out of line, he'll hear it from the chancery office.

At the present time, the pastor often relates to the council partly from his pastoral office and partly from his ordination. Again, that relationship is very much in process. It may change. But that's where the pastor is "coming from" in many parishes today. Fr. Orville Griese has summarized the state of the pastor's relationship to the council in three basic pre-suppositions:

1) There can be but one head of the parish; the pastor shoulders that blessed burden.

2) The pastor does not work *for* or *under* the parish councils; the parish council does not work *for* or *under* the pastor.

3) Both pastor and parish council are to work *with* one another *for* 'Thy kingdom come' on the parish level and beyond.[4]

The Pastor's Personal Skills

As one clerical wag puts it, pastors are a lot like people. They come in various shapes and sizes. Each has his own history, experience and personality. Each has a different level of competence or incompetence. Each is "gifted" with different talents and charisms. Each is also flawed by the mystery of evil still at work in his life and world.

Some "don't give a hoot" about administration; others love it. Some actually like meetings; others hate them. Some are good catechists for children; others are a disaster. Some have a great need to do everything themselves; others delegate freely. Some are rigid and legalistic; others "hang loose." Some are easily threatened by articulate laity; others are glad the lay people are finally speaking out. Some are shy and reserved; others are the life of the party. Some seem holy and prayerful; others seem worldly. Some are good preachers but poor builders; others are good builders but poor preachers. And so it goes.

Pastors, in other words, do not come from the seminary in set molds, like cars from an assembly line. Since Vatican II it should be plain to everyone that pastors, like the rest of humans, cannot be lumped into any kind of stereotype. Whatever the pastor's strengths and weaknesses, his personal skills and his personality become part of his role in the council and in the parish. One would hope that the council would be an accepting and supportive community which would maximize his strengths and shore up his weaknesses. He is, after all, a responsive human being who is susceptible to change. He isn't immune to the human and divine dynamism of a faith community. Shared prayer and shared pizza can do wonders for the most neanderthal pastor.

Unless the pastor is very new, he'll probably know more about running the parish than the average councilor. He has received at least four years of graduate training in theology. Over the years, he has picked up a lot of practical know-how about "pastoring." After all, he's full-time. He lives at the control center of the parish. His nose can quickly detect the more bizarre religious behavior. He also knows where the roof leaks and where the extra altar linens are.

To summarize--the pastor, as pastor of the parish, gets his role from the pastor's office, from ordination and from his personal skills. It remains now to discuss how the pastor relates to the parish council.

The pastor relates to the council first as *ratifier* of the council's recommendations and second, as a *member* of the council with his own unique ministry of pastoral leadership.

The Pastor as Ratifier

When parish councils first started, they spent all kinds of time discussing their competence and authority. Were they merely advisory to the pastor? Or were they decision-making? Unfortunately, the whole discussion was narrowly focused in either/or terms. The question came out of a legal, preconciliar mentality. Then too, there was an atmosphere of mistrust. Both priest and laity were anxious to get it all down in writing, in a constitution. After all, "the council might get out of hand."

Such attitudes were understandable. Pastors knew enough church history to have some fears about a recurrence of the lay trusteeism of the 1840's. And they were conditioned to see authority (jurisdiction) coming "from above." They were the bishop's helpers. They were accountable to him alone.

Most pastors, therefore, answered the simplistic, either/or question in favor of themselves. The council would be advisory only. And many laypersons were quite willing to accept a merely advisory status. After all, whether it was in the confessional or in the pulpit, many laity were conditioned to accept final answers from their pastors. Then too, many laity felt advising the pastor was better than nothing. It was quite a promotion from the "pay, pray and obey" status of yesteryear.

If the council was merely advisory, then everything hung on the pastor's veto power. The council had to come up with the pastor's answer. Otherwise, he would say "No." The possibility, if not the threat, of veto hung as a spectre over all council discussion. It was not exactly conducive to mutual trust or to shared responsibility.

Fortunately, most councils have moved beyond the legalism of their early days. Pastors and laity have begun to trust one another. They also have acquired a deeper appreciation of what it means to be partners in a Christian community. They are more ready to understand their relationships in terms of a sharing faith community.

Advise and Decide

If a council is going to be a true Christian partnership (Chapter 4), it will be *both* advisory and decision-making. In a marriage partnership there are times when the husband is advisory; other times he is decision-making. And there are times when the wife is advisory; other times, she is decision-making. What marriage could be described as a true, trusting partnership if the husband is always the decision-maker and the wife always the advisor, or vice versa?

For certain theological topics like liturgy and canon law, the council may indeed be *mainly* advisory, but hardly *merely* advisory. In other words, one could rightly assume that the council's discussion would have at least some influence on the ultimate decision. And since refusal to ratify is a rare occurrence, there is no reason why councils cannot be *primarily* decision-making. (See definitions of parish councils in the previous chapter.)

Karl Rahner suggests that the time has come for lay people to have deliberative participation in the decision-making process of the church. He wants them to have a share in policy-making decisions. He writes:

> . . . there must today be a right on the part of priest
> and lay people to cooperate in varying degrees and

in forms appropriate to the matter at hand, in a deliberative and not merely,consultative way in the church's decisions. . . . Anyone who opposes a deliberative collaboration should be asked why he does so, although it is not in principle contrary to what is properly the constitutional law of the Church, or why he wants to restrict this collaboration to as few and as trivial questions as possible.[5]

Walbert Buhlmann discusses the use of the democratic model in the decision-making process of the church:

Even if the democratic model cannot be applied in all points to the Church (because here all authority does come ultimately from Christ) and even if the voice of bishops carries a weight qualitatively distinct from that carried by any vote taken among the faithful, this by no means implies that the faithful and the priests have a merely consultative function in the pronouncements and decisions of the Church[6].

A council, which in its decision-making process, does not witness, to some extent, to the basic equality of the Christian partnership, publicly falsifies the meaning of the Christian community. As a body, it has lost its right to act in the name of the parish.

A council which is *merely* advisory to the pastor is a denial of almost everything contained in chapters three and four. Such a council can hardly contribute to the growth of adult Christian responsibility. It reduces councils to a child/father relationship. By structuring such a relationship, a council may even do more harm than good.

In spite of all the above, however, the diocesan church needs to retain the right of ratification over *some* council decisions. It would, of course, be helpful if dioceses would list the *general* areas in which councils do not have the final say. In this way, a diocese could prevent confusion and unrealistic expectations at council meetings.

For instance, the diocese of Fort Worth, Texas, in its council guidelines, speaks to the problem directly: Parish councils are to be decision-making in all matters of the parish--spiritual, educational, financial--except "where specifically *limited* by *Church law,* by written or established policy of the Diocese or Vatican II."[7]

The principle of ratification flows, in a sense, from the very nature of the church. In the first place, the gospel which is proclaimed by the priest in the parish is not subject to vote. The gospel does not evolve out of the opinions or consent of the parishioners. The preached gospel is the Lord's word, not man's. It includes the truth of the apostolic tradition, the truth of the historical Jesus. Thus the main message of salvation comes from the Easter community of the New Testament. It has an historical transcendence. It is the Good News which the herald brings "from outside" into the parish community. It is an announcement, a proclamation. Neither its truth nor its power "wait on" a majority vote by the parish council.

Second, the church as a community of salvation, historically antecedes the faithful and constitutes them, i.e., brings them into existence as believers. The baptismal font with its power exists before the baptized faithful. The church precedes the faithful in Christ in three essential points: 1) By the revelation of the mystery of the Trinity and of the Kingdom of God, Jesus established the messianic people in respect to their faith; 2) By his baptism, by his celebration of the Lord's supper, by his other priestly acts, he instituted the sacramental life by which the faithful enter into a true communion with Jesus and with one another; 3) By calling his disciples and by sending them forth, he gave the messianic community an apostolic ministry. So before any vote is taken, the church possesses the treasure of faith, the treasure of the sacramental life and the treasure of the apostolic ministry. These are the Lord's gifts which bring a new community into existence.

The diocese's right to ratify also flows from two other theological principles: 1) the need for the parish to retain its doctrinal communion with the diocesan church; and 2) the need for the parish to witness to the truth that it is a smaller, dependent community within the larger, more independent diocesan church. A few words about each principle may be helpful.

The parish and its council need to build up a living communion with the diocesan church. As the head is one with the body, so the parish is one with the diocese. The parish witnesses to its union with the diocese by professing the same faith, by following the same Lord, by obeying the same gospel, by celebrating the same baptism, by breaking the same bread and sharing the same cup. When the pastor ratifies the council's recommendation, the *whole council* is sharing in a sign of unity which, like breaking bread, witnesses to the diocese's communion with the parish.

The diocesan church builds up unity by ratifying council decisions in four areas: 1) faith, 2) morals, 3) liturgy and sacraments, and 4) general and diocesan law.

Here are a few examples of council decisions which the diocese could *not* ratify: 1) In matters of faith--a council decides to reject the infallibility of the pope; 2) In matters of morals--a council decides to move adultery from its list of sins; 3) In matters of liturgy--a council decides to use beer and pizza for the eucharist; 4) In matters of general and diocesan law--the council authorizes a Baptist minister to preside over the Sunday eucharist.

In all of these examples, the diocesan church, through the pastor, could rightly withhold ratification. The reason is that the council by its decision, at least in part, severs its unity, its communion, with the diocesan church.

The second principle for ratification is the truth that, in the Roman Catholic tradition, the parish is a smaller, dependent cell in the larger body that is the diocesan church. The Catholic parish is not a Congregationalist church. It's neither autonomous nor independent.

The diocese is not merely "the bishop" or the chancery office. Nor is it merely an organizational linkage of small, independent congregations called parishes. The diocese is church in its own right. It's a portion of the People of God constituting "a particular church in which the one, holy, Catholic, and apostolic church of Christ is truly present and operative." It can ordain all the ministers it needs. It can celebrate all the sacraments.

The parish, on the other hand, is dependent on, and relative to, the diocese, just as the hand is dependent on, and relative to, the body. All council decisions, therefore, need to remain open to the body of the diocesan church. Ratifying a council decision is one way of expressing that openness to the diocese.

Remaining open to the diocese in a positive way isn't easy for many parishes. Often they have absorbed a Congregationalist attitude. The diocese is the "enemy." The parish is "where the action is." Because the diocese is usually too large, it is seen more as an impersonal, administrative bureaucracy than as a warm, loving, Christian community. As a result, parishes often become parochial, like isolated cells in the body of the diocesan church. Such parochialism is, of course, detrimental both to the parish and to the diocesan church.

While remaining in doctrinal communion with the diocesan church, a council can still be *primarily* decision-making. At least four reasons can be listed. *First,* the council, as explained in Chapter 4, is a true Christian partnership. If its members are not partners in the decision-making process, they can hardly be called partners at all.

Second, the Spirit is in the church, i.e., the whole people of God. And no one can, in advance, restrict the Spirit's activity to legal categories like advising and decision-making. The Spirit is one. He will not be divided up. He is present and active in the church and in the council according to the measure of faith. He is not present as only advice-giver in one part of the church and as only decision-maker in another.

Third, all the faithful, in virtue of baptism, share in the priestly, prophetic and kingly mission of Christ. Sharing in the church's apostolate is *not* a participation in the apostolate of the hierarchy, but in the apostolate of Jesus Christ. Such participation is part of Christian life as such and it cannot be reduced to giving advice.

Fourth, the laity in our country are conditioned by democracy and participative decision-making. Many have considerable experience in the shared decision-making of corporation boards and modern management systems. If they are reduced to the level of mere advice-givers on their council, they will soon be "too busy" to run for election. Their time is too valuable to waste at meetings which have no power to make real decisions.

It should be clear from all the above that it's impossible to define precisely, in bylaws or constitution, what is merely advisory and what is decision-making. The whole matter is too complex to be reduced in legal fashion to an either/or category. The church is mystery. And so is the Christian community. Many grey areas will remain.

Suffice it to say, that the grey areas need to be discussed and resolved on a case by case basis in an atmosphere of trust, prayer, study and discernment. If a council does not first become a true Christian community, no constitution, however precise, will be any help.

As councils grow and develop, there will be less and less emphasis on the either/or approach to decision-making. The either/or dilemma is a problem created by a preconciliar, legalist mentality. The more councils begin to see themselves as primarily faith communities, the more they will trust and use the consensus decision-making process (Chapter 10). Then the divisive, either/or debate will, thanks be to God, subside and vanish into history.

In present practice, however, the pastor, as delegate of the diocesan church, often ratifies the council's decisions. Since ratification is in the name of the diocese, it should be an explicit and distinct act. It should not be done by silence alone.

One should not assume that ratification is the pastor's responsibility alone. For all members share in the parish's responsibility to maintain doctrinal communion with the diocesan church. For this reason, the whole council should be sensitive to what can, and what cannot, be ratified. Then it will never recommend that beer and pizza replace wine and bread in the liturgy.

The pastor is the official representative of the diocesan church. It is only natural, therefore, that he serve as ratifier of council decisions. One should not assume that the power to ratify goes with ordination. With the growing shortage of priests, bishops may soon appoint lay pastors as administrators of parishes. Such lay persons may then represent the diocese and may serve as ratifiers of the council decisions.

In the normal course of events, withholding ratification will be rare. This is especially true if the council uses consensus decision-making. If a pastor or lay administrator feels he/she

cannot ratify a council decision, he needs to explain his reasons
to the full council. After hearing the reasons, and after further
discussion, the council can, by two-thirds vote, appeal to the
appropriate diocesan office or committee to resolve the dispute.
This process of appeal is further explained in Chapter 14.

It hardly needs saying that the pastor cannot give up the
power of ratification without giving up the pastoral office itself.
He may not abdicate his responsibility in a false move toward
equality. The council is not meant to bring about a grand leveling of all the members. It is meant to support all the diverse gifts
and ministries, including the unique ministry of the pastor.

If each council member sees him/herself as having a unique
ministry, it is a waste of time and energy to argue about who
has the most authority or whose voice carries the most "weight."
The "amount" of authority will depend on each person's gift
and on the issue being discussed. On an educational issue, the
gift of the teacher may have the most authority. On a family
issue, the gift of the mother of a family may have the most
authority. On a farm issue, the gift of the farm worker may
have the most authority, etc.

For the foreseeable future, the unique ministry of the pastor,
in the model just described, will probably be in tension with the
concept of shared ministry as outlined in Chapter 4. There are
no simple formulas for resolving that tension. In actual practice, pastors and council members may have to deal with that
tension on a day to day basis.

Tension is, of course, a sign of life and growth. Both pastor
and council members need to accept this tension with a positive
attitude, praying and hoping that the Spirit will use it to give
birth to new forms of ministry both for the pastor and for
council members.

The Pastor's Ministry of Leadership

As new ministries converge in the council, the pastor needs
to adjust his pastoral role. He needs to evaluate his own ministry and its relationship to these new ministries. The parish
council is an excellent, experimental laboratory for reflecting
on the new directions in the pastor's ministry.

Today's pastor can be grateful that the Spirit is superabundant in his gifts. Ministries are "bustin' out all over." A new

Pentecost is indeed occurring. The Spirit continues "to equip the saints for the work of the ministry for building up the body of Christ" (Eph. 4,12). So, the pastor can relax. He doesn't have to do "everything" anymore. He can give up some of the hats he's been wearing. He never was able to wear them all anyway. But now, he doesn't even have to try. The administration committee can balance those books. Sister Joan can take that wake service over at the funeral home.

On the other hand, even through he no longer does everything himself, the pastor needs to place high priority on the ministry of presence. He will not learn to relate to other ministries unless he's present to them. Besides, by absence the pastor conveys the subtle message that his priestly ministry is really more important than the other ministries. He gives the impression that he is entitled to pull rank. The lay ministers on the council may have equally compelling reasons for being absent.

Today's pastor needs to minister in the context of accountability. Secrecy, hidden funds, arbitrary and unilateral decisions are over. The pastor is a model of trust and openness. He takes the council in his confidence. He constantly reports back to it. Whether it's closing the school or launching a building campaign, the pastor first discusses it with the council. Sometimes this open style brings the pastor into conflict with diocesan procedures. But that may be a fine opportunity for the parish to give an example to the diocese about accountability and shared ministry.

The pastor also needs to see himself in a positive and supportive relationship to the council's ministries. This means he creates an atmoshpere in which lay ministers feel free to risk, to test, their ministries. He is always available to help councilors reflect on "mistakes" and turn them into learning experiences. He affirms and encourages them.

He would do well, in this connection, to practice the principle of subsidiarity. He could model a decision-reaching process whereby issues are dealt with and policies are established at the lowest level of responsibility and competence. Thus, he could encourage the education committee really to deal with the educational issues, rather than allowing them to "spill into" the meetings of the parish council. In this way, the committee's ministries would grow toward maturity, because they would be encouraged to exercise real responsibility.

He has to be aware, too, that councils, like growing children, "will go through phases of contrariness in order to acquire their own personalities."[8] They may indeed take a stand against him and everything he says just to assert their own individuality and their own new found authority. They are going through a period of adolescence. They'll grow out of it. In the meantime, the pastor has to be patient and not take the council's opposition personally. He has to realize that it takes time to train leaders. But that's his job—training leaders who can assume responsibilities without being dependent on himself. When he has completed his task, the Lord will call him elsewhere to begin the same task all over again.

The pastor needs to challenge the councilors to adopt a broader vision of the church and its mission in the world. Lay councilors tend to concentrate on *their* school, *their* C.C.D. program, *their* bingo, *their* athletic program, *their* parish. So the pastor delivers the council from its parochialism and opens it to the diocese, to the church and to the world. Then, too, he needs to be vulnerable to be ministered to. He needs to be seen as a man who is human enough to own his real needs and failings and to be accepting of the ministry of others. He can't walk on water. He needs to *receive* as well as give. That's what shared ministry is all about.

The pastor is called to build an atmosphere of faith and prayer. And that means more than "saying a prayer" before and after the meeting. In times of conflict the pastor can interject: "Could we all pray about this matter for a few minutes?" Or: "Let's see what the gospel has to say about this."

It's easy for councilors to get lost in financial and administrative details. The pastor, by guiding the preparation of the agenda and by appropriate questions during the meeting, can lead the councilors to reflect on the issues in the light of faith. Christian ministry, after all, flows out of faith and prayer.

It's in the context of faith and prayer that the pastor serves as a minister of healing and reconciliation. During the beverage break and before and after meetings, the pastor listens to the councilors' hurts and gripes. He makes room for different opinions in a pluralist church. When discussion generates more heat than light, he leads the way in reconciling the dispute. The ministry of reconciliation is not limited to the words of sacramental absolution.

As new ministries emerge, the pastor needs to be on guard that he doesn't spread his sacramental ministry, as a wide umbrella, over all the other ministries. Historically, the ordained ministry tends to overwhelm and absorb all the other ministries. Rather than being the master of the ministries, he is merely one among many of the Spirit's enablers of ministries. He should not assume that his cultic ministry is so sacred that he is exempt from the questioning and challenging process that goes on during the meetings. He has to remember that he is not one *over* many but one *among* many. The pastor's ministry, like all ministry, is always in need of feedback and evaluation. He needs to build a climate which makes it easy for councilors to offer that feedback.

The pastor also needs to hold up high ideals for the councilors. Since all ministry is for the public good and in the name of church, he can require that councilors be adequately prepared and that they meet certain standards of performance. The bus driver and airline pilot have to pass examinations and possess certain qualifications. They must have good physical and mental health. They need to know the rules of the road or of the sky. Only then are they allowed to "minister" transportation to the public.

All *public* ministry, whether ordained or not, requires faith, skill, knowledge and competence. Good will isn't enough. Lay readers, deacons, pastors, councilors, and ministers of the eucharist need to be evaluated. They need to meet certain standards of performance. The needs of the common good (the People of God) have priority over the needs and desires of the individual minister. If a lector doesn't pass the test, if he doesn't read well, then he should not be allowed to minister the Word of God. For the People of God's right to hear the Word of God has priority over the lector's personal desire to serve as lector. In the same way, if a ministering councilor promotes division, if he's incompetent, or if he refuses to study the issues in the light of the gospel and the mission of the church, then he should not be allowed to minister as a councilor.

Now all this emphasis on skill and competence doesn't mean that the council is supposed to be an exclusive group of skilled and educated elite. The council must always be open to the "hidden" gifts of the Spirit given to the poorest and humblest parishioner. But it does mean that even the humblest gift may have to be formed and developed according to some standards which grow out of the discernment of the larger community. (Chapter 9 contains a list of qualifications for ministering on the council.)

The pastor has a difficult leadership role because he shares in a special way in the prophetic mission of Christ. Sometimes the pastor must offer the service of "brotherly against." This means he may have to take a stand against the community he leads.[9] He has to challenge it to obey the gospel even if it means giving up his pastoral office or his life. He has to confront the conscience of his council on racial and sexual discrimination, on its insensitivity to poverty, world hunger, social justice, etc.

In these areas, the pastor's prophetic ministry will be all the more difficult in view of the empirical evidence (Andrew Greeley) that the majority of American Catholics reject the right of the church to teach them both on sexual and social morality. The pastor is not a man who merely responds, in political fashion, to the likes and dislikes of his parishioners. He serves their *real* needs precisely by remaining faithful to the often unpopular and painful demands of the gospel and of the church.

In today's church, the pastor may need to improve his leadership skills by learning a lesson from group dynamics and from management theory. Chris Agris of the Labor and Management Center of Yale University, after studying the leadership qualities of many higher executives, believes that they rate high in these characteristics:

1) Do not "blow up"--or sulk--when things don't go as hoped. Can hold feelings in check without interfering with ability to work. Able to work enthusiastically for some long-range goal.

2) In reaching decisions, they welcome participation by others rather than insisting on the acceptance of their

own ideas. "A man of decision" comes to mean a man who leads others to reach a decision.

3) Look for mistakes in their own methods of thinking, but do not become upset over all blunders. Try to understand their own prejudices better than most people.

4) Enter into the competition without a feeling of hostility. Can take hostility shown them without indulging in self-pity.

5) Can take hostility from others without trying to get even with the instigator. Let the other person know that they realize what he is up to, but do it without showing personal hatred.

6) A setback on one goal does not cause them to give up on other goals.[10]

Today, more than ever, pastors and all ordained ministers may need to internalize the truth that the *ministry of enablement* is one of their primary ministries. This form of ministery is described rather well by James Fenhagen. It's a ministry which gives top priority to the following four values:

1) It is more important for the ordained ministers in a congregation to enable others to identify and carry out their ministries than to do it themselves.

2) Recruiting persons for ministry is only half the task. Without consistent and ongoing support--the hard follow-through--enablement will not take place.

3) Interdependence is preferable to dependence.

4) The greatest gift a pastor has to give to another is not the right answer but the authenticity of his or her own search.[11]

Now finally, here are some brief practical applications for the pastor and the council:

1) If a voting system is used, the pastor should be a voting member of the council. This follows from his dual role on the council, as explained in this chapter.

2) The pastor should not identify his role with ratifying or non-ratifying the council's recommendations. He should not narrow his ministry to one function.

3) If the council develops a conflict and becomes split into two factions, the pastor has to be careful he doesn't become identified with one faction (liberal?) or the other (conservative?). If he does, he'll lose his power to reconcile the two factions. He has to keep enough distance so that neither side can claim him in order to prove the rightness of their position against the other. He has to remain free enough and "objective" enough to minister healing and reconciliation to *both* sides.

4) The pastor has to be careful he doesn't present the diocese, the diocesan office or "downtown," as the "bad guy." In virtue of his unifying ministry, it's his special responsibility to build up positive feelings between the diocesan church and the council. He's not doing much to foster unity, for instance, when he introduces a diocesan program by saying: "Now I don't like this anymore than you do, but the diocese says we have to do it (stewardship, liturgical changes), so we better do it." Speaking and acting as if there is a conflict between the diocesan church and the parish doesn't build up the church, either diocese or parish. Then, too, if the diocesan church loses its credibility because of negative image-making, it will not be able to offer a mediating ministry when the council needs outside help to reconcile a dispute.

5) Finally, the pastor needs to be on guard lest he foster competitive spirit between "his" council and those of neighboring parishes. He may be doing just that when he says: "We've got the best council in town," or "We're way ahead of all the other councils in the diocese." Such remarks are often not based on actual knowledge of the neighboring councils. But more importantly, they foster the notion that "his" council has nothing to learn from the neighboring councils. They build a spirit of competition rather than cooperation.

Now that we have a clearer understanding of the unique ministry of the pastor, we can move on to outline the ministries of the various council committees.

Footnotes

1. *Documents of the Christian Church,* Henry Bettenson, ed. (New York: Oxford University Press, 1943), pp. 93-94.

2. W. Telfer, *The Office of Bishop* (London: Darton, Longman & Todd, 1962), p. 202.

3. Ibid., p. 204.

4. "Pastor-Parish Council Collaboration," *The Priest,* 33 (Feb. 1977), p. 20.

5. *The Shape of the Church to Come* (New York: Seabury Press, 1974), p. 121.

6. *The Coming of the Third Church* (New York: Orbis Books, 1977), p. 178.

7. *Your Parish Council* (Fort Worth, Texas: Diocese of Fort Worth, n.d.), p. 17.

8. *The Coming of the Third Church,* p. 273.

9. E. Schillebeeckx, "The Catholic Understanding of Office," *Theological Studies,* 30 (December, 1969), p. 572.

10. *Parish Council, Diocesan Guidelines* (Pittsburgh, Penn.: Diocese of Pittsburgh, 1972), p. 20.

11. *Mutual Ministry* (New York: The Seabury Press, 1977), p. 105.

Chapter 7

The Mission of the Parish and its Council

As mentioned in the introduction to the previous chapter, councils in the past ten years have often concentrated on budgets, maintenance, and "running the plant." The minutes of the meetings show that councils devoted most of their time to the crisis of the moment. There's little evidence of long-range, pastoral planning regarding the mission of the parish.

Bishop Frank Rodimer, the former chancellor of the diocese of Paterson, N.J., reports the results of a brief survey of 21 councils in his diocese.[1] He asked: "What major issues did the council deal with last year?" A summary of the responses reveals the following:

Finances 12
Property maintenance 11
Social Life calendar 4
Religious Education Program 3
Liturgy 3
Community or social programs 2
Census 1
Spiritual Renewal 1
Communications (Newsletter) 1

No doubt many priests will agree with Bishop Rodimer's conclusion: "In some ways we're still off track." The question is, how do we get on the right track? If councils don't deal with finances what should they deal with? What should be on the agenda? What should the councilors' ministry be ministering? What kinds of committees should councils have? In brief, what is the mission and ministry of the council?

Once a council knows where it's supposed to go, it will be easier to decide how to get there. Once a family knows it's going to Florida, it knows it has to fix the camper, gas up the car, get permission to take the kids out of school, etc. Once a goal has been determined, the specific tasks fall into place.

To determine its goal or mission, the council needs to ask two very basic questions: What is a Christian community called *to be*? What is it called *to do*? Once these two questions have been answered, the council will be ready for a third, viz., What committee system should be set up to carry out the mission of the parish? This chapter will discuss the first two questions. The next chapter will take up the third.

Of course, one ought not to assume that the Christian community will discharge its responsibilities to the world only through "churchy" activities like parish councils. The greatest challenge to the Christian usually comes in his/her daily life in the civic and secular society. In a sense, it's the main business of the council to get the People of God "out of the church" and into the world where Christian witness is needed most. The parish council is only one of many ways in which the Christian shares in the mission of Christ. It may not be the best way for everyone. And, as a form of Christian ministry, it may be a very temporary commitment. One ought not to assume that those who are not involved in the parish council activities are therefore not involved in Christ's mission. Whatever the *form* of involvement, however, the Christian constantly needs to ask: What does the Lord call me *to be*? What does he call me *to do*?

What is a Christian Community called to be?

The first item on the agenda of every council meeting should be: How do we become a true Christian community? A person has to *be* in good mental, physical and spiritual health before he *does* anything. So too, the council should try to become a healthy Christian community before it moves into action. "So every sound tree bears good fruit, but the bad tree bears evil fruit" (Matt. 7,17).

To be an authentic Christian community the council needs to become a true partnership (Chapter 4). To remain a member of this partnership requires an equal willingness to give and an equal willingness to receive. A true partnership doesn't exist if all the helping is going one way, in the direction of the pastor. It has to be a *communion* of services. This partnership of services is always reaching outward. It exists *not only for itself, but for the world.* Like Christ, it is always laying down its life for the world.

This Christian community, and therefore the council, is called, first of all, to be a partnership in *faith.* The council is not merely a team working together, like football coaches or a management board. It becomes a true partnership because the members are "bonded together" by a deep personal faith in Jesus/Lord. They do everything in *his name.* They believe together before they work together. The risen Lord, who unifies and reconciles, makes the partnership.

Because of their faith in the risen Lord, the members of the partnership become capable of a living, trusting, working relationship with one another. The partnership, therefore, doesn't come about: because all the members are in a negative protest, e.g., against the Protestants, against the neighboring parish, against the chancery office, etc.; or because they all submit themselves to the same law or constitution; or even because they all like and admire their pastor, Fr. Joe Smith. Paul vigorously rejects a partnership based on a personality (1 Cor. 3: 5-6). The partnership of 'a council can be based on no other foundation than faith in Jesus Christ (1 Cor. 3:11).

Second, the council, before it does anything, is called to holiness. Vatican II's *Constitution on the Church* teaches:

> The Church...is held, as a matter of faith to be unfailingly holy...Therefore, all in the Church, whether they belong to the hierarchy or are cared for by it, are called to holiness...All Christians in any state or walk of life are called to the fullness of Christian life and to the perfection of love, and by this holiness a more human manner of life is fostered also in earthly society.[2]

For Paul the church is a communion of "those sanctified in Christ Jesus, called to be saints..." (1 Cor. 1,2). As lectors the "saints" minister the holy Word of God; as "saints" they minister the holy sacrament of baptism, in emergencies; as ministers of the eucharist, they serve the holy body and blood of the Lord to the people. By their holiness of life, "the saints" are signs or "sacraments" ministering holiness to the whole parish. (More about this in Chapter 12.) So it's the business of the council to help its members to grow in holiness. If it misses that, it has missed it all.

It hardly needs saying then that a council must be a *praying* community. Bishop Rodimer's comments are pertinent: "The first thing a council must do is pray. The parish council is not a board of directors, not a blue ribbon panel, not a house of representatives...Council members are a group of people trying with the grace of God to discern the voice of the Holy Spirit, trying to be one with Christ, trying to acknowledge his presence in their midst."[3] At every meeting, therefore, the councilors need to devote some time to shared prayer. The council, if it hopes to stay on the right track, needs to be in dialogue with God, searching for his will.

The council also needs "a conversion to a sense of community, to an understanding of the parish as a community...The understanding of the church—and of the parish—as a community is not dominant or primary in most people's minds. The parish, as an institution, is—that's why most parish councils consider their main area of activities to be finances, properties and schedules."[4]

Third, the parish council, as council, is a communion of disciples. All the baptized are called to be disciples of the Lord. This is the basic Christian vocation. No one lays hold of discipleship merely by entering a certain state of life, i.e., by becoming a sister, a brother, or a priest. Discipleship is never a question of religious garb, of titles, of grades, of status, of privilege or even of the celibate state. There are no degrees of discipleship. (A priest is not more of a disciple than Sister Margaret merely because he's a priest.) All are still in the process of becoming more perfect disciples. St. Ignatius of Antioch (c. 107), looking forward to his martyrdom, writes to the Romans:

"Then shall I be truly a disciple of Jesus Christ, when the world shall not so much as see my body."

Fourth, the council is a community endowed with the common possession of the Spirit. "I will pour out my Spirit on all flesh" (Acts 2:17). Paul writes: "Now there are a variety of gifts, but the same Spirit...to each is given the manisfestation of the Spirit for the common good" (1 Cor. 12,7). In 1 Cor. 12, Paul gives a list of these gifts. Of course, Paul never intended to give a closed list of all gifts for all time. Because of the Spirit's continuing activity in the church, each parish is the fertile soil for the flowering of *new* and *diverse* ministries. They are formed partly by the faith of the community and partly by the concrete response to the local needs of the parish and the civic community. The council is called to foster, nurture and develop the gifts given "to each," both in the council and in the parish.

Fifth, if the parish council is truly carrying out the mission of Christ, it will be a community which ministers healing. In Matt. 4,24 we read: "So his fame spread throughout all Syria and they brought him all the sick, those afflicted with various diseases and pains, demoniacs, epileptics and paralytics, and he healed them." The society in which we live is geared at a hectic pace to production and consumption. It is focused more on *things* than on *people*. For this reason, many people suffer despair, mental illness, neurosis, estrangement and loneliness. The pressure of a competitive, success-oriented society drives many to sex, drugs, alcohol and suicide. In every parish and civic community, many people also suffer physical pain and sickness. They may be in clinics, hospitals, convalescent homes or in their own homes.

The parish council, as the model of a ministering community, is called to minister the healing power of Jesus/Lord—to promote life in all its richness. It is called to be a healing, humanizing community, offering warmth, acceptance and compassion to those who have fallen by the wayside in a cold, mechanical, "number" society. For example, one parish adopted a prostitute. It offered her a warm, accepting community in which she could start a new life. Three times she attempted suicide. Each time the members of the community took turns sitting by her bedside, offering care, compassion and understanding. They became the healing environment which enabled her to build a new life. All council members, therefore, are called to support a ministry to the sick, especially the poor. They can do this by visiting the sick personally. But they can also set up a committee on health care. Such a committee would be concerned, both on the state and the national level, about legislation promoting health care.

In summary, then, a council is called to be a community of disciples who, in faith and prayer, respond to the Spirit, strive for holiness and minister healing to the sick in the church and in the world. In this way, it serves as a model for what the whole parish is called to be.

What is the Christian Community called to do?

In determining the number and kinds of council committees, it is often assumed that the council must serve the needs of the parish and the community. When the council's committees are formed, they are often a response to the "need" crisis of the moment, e.g., finances. Or, they are a response to the *felt* needs of those who lobby for a particular point of view, e.g. the parish school. Thus, the committee system sometimes reflects more what *is* than *what ought to be*. Other times, it is nothing more than a reorganization of parish societies with a heavy focus on institutional needs, e.g., the members' concern for education for their children, for comfortable physical facilities, etc.

If the council is going to get on the right track, it needs an order of priority in assessing needs. Of course, the needs which relate us to God come first. Thus, we need to praise God. So the council first needs to devote itself to prayer and worship. The gospel needs to be proclaimed in word and deed. So the council needs to proclaim the gospel through some kind of evangelism. The church, and therefore the parish, needs to be catholic. Therefore, the council needs a *world* vision. The church needs to be missionary. Therefore, the council needs a missionary thrust, etc.

All these needs come before the *felt* needs of the parishioners or the needs of the various special interest groups in the parish.

For this reason, the mission of the parish and of the council must respond to: 1) God's "needs," 2) the church's needs, and 3) the people's needs. Of course, the council doesn't need to set up a special committee to respond to every need. The council as a whole can respond to some needs. And one committee can very well respond to a whole series of different needs. More about this in the next chapter.

The main point is that a committee system ought to reflect the truth first, that God's "needs" are primary, and second, that the council is concerned not only about where the parish *is*, but especially where it ought *to go*. Thus the committee system may challenge and discomfit many plant-oriented Catholics. For instance, in spite of numerous social encyclicals and bishops' pastoral letters, many Catholics can't figure out why a council should have a committee on justice and peace or social concerns. In this area, many parishioners have a need to be challenged by a specific committee even though they don't know it, and do not *feel* they need it. In view of the priority of needs explained above, the mission of the parish and its council can be described under the following ten headings:

1) *To proclaim the gospel.* The first business of the council is to herald the kerygma, i.e., to announce the Good News of salvation *to those who have not heard it.* Its first mission is to the *non-baptized* in its own territory and in the world. It is called to reach out to the vast numbers who have never really heard or seen the Jesus/Lord event. Councils might respond to this need by instituting a program or a committee on evangelism.

2) *To establish the baptized believers in the faith.* There is a constant need to deepen, to intensify the faith of those who are already baptized. The parish usually responds to this need through Sunday homilies, Catholic schools, C.C.D., family and adult education programs.

3) *To offer the liturgy of prayer, praise and thanksgiving to God.* The Christian community by definition is a "thanking" and praying people. The council is called to respond to the community's need to sing God's praises for his mighty saving deeds. The council might respond to this need by offering the

liturgy together, (perhaps in the home of the chairperson) by shared prayer during meetings and weekend retreats, or by giving high priority to a committee on worship or liturgy.

4) *To build up the Christian community.* The mystery of evil is at work until the Lord comes again. It reveals itself in the effects of original and personal sin. For this reason, sin, selfishness and factionalism tend to divide the Christian community. Building up the community means an ongoing concern about unity, reconciliation and ecumenism. The hurts, wounds, factions and divisions, both within the Christian and within the secular communities, need to be healed. As many grains of wheat become one bread, so the Christian community is always in the process of becoming one. The council, as model for the whole parish, is called to witness to the Lord's call to unity by building bonds of dialogue and prayer with members of other faiths and with the civic and secular communities.

5) *To offer diakonia or service.* The Christian community offers a threefold service to the gospel, to the Lord and to the world. The council, like Christ, is always in an attitude of self-giving. A council which is turning inward, geared primarily to preserve itself and its institutions (even its own school), is betraying its call from the Lord to lay down its life for the world. The council is called to feed the hungry, to give drink to the thirsty, to clothe the naked, to accept the sinner and to visit those in prison. The council goes especially there where the city, state and government workers do not go.

6) *To be missionary.* The Christian community is missionary by its very nature. "It is clear, therefore, that missionary activity flows immediately from the very nature of the church."[5] The parish council, again as model for the parish, is called to assume its responsibility to carry the gospel to the ends of the earth. Needless to say, this responsibility is not discharged by pitching a few bucks into the collection basket on Mission Sunday. As a segment of an orange reflects the nature of the orange, so the council must constantly reflect the nature of the church as missionary.

7) *To discern the Spirit and his many gifts.* In 1 Cor. 12:10 we see that discernment is one of the many gifts the Spirit gives to *each* believer for the common good. We can assume that the Spirit is superabundant in allotting his gifts. These gifts are given not only for the individual, but especially for the church. The gifts, therefore, become a variety of ministries. Every parish has them. They need to be discerned. This is the most challenging task of the council.

8) *To read the signs of the times in a particular time and place.* Vatican II teaches: "At all times the church carries the responsibility of reading the signs of the time and of interpreting them in the light of the gospel, if it is to carry on its task... We must be aware of and understand the aspirations, the yearnings, and the often dramatic features of the world in which we live."[6] Our age is characterized by power, wealth, violence, poverty, urbanization, interdependence, disintegration of the family, electronic communications, the alienation of youth, racial and sexual discrimination, the explosion of knowledge and the challenge of the "new" morality. These "signs of the times" change constantly. The council is living in a rapidly changing culture and society. No outsider can program the council's response in advance. To respond to the changing signs of the times, the council might institute some *ad hoc* committees. Such committees might be called youth ministry, Mexican-American ministry, family life ministry, etc. Because of the seriousness of the need in a particular time and place, such *ad hoc* committees might even become standing committees.

9) *To be a sign of the inbreaking of the kingdom of God in a particular time and place.* In a world where there is discrimination, the council is called to witness to the kingdom of God where there is neither Greek nor Gentile, neither slave nor free, neither male nor female. In a world of hate, revenge and "balance of terror" the council is called to be a sign of love. In a world of mistrust and triple locked doors, the council is called to be a sign of trust. In a world of harsh and unequal justice, the council is called to be a sign of God's forgiveness and healing mercy. In a world of creeping despair and pessimism, the coun-

cil is called to be a sign of a "new heaven and a new earth" where there is honesty and freedom, "truth and life, holiness and grace, justice, love and peace" (Preface of Christ the King). The council's service to the inbreaking of the kingdom can't be reduced to a specific committee or program. For all committees, all forms of Christian discipleship, are so many different responses to the power of the kingdom breaking into the present world. For the kingdom comes on God's terms, not man's. Visible here and there to the person of faith, it, nevertheless, remains mystery.

10) *To exercise Christian stewardship over the material goods of the parish community.* Already in the New Testament Christians were involved in financial and material affairs. Paul writes: "...I am going to Jerusalem with aid for the saints. For Macedonia and Achaia have been pleased to make some contribution for the poor among the saints at Jerusalem" (Rom. 15,26). "...and they sold their possessions and goods and distributed them to all, as any had need" (Acts 2,45). In 1 Cor. 12,28 Paul lists "administrators" among the gifts given to the body of Christ. One scripture scholar thinks Paul himself was a fulltime tentmaker and *part-time* preacher of the gospel.

In his resurrection, Jesus has redeemed and sanctified the world in its material form. All of creation, including money, is holy again. The council is called to witness to the truth that Christ has eliminated the distinction between the sacred and the profane. Just as bread, wine, water and oil are holy enough to "minister" the liturgy, so too money, buildings and properties are holy enough to "minister" the mission of the church. Those who administer the finances and properties of the community are engaged in a holy ministry. In 2 Cor. 9:12 Paul calls the collection itself a *diakonia,* i.e., a ministry.

Now that we have a clearer picture of what the Christian community is supposed to be and what it is supposed to do, it will be easier to figure out what kinds of committees the council might set up. That will be the task of the next chapter.

FOOTNOTES

1. *Origins*, Vol. 6. (May 5, 1977), p. 727.
2. "Dogmatic Constitution on the Church," in *Vatican Council II*, pp. 396-97.
3. *Origins*, Vol. 6, p. 728.
4. Ibid.
5. "Decree on Missions," p. 820.
6. "Church in the Modern World," p. 905.

Chapter 8

A System of Committees

At an early stage in its development, the council will have to figure out what kinds of committees it will set up to carry out the mission of the church in its parish. Of course, there isn't any standard system of committees which can simply be adopted by every parish. The committees and their specific responsibilities will be the fruit of a discernment process (Chapter 10) by each parish community. On the other hand, one would hope that, in view of the previous chapter, each council's committee system would be a real response to the call of the Lord, the demands of the gospel and the mission of the church, as well as the unique needs of the parish community. Thus, every council needs a committee on worship but every council doesn't need a committee for the Mexican-American apostolate.

In setting up its committee system, the council would often do well to look to the diocesan church. Does the diocesan pastoral council have a committee on family life? If so, the council might show its unity with the mission of the diocesan church by also setting up a committee on family life. In this way, the council could open up a two-way channel of communication between the diocese and the parish on family life. Does the diocese have an office or department on justice and peace? Then the council might also set up such a committee. In this way, the council committees would get on the diocesan mailing list and receive newsletters and materials for their own programs. At the same time, they would bring about an organic unity with the mission and priorities of the diocesan church.

Before going any further, however, it may be helpful to clarify the *terms* which describe the committee system. Some councils use *commission* to designate their four or five standing committees. They use *committee* to designate those committees which serve under the commissions. They use *subcommittee* for those committees which serve under the commission's committees. They use *ad hoc committee* to designate any committee which is set up on a temporary basis for a specific task or purpose. Often both *ad hoc* committees and subcommittees can be responsible either to the full council or to one of its standing committees or commissions. Other councils use *committee* to designate their four or five standing committees. They use *subcommittee* for any committee responsible to a standing committee. They use *ad hoc committee* as defined above. *Subcommittees* are responsible either to the full council or to a standing committee.

In this chapter and in the rest of this book, unless otherwise noted, *committee* will indicate a standing committee of the council. *Subcommittee* will indicate any committee responsible to a standing committee or to the full council. An *ad hoc committee* will be any committee set up on a temporary basis to accomplish a specific task or purpose. It can be responsible either to the full council or to a standing committee. The number and kinds of committees varies from diocese to diocese and from council to council. In general, councils rarely have less than four or more than seven. With too few, the council may miss an important aspect of the mission of the church; with too many, the mission of the council becomes too scattered and the meetings, with their numerous reports, become too long, unwieldy and cumbersome. Besides, if the meeting time is used up with long reports, the council has no time left to do its main job i.e., to plan, to think creatively about the mission of the parish.

Councils will work best if they have no less than four and no more than six committees. If more are needed, they can be set up as subcommittees reporting to one of the committees. If the council is going to carry out the mission of the church, it will need at least the following kinds of committees: 1) *Liturgy or Worship* 2) *Education* 3) *Christian Service* 4) *Administration*.

These will make up the core committee system. In partnership with the full council, they will oversee and coordinate all the other subcommittees which will have more specific responsibilites.

Since the needs and organizational patterns vary so much from parish to parish, it will be up to the individual councils to decide both the number and the kinds of committees. They also have to determine the number and kinds of subcommittees and what subcommittees relate to what committees. The council structure will work best if it is the fruit of the communal discernment of the actual needs in a specific parish, united to the larger church.

As an aid to that discernment process, this chapter offers a rather long list of possible committees. The hope is that this rich smorgasbord of options will be some help to councils who wish to set up a committee system or who wish to evaluate the one they have. Of course, each council will need to make its own selections and then decide which committees can be combined and which shall serve as *standing*, and which, as *sub*-committees. Councils are certainly not expected to adopt all the committees listed here nor to accept without change and adaptation the lists of specific responsibilities given under each committee. The list of committees with their responsibilities is offered as a thought-starter in the hope that it will assist the discernment process of the council and its committees. It's also an effort to respond to the question new councilors often ask, viz., "What are we supposed to be doing?"

It hardly needs saying that whatever committee system is adopted, it will need to be evaluated on a rather regular basis. The council has to remain open to eliminating some committees and establishing new ones as the gospel makes new demands in view of new needs. To avoid committee bureaucracy, it could eliminate one committee every time it starts a new one. The council's committee system must, therefore, be flexible and adaptable. Constitutions and bylaws should not bind the council in such a rigid system that it can't respond to floods, earthquakes, tornadoes, Vietnamese refugees, undocumented aliens, etc. No matter what committee system the council adopts, it needs to retain its policy-making role. It assigns portions or specific goals of the total parish mission to the proper committees. *Then it holds them accountable.* The committees are the working arms of the council. They do not make parish policies on their own. They only carry out the *council's* policies.

The council has to coordinate and monitor the activities of the various committees; otherwise they may soon be running off on their own, overlapping and even competing with one another. The committees need to relate to the council and through the council to one another, as arms and feet relate to the body and through the body to one another.

At the same time, the council needs to keep a good grip on its own identity as a council. Its main functions are listed in chapter 5. It needs to be careful it doesn't get caught in the activity trap, assuming that, if it has handed over its activities to the committees, it has nothing more to do. The council *as council* needs to remain sharply focused on its own main tasks—to pray, to think, to reflect, to study, to learn, to share information, to build a community of faith, to plan, to develop skills, to develop the broad policies of the parish. At least two times a year, the council should devote a whole meeting to prayer, brainstorming and planning. (No committee reports). It could well establish a planning cycle: planning in March and September; evaluating in December and May. It could devote at least one meeting a year to answer the question: who are we as council ministers? The toughest job of the council is to dream dreams, to lay out the broad vision. It would be far easier to serve on a council committee. There, the tasks are often simple and neatly defined.

Naturally, each committee should also do what the full council does, viz., set aside some meetings each year just to pray, to dream dreams, to reflect, to plan. It too can be caught in the activity trap. Church activity is not Christian just because it's church activity. Committees need to make time for the reflective spirit so that their activity will flow from an inner Christian life rather than become an obstacle to that life. Now that we understand these general principles about the role of the council and the role of the committees, we are ready to discuss the various ministries of the individual committees or subcommittees.

The Committee on Evangelism

Born Catholics often feel that evangelism and evangelization are Protestant words. To them they evoke an image of the Jehovah Witnesses going from door to door in a rather aggressive style. And Catholics will have no part of that. So, before we go any further, let's define *evangelization*. The Archdiocese of Cincinnati has published a report prepared by its task force on evangelization. The task force defines evangelization this way:

> Evangelization is any activity that seeks to permeate human society with the gospel's values. Through the power of the Holy Spirit the Good News of Jesus is proclaimed and lived, transforming individuals, communities and their structures, liberating them from sin and all that oppresses. This communication of the gospel by witness of life through word and sacrament and by service for justice and peace initiates or deepens commitment to Jesus and active membership in the Christian community.[1]

Evangelization may be a big word. But all it means is living the gospel in word and deed. And Jesus himself told us to do that: "Go into the world and preach the gospel to the whole creation" (Mark 16:15). Now, the problem is that most lay councilors figure that it's the job of the priests and missionaries to preach the gospel. They are quite ready to support the priests in *their* work but they don't feel *they* should get out there and do any evangelizing themselves. On this point, many lay councilors may have to shift gears and change their attitude. The Synod of Bishops (1974) asks *all* baptized Christians to do their part in the mission of evangelization: "Therefore, the duty to proclaim the gospel belongs to the *whole people of God,* gathered by the Holy Spirit in the church through the word of God and the eucharist. *No real Christian may absent himself* from this duty which he must carry out in keeping with his state and in communion with his pastors."[2] (Italics mine)

No doubt Pope Paul VI will be remembered in history for the many times he urgently called the whole Catholic world to evangelize: "Those who have received the Good News and who have been gathered by it into the community of salvation can and must communicate and spread it . . . Evangelizing is in fact the grace and vocation proper to the church, her deepest identity . . . Thus it is the whole church that receives the mission to evangelize and the work of *each individual* is important to the whole"[3] (Italics mine). Proclaiming the gospel is not merely a question of sending missionaries to foreign lands. Again, Pope Paul writes:

> . . . for the church it is a question not only of preaching the Gospel in even wider geographic areas or to even greater number of people, but also of affecting and *as it were upsetting,* through the power of the Gospel, mankind's criteria of judgment, determining values, points of interest, lines of thought, sources of inspiration and models of life which are in contrast with the Word of God and the plan of salvation"[4] (Italics mine).

Responding to the Synod of 1974 and to the call of Pope Paul, the American Bishops set up a committee and an office for evangelization in Washington, D.C. This committee decided that its first task would be to minister to the alienated Catholics and to the churchless in the United States. Here are just a few of its stated goals:

1) to minister to those who have never been a part of any church and to minister also to those who have become alienated from the faith they once held.

2) to invite individual dioceses and Catholic organizations, both lay and religious, to join with the American Bishops . . . to help them raise public awareness to the reality of eighty million churchless . . .

3) to provide a central service for resource materials selected from many sources as an aid to dioceses, organizations, parishes and individuals anxious to engage in this challenging aspect of the over-all mission of the Catholic community.[5] (See Resource List at the end of this chapter.)

It may be helpful to know who the bishops are talking about when they call for an apostolate to the churchless or the unchurched. Russell Hale divides the unchurched into the following types:

1) *The Anti-institutionalists.* This category includes those persons who are defectors from the church on the basis of what they perceive to be the church's preoccupation with its own self-maintenance. 2) *The Boxed-in.* These are the ones who have once been church members and have left. 3) *The Burned-out.* These feel their energies have been utterly consumed by the church. 4) *The Cop-outs.* These were never really committed to the church in the first place. 5) *The Happy Hedonists.* These feel they find fulfillment in the momentary pleasures or a succession of pleasure-satisfying activities. 6) *The Locked-out.* These are the ones who feel the churches have closed their doors against them. 7) *The Pilgrims.* These are the ones who describe their religious beliefs as in process of formation. 8) *The Publicans.* These perceive the churches to be primarily populated by Pharisees. 9) *The Scandalized.* These reject the church on the basis of the church's disunity. 10) *The True Unbelievers.* These are the atheists, agnostics, deists, rationalists, humanists and secularists. 11) *The Uncertain.* These have no reason for their lack of church affiliation.[6]

With this basic orientation to evangelization, it may be a little easier now to understand why a parish council could consider forming a committee or subcommittee on evangelism. Of course, forming such a committee doesn't relieve each individual from his/her responsibility to evangelize. Such a committee does, however, witness to the fact that the council is trying to fulfill its collective responsibility. At the same time, the very existence of the committee prods the conscience of the whole parish to assume its duty to evangelize.

Without attempting any priority in the following listing, and without intending to be in any way exhaustive, the responsibilities of the committee on evangelism can be listed as follows:

1)   Conducting a public inquiry class

2) Cooperating with the liturgy and education committees in conducting the catechumenate

3) Overseeing the apostolate to alienated Catholics and to the unchurched

4) Conducting a parish open house

5) Conducting a Day of Prayer for World Evangelization

6) Sponsoring a radio program

7) Conducting a survey of religious attitudes and affiliation

8) Training evangelizers

9) Conducting a parish census with follow-up visits

10) In conjunction with the diocesan office of communications, promoting a television apostolate

11) Evaluating the parish's religiosity and superstitious practices in the light of gospel, i.e., use of candles, medals, shrines, devotions, etc.

12) Sponsoring a mission to nonbelievers, agnostics, atheists, etc.

13) Forming small prayer groups which listen to and reflect on the gospel

14) Writing letters about gospel values to the journals of politics, economics, arts and sciences.

A committee which is really sensitive to the gospel will try constantly to discover the prime moments for evangelization. Some of these moments may be Thanksgiving Day, Christmas, Good Friday, Mother's Day and the feast of St. Patrick. Others may be death, weddings, ground breakings or tragedies in the community, such as fires, tornadoes, auto accidents, etc. It's up to this committee to discern when and where the gospel speaks to the pain and the joy, the tears and laughter of the human pilgrimage. As in the gospel itself, deeds will speak louder than words.

The Committee on Missions

Diocesan guidelines for councils rarely make provision for a committee on missions. Yet in view of Vatican II's "Decree on the Church's Missionary Activity," one could rightly expect a concrete form of missionary activity at the parish level. The "Decree" states: "Since the people of God live in communities, especially in dioceses and parishes . . . it belongs to such communities to bear witness to Christ before the nations. The grace of renewal cannot grow in communities unless each of them expands the range of its charity to the ends of the earth and has the same concern for those who are far away as it has for its own members."[7]

In another place, the same "Decree" states: "In lands which are already Christian lay people can cooperate in the work of evangelization by fostering knowledge and love of the missions in themselves and others, by encouraging vocations . . . by offering aid of any description, so that the gift of faith which they have received freely might be bestowed on others."[8]

The committee on missions will, of course, be closely related to the committee on evangelism. (In fact, in small parishes a council could well combine the two committees.) It's possible, however, to list the following distinct functions for a committee on missions:

1)   In cooperation with the diocesan office, to promote the work of the *Propagation of the Faith.*

2)   In consultation with the diocesan office or Maryknoll, to adopt a mission parish in Korea, South America, etc. In cooperation with the diocese, to adopt a poor parish in the inner city.

3) In cooperation with neighboring parishes, to sponsor a lay missionary (nurse, teacher) for the foreign missions. This can be arranged through Lay Mission Helpers, The Catholic Medical Mission Board or International Liaison (Lackawanna, N.Y.).

4) To develop lay ministries.

5) To sponsor *Bread for the World.*

6) To sponsor a parish forum on the missions with a visiting missionary.

7) To prepare publicity and a special liturgy for the annual mission week in October.

8) To oversee educational programs on the missions both in the Catholic school and in the non-school religious education programs.

9) To keep an adequate supply of current books and magazines on the missions in the parish library. Books from Orbis (Maryknoll, N.Y.) will be especially helpful.

10) To sponsor a dance or parish supper for the benefit of the missions.

The Christian Service Committee

Many diocesan council guidelines suggest the formation of a Christian Service Committee. In so doing, they are implementing the teachings of Vatican II's "Pastoral Constitution on the Church in the Modern World," the 1974 Synod of Bishops' "Declaration on Justice in the World," numerous papal encyclical and pastoral letters of the American bishops. For instance, the 1974 Synod declared: "The members of the church, as members of society, have the same right and duty to promote the common good as do other citizens . . . They should act as a leaven in the world, in their family, professional, social, cultural and political life. They must accept their responsibilities in this area under the influence of the Gospel and the teaching of the church."[9]

In 1976 the U.S. bishops declared: "As a leaven in the world, the church is called to participate in human affairs and to recognize in the poor, the afflicted and the oppressed the presence of the Lord summoning the Christian community to action."[10] In August 1974 the Bishop's Committee on Social Development and World Peace wrote: "Together in our preaching and actions, we are moved to pronounce God's judgment on the side of powerless life whether of the unborn child, of the elderly without care or security, of the overtaxed citizen, or of the poor in the barrios of Latin America."[11]

The responsibilities of the Christian Service Committee can be listed as follows:

1) Campaign for Human Development

2) Prison Reform

3) Job Discrimination

4) Welfare and Child Care

5) Drug and Alcoholism

6) Aid to the Retarded and Handicapped

7) Migrant Workers

8) Interracial Issues

9) Big Brother

10) Transportation for the Needy

11) World Hunger

12) Voter Registration

13) IMPACT — an Interfaith Legislative and Action Network

14) Senior Citizens

15) Poverty

16) Consumer Protection

17) A Balanced Look at Energy and Environmental Issues

18) Housing

19) Food Cooperatives and Credit Unions

20) Undocumented Immigrants

21) Battered Spouses

22) Health Care

23) Separated and Divorced Persons

24) Hospitality for the Newcomer

25) Human Rights

26) Visiting the sick, lonely and the shut-ins.

In most cases, this committee can work with the diocesan Office of Justice and Peace or Catholic Charities. The diocesan office may know from experience what form the local apostolate should take.

The Worship Committee

Since Vatican II, we've come to realize more clearly that the liturgy is not the property of the priest but that it belongs to the church i.e., the People of God. For this reason, it's altogether

fitting that members of the parish community share, not only
in the actual celebrations but also in their preparation. The
Sacred Congregation of Rites (1964) lays down the following
principle: "They (pastors) should take special care that members of religious associations of layfolk be instructed in the
liturgy and take an active part in it. It is the role of such associations to share more intimately in the life of the Church and
to assist pastors in organizing the liturgical life of the parish."[12]

The *General Instruction on the Roman Missal* (1970)
recommends: "It is therefore of the greatest importance that
the celebration of the Mass, the Lord's Supper, be so arranged
that everybody—ministers and people—may take their own
proper part in it . . . The best way to achieve this will be to consider the particular character and circumstances of the community, and then to organize the details of the celebration in
a way that will lead them to full active and conscious participation."[13] In another place, the same *Instruction* continues:
"The ceremonies . . . for every liturgical celebration, should be
prepared with care and the cooperation of those concerned."[14]
"Nothing should be left for a hurried last minute decision. A
well-considered and carefully prepared celebration can do
much to dispose the faithful to take their full parts in the
Mass."[15]

The responsibilities of the worship committee can be listed
as follows:

1) Liturgical studies

2) Planning for liturgical celebrations

3) Liturgical art, banners, etc.

4) Liturgies for children

5) Church architecture

6) In cooperation with the education committee, prepa-
    ration for sacraments of baptism, confirmation,
    marriage, first penance and communion

7) Lectors—selection, training and evaluation

8) Auxiliary ministers of eucharist—selection, training, and spiritual formation

9) Ushers—selection, training and evaluation

10) Choir, cantors, organist, musicians, guitarists, congregational singing

11) Altar servers

12) Offertory gifts

13) Special events, Thanksgiving Day, Mother's Day, Reconciliation, Communal Anointings

14) Home Mass Programs

15) Sacristans, altar decorations

16) Evaluation of liturgical celebrations, including homilies.

More and more parishes now have a full-time minister of the liturgy. Many parishes have discovered that the responsibilities listed above are too much for a volunteer committee. Good liturgy is no accident. It requires skill, money, talent, knowledge and competence. Since the parish is defined in terms of the altar, it is understandable that the council would give the parish liturgy high priority ". . . the liturgy is the summit toward which the activity of the church is directed: it is also the fount from which all her power flows."[16]

The Education Committee

Perhaps the most challenging task of the parish council is to define and plan the educational mission of the parish. *To Teach as Jesus Did* indicates the scope of the council's task:

"Educational needs must be clearly identified; goals and objectives must be established which are simultaneously realistic and creative; programs consistent with these needs and objectives must be designed carefully, conducted efficiently and evaluated honestly."[17] The bishops' pastoral message clearly teaches that the whole Catholic community has responsibility for the educational mission of the church:

> Under the leadership of the Ordinary (bishop) and his priests, planning and implementing the educational mission of the church must involve the entire Catholic community. Representative structures and processes should be the normative means by which the community, particularly Catholic parents, addresses fundamental questions about educational needs, objectives, programs and resources. Such structures and processes, already operating in many dioceses and parishes in the United States, should become universal.[18]

In some parishes, there has been some confusion whether the council or the school board is the official and final "representative structure" for overseeing the educational mission for the entire Catholic community. Often there has been tension between the council and the school board because in many parishes school boards came first. These boards were not disposed to "step down" in favor of the emerging parish councils which defined themselves as the top policymaking body for all parish programs and activities. In most cases, this tension has been resolved. Perhaps the best solution for this tension (at least on paper) is contained in the *Parish Council Guidelines* of the Archdiocese of Newark:

> In those parishes where a school board, religious education (CCD) board, or adult education board has been established, the board should act as a subcommittee of the parish council's Education Committee since the council should be concerned with the total educational needs of the parish. Plans and budgets of all subcommittees should be incorporated into the programs of the full Education Committee which is subject to parish council approval.

No subcommittee may act as an autonomous body: each is a member of the one body, the parish Education Committee. Once the total program is approved, however, the committee and subcommittees should freely administer their portions of the plan. Following the principle of subsidiarity, the council should not assume the role of the special subcommittees, especially in areas of professional expertise and competence.[19]

As is the case in Newark, the education committee can be divided into three subcommittees: adult education, C.C.D., and school board. The responsibilities which are listed below can be distributed to the three committees according to local needs and situations:

1) C.C.D. teachers—selection, training and evaluation

2) Preschool organization and programs

3) Recommendations for members for adult education, C.C.D. committees and board of education

4) Recruiting of catechists and substitute teachers

5) Supervision of parish library

6) Coordinate regional education programs and services to the parishes

7) Adult Education—organization and programs

8) Family centered religious education programs

9) Relationship with neighboring public school system

10) Training and spiritual formation of catechists

11) Search committee for Religious Education Director

12) Training leaders for adult education discussion groups

13) Liaison with diocesan office of education

14) Evaluation of school and all religious education programs

15) Programs for young adults/singles

16) Sponsoring parish lecture forums

17) Overseeing Newman apostolate for college students

18) Sacramental preparation programs, baptism, eucharist, etc.

The Family Life Committee

The purpose of the family life committee is to promote a holy, wholesome and Christian family life both in the parish and in the world. Vatican II often speaks of the important role of the family in the church and in society: "The mission of being the primary vital cell of society has been given to the family by God himself."[20] "The well-being of the individual person and of both human and Christian society is closely bound up with the healthy state of conjugal and family life."[21] "Christians, making full use of the times in which we live and carefully distinguishing the everlasting from the changeable should actively strive to promote the values of marriage and the family; it can be done by the witness of their own lives and by concerted action along with all men of good will."[22]

The "Decree on the Apostolate of Lay People" indicates what form this "concerted action" might take:

> Among the various works of the family apostolate the following may be listed: adopting abandoned children, showing a loving welcome to strangers,

helping with the running of schools, supporting
adolescents with advice and help, assisting engaged
couples to make a better preparation for marriage,
taking a share in catechism teaching, supporting
married people and families in a material or moral
crisis and, in the case of the aged, not only providing
them with what is indispensable but also procuring
for them a fair share of the fruits of economic
progress.[23]

The family life committee could first educate itself regarding
the Christian view of marriage and family life. Then it could
study the needs of the parish and the community. Finally, it
could set up new programs or support existing programs which
promote quality family life for all the People of God. The responsibilities of this committee can be listed as follows:

1) Marriage Encounter

2) Compiling a director of family services available in
the community

3) Arranging for foster homes for orphans and refugees

4) Programs for Catholic divorcees with children

5) Retreats for couples

6) Right to life programs

7) Christian Family Movement

8) Sex education

9) Help for widows and widowers

10) In cooperation with the liturgy committee, sponsoring
Passover suppers

11) Adoptions

12)   Outings for the elderly

13)   Marriage preparation

14)   Parents without partners

15)   Visiting sick and shut-ins

The Committee on Ecumenism

The call to participate in the work of ecumenism has been issued many times by both popes and bishops. This call is especially urgent in the U.S. where we have numerous "churches" and where, especially since Vatican II, conditions for ecumenical cooperation have become more favorable. Vatican II set the tone for the Catholics' involvement in ecumenism: "There can be no ecumenism worthy of the name without interior conversion . . . St. John has testified: 'If we say we have not sinned we make him a liar, and his word is not in us' (1 Jn. 1:10). This holds good for sins against unity. Thus, in humble prayer we beg pardon of God and of our separated brethren just as we forgive them that offend us."[24] "Christ summons the church, as she goes on her pilgrim way, to that continual reformation of which she always has need insofar as she is an institution of men here on earth."[25]

Vatican II urges all Catholics to share in the church's ecumenical activity:

> The sacred Council exhorts, therefore, all the Catholic faithful to recognize the signs of the times and to take an active and intelligent part in the work of ecumenism . . . In ecumenical work, Catholics must assuredly be concerned for their separated brethren, praying for them, keeping them informed about the church, *making the first approaches toward them.* But their primary duty is to make a careful and honest appraisal of whatever needs to be renewed and done in the Catholic household itself, in order that its life may bear witness more clearly and faithfully to the teachings and institutions which have been handed down from Christ through the apostles"[26] (Italics mine).

Vatican II also lists some possible areas of cooperation in common Christian concerns:

> Cooperation among Christians . . . should contribute to a just appreciation of the dignity of the human person, to the promotion of the blessings of peace, the application of Gospel principles to social life and the advancement of the arts and sciences in a truly Christian spirit. It should use every possible means to relieve the afflictions of our times, such as famine and natural disasters, illiteracy, poverty, lack of housing, and the unequal distribution of wealth.[27]

In may 1967 Rome issued a *Directory Concerning Ecumenical Matters.* It calls for the establishment of a council, commission or secretariat either for several dioceses or "in each diocese, charged to promote ecumenical activity . . ."[28] Some of its duties are listed as follows:

1) Put into practice, according to local situations, the decisions of Vatican II on ecumenical affairs.

2) Promote friendliness, cooperation and charity between Catholics and their brothers who are not in their communion.

3) Initiate and guide dialogue with them.

4) Cooperate in such areas as education, morality, social and cultural matters, learning and the arts.

Naturally, the ecumenical cooperation needs to be given concrete form at the diocesan and parish levels. The diocese of Worcester, Mass. in its parish council handbook, recommends the following activities for its council committee on ecumenism:

1) Open house and tour of the parish during which belief and practices can be informally discussed

2) Group visits to other churches, including synagogues

3) Ecumenical supper

4) Seder or Passover dinner with members of neighboring synagogue, including a Jewish speaker

5) Ecumenical Dialogue or study groups

6) Informational programs on religious customs i.e., Holy Days, dietary laws, etc.

7) Women participating in Church Women United

8) Cooperate with neighborhood churches and synagogues in establishing an ecumenical library with books, periodicals of an ecumenical nature and interest.

9) Participate in local conferences sponsored by church groups such as Y.M.C.A., Y.W.C.A.

10) May Fellowship Day

11) Membership in Ministerial Associations

12) Prayer in Common on special occasions such as:

    a) Thanksgiving Day

    b) Bible Vigils for Christian Unity; for peace, in time of public need; in time of mourning for a public official

    c) Week of Prayer for Christian Unity in January

    d) World Day of Prayer

    e) Private prayer groups

The Communications Committee

Vatican II issued its "Decree on the Means of Social Communication" Dec. 4, 1963. As a follow-up on that "Decree", Pope Paul VI issued a *Pastoral Instruction on the means of Social Communication* on Jan. 29, 1971. The Foreword to this *Instruction* declares:

> The unity and advancement of men living in society: these are the chief aims of social communication and of all the means it uses. These means include the press, the cinema, radio and television. The constant improvement in the media puts them at the disposal of more and more people who in their daily lives make increasing use of them. More than ever before, the way men live and think is profoundly affected by the means of communication. The church sees these media as 'gifts of God' which, in accordance with his providential design, unite men in brotherhood and so help them to cooperate with his plan for salvation.[29] "A proper use of the means of social communication is the responsibility of the entire People of God."[30]
> "The People of God . . . commit themselves . . . to give support to the initiatives of men of goodwill everywhere, so that the means of social communication may be used for justice, peace, freedom and human progress."[31]

The purpose of the communications committee is threefold:

1) To establish and maintain communication systems and media for the dissemination of information about issues and programs of concern to the parish and the various communities it serves;

2) To assist parish organizations in promoting and publicizing programs;

3) To develop and implement special projects and programs designed to build community within the parish, and otherwise foster enthusiasm and good will.

The responsibilities of the communications committee can be listed as follows:

1) To identify the communication needs of the parish

2) To determine communication goals, objectives and priorities that will enable the parish to fulfill its mission

3) To prepare, and periodically publish information about council activities, e.g., agenda, highlights of minutes, etc.

4) To assist council committees and other parish organizations in publicizing their activities and promoting their programs

5) To develop good working relationships with local radio, television and newspapers (including the diocesan paper) and to inform them of newsworthy parish activities

6) To provide information on issues and events affecting the community

7) To provide a means for parishioners to voice their concerns or otherwise bring their suggestions and ideas to the parish council

8) To periodically survey the composition, attitudes and concerns of the parish in order that the council may effectively plan its goals, objectives and priorities

9) To work with the diocesan office of communications in the use of radio and T.V.[32]

10) To evaluate the parish bulletin and make recommendations for improvement

11) To organize a telephone committee to notify parishioners regarding special events

12) To keep an up-to-date calendar of civic and parish
     events.

The Administration Committee

This committee offers the service of administration to the
council and to the parish community. As mentioned earlier,
administering is one of the ministries given to the church by the
Spirit for the common good (1 Cor. 12:28). Like the rest of the
committees, the administration committee is accountable to
the full council. And it has no more authority than the other
committees. While it prepares the budget, it does not approve
it. Only the full council can do that. Nor does the administration committee determine parish priorities. That too, is reserved to the full council. (It's no secret that the administration
or financial committee tends to become the tail that wags the
dog.) This committee's main service is to support all the other
committees to see that they have the money, the personnel and
facilities they need.

The administration committee is concerned with parish
resources, parish budget, parish support and the effective use
and maintenance of parish facilities. It's often divided into
three subcommittees: finance, maintenance, and development.
The following responsibilities can be listed for each of the
three subcommittees:

1) *Finance:*
    a) In cooperation with the other committees, to prepare
        and present an annual budget for both operating and
        capital expenditures based upon the goals and objec-
        tives determined by the entire parish council. This
        approved budget is published and made available to all
        parishioners.
    b) To periodically review income and expenditures to
        determine if the parish is operating within the approved
        budget.
    c) To provide parishioners with periodic (quarterly, semi-
        annual, or annual) reports on the financial position of
        the parish.
    d) To approve financial statements for submission to the
        chancery

e) To assist parish council committees and subcommittees in preparing and submitting annual budgets

f) To study parish revenue and make recommendations to the parish council for maintaining or increasing revenues to meet parish objectives and priorities.

g) To educate parishioners to the need for church support

h) To coordinate all fund-raising programs such as pledges, raffles, bingo, socials, campaign for human development, mission appeal, catholic relief services, annual diocesan appeal, etc.

i) To coordinate parish business and financial activities with the Diocesan Office of Finance or Office of Administration

j) To establish a program of job classification and salary administration for all employees of the parish

k) To review and approve all banking arrangements, capital expenditures and long term contracts.

2) *Maintenance:*

a) To periodically inspect all parish properties and review and recommend additions or repairs according to the priorities established by the committee

b) To prepare an inventory of all parish equipment, furnishings and facilities along with a schedule of replacement or servicing

c) To prepare guidelines concerning use of parish facilities, lighting, security, heat and janitorial needs

d) To procure qualified engineers or professionals for maintenance and custodial personnel

e) To develop teams of parishioners, skilled and unskilled, who will donate time and talents for parish maintenance tasks

f) To promote economical preventive maintenance practices concerning parish grounds and facilities

g) To study parish needs for heat, lighting, and air conditioning with the aim of conserving energy

h) To check whether rental and leasing of parish buildings complies with the laws of the state and the diocese.

3) *Planning:*

This subcommittee is primarily concerned with the long-range planning for the financial and physical needs of the parish and the use of its building facilities. Its specific functions are:

a) To inspect all parish properties periodically, evaluate current needs and plan for future requirements

b) To analyze the feasibility of financial investments, purchase of land, new building projects and the sale or rental of land and buildings

c) To study the insurance needs of the parish and make recommendations to the parish council, with special reference to diocesan insurance policies

d) To inspect the facilities annually for fire, safety and security hazards

e) In consultation with the diocesan building commission, to review plans for new buildings, to present alternatives, etc.

f) To recommend to the parish council necessary maintenance personnel and services for the parish properties

g) To work closely with the finance and maintenance subcommittees and other committees of the parish council to adequately plan for and care for the needs of the parish.

As mentioned earlier, the finance committee has to be careful it doesn't become the dominant committee on the council. Ordinarily, it should not get more time on the council agenda than other committees. The annual approval of the parish budget is, of course, an exception. Once a council has set up its committee system it will be easier for the parishioners to run for election. They will have a much clearer picture of what it is they are getting into. They will have a better idea about how their particular skills and talents fit into the council system. And that's one of the purposes of election—to fit the skills and charisms of the parishioners to the various parts of the council's task in carrying out the mission of the parish. It's time, therefore, to move on and figure out how the council will select its members to do the job.

Footnotes

1. Archdiocese of Cincinnati. *Witness to Christ, Report of the Task Force on Evangelization* (Cincinnati: March 27, 1977), p.3.

2. "Declaration on Evangelization," *The Catholic Mind*, Vol. 73 (1975), p. 53.

3. U.S. Catholic Conference, "On Evangelization in the Modern World," (Washington, D.C.), pp. 12-13.

4. Ibid., p. 16.

5. Bishops' Ad Hoc Committee on Evangelization, "The National Conference of Catholic Bishops Welcomes You" (Washington, D.C.), n.p.

6. *Who are the Unchurched?* (Washington, D.C.: Glenmary Research Center), pp. 38-44.

7. "Decree on the Church's Missionary Activity," *Vatican Council II.* op. cit., pp. 850-51.

8. Ibid., pp. 854-55.

9. *Justice in the World* (Washington, D.C.: National Conference of Catholic Bishops), p. 43.

10. *People on the Move* (Washington, D.C.: National Conference of Catholic Bishops), p. 2.

11. "Development" (Washington, D.C.: National Conference of Catholic Bishops), p. 6.

12. "Instruction on the Proper Implementation of the Constitution on the Sacred Liturgy," *Vatican Council II*, op. cit., p. 50.

13. Ibid., p. 162.

14. Ibid., p. 183.

15. Ibid., p. 199.

16. "The Constitution on the Sacred Liturgy," op. cit. p. 6.

17. "To Teach as Jesus Did: A Pastoral Message on Catholic Education" (Washington, D.C.: U.S.C.C./N.C.C.B. Publications, 1972), p. 38.

18. Ibid.

19. *Parish Council Guidelines* (Newark, N.J.: Archdiocese of Newark), p. 22.

20. "Decree on the Apostolate of Lay People," op cit., p. 779.

21. "The Church in the Modern World," op cit., p. 949.

22. Ibid., p. 957.

23. Op. cit, p. 779.

24. "Decree on Ecumenism," op. cit., p. 460.

25. Ibid., p. 459.

26. Ibid., p. 457-58.

27. Ibid., p. 463.

28. *Vatican Council II.* op. cit. p. 484.

29. Ibid., p. 293.

30. Ibid., p. 294.

31. Ibid., p. 325.

32. *Parish Council Guidelines,* Archdiocese of Newark, p. 32.

Resources

Anyone in pastoral work knows that there are almost too many excellent sources for helpful materials to aid people in various church ministries. Because publishers' lists continue to grow and change with their continuing publishing schedules, it is impossible to list all the helpful sources here. Thus, we have selected several publications and publishing companies providing constant updating and a continuous flow of new material to help parish council members, committee people, parish staff, and the clergy. Although the Bible is not listed specifically, it is hoped that each council member owns and uses a Bible regularly. It is also presumed that council and commission members be provided with the continuing education materials needed for their tasks such as personal subscriptions to magazines or periodicals relating to their ministry. Helpful leads for good material may be found in the bibliography of sources consulted in the writing of this book. These titles are listed prior to the Index. Diocesan offices frequently publish their own resource materials, especially in the area of liturgy. Many dioceses provide resource lists in the areas of Christian service, education, family life, evangelization and liturgy.

Basic Sources

A single source book which is basic for all people in parish ministry is
Documents of Vatican II, edited by Austin P. Flannery. Available from Costello Publishing Company, Box 9, Northport, N.Y. 11768 and Wm. B. Eerdmans Publishing Co., 255 Jefferson Ave., S.E., Grand Rapids, Mich. 49502. Over 1000 pages, this paperback contains a new translation of the Conciliar documents plus Post Conciliar papers and commentaries. The appendix and index readily lead the reader to the desired section of the book for background reading for such ministries as worship, education, family life, ecumenism, communications, administration, evangelization, missions, Christian service, etc.

For resource lists and catalogs of publications covering all phases of church ministry and "official documents and statements", write
Publications Office, United States Catholic Conference, 1312 Mass. Ave., N.W., Washington, D.C. 20005 and *Publications Service of the Canadian Council of Catholic Bishops,* 90 Parent Avenue, Ottawa, Ont. KIN 7BI Canada.

Magazines and Periodicals

Aim (Aids in Ministry), J.S. Paluch Co., 1800 West Winnemac Ave., Chicago, IL 60640.
Published quarterly. Contains material based on the liturgical year, lectionary readings, music advice, articles. Helpful for worship committees.

Bread for the World, 207 East 16th St., New York, N.Y. 10003.
Monthly newsletter containing information about world food issues and organization aids to raise consciousness on the local level. Of great service to social action committees.

Catechist, 2451 E. River Road, Dayton, OH 45439.

Published eight times a year. Features short articles on catechetics for teachers of all grades. Reviews of current materials and advertising from other publishers included. Bulk discounts available.

Ecumenical Trends, Graymoor, Garrison, N.Y. 10524.

Published monthly. Documents news and developments of interest for people in inter-Church activities.

The Living Light, 11 Park Place, New York, N.Y. 10007.

Published quarterly as the official publication of the Dept. of Education of the U.S. Catholic Conference. Provides a professional forum for reporting on research, identifying problems and issues in religious education and pastoral action. Includes book reviews and advertising.

Liturgy, The Liturgical Conference, 810 Rhode Island Ave., N.E., Washington, D.C. 20018.

Published bimonthly. Includes prophetic articles on liturgy and church worship events, art, music, dance, etc. as well as book reviews and news and notes.

Marriage and Family Living, Abbey Press, St. Meinrad,IN 47577.

Monthly magazine of help to family life committee members and staff engaged in marriage preparation and counselling. Articles, columns, reviews and advertising all relating to marriage and family life.

Modern Liturgy, Resource Publications, 7291 Coronado Drive, San Jose, CA 95129.

Published eight times a year. Contains articles of great help to worship committees, musicians, liturgists, in general. Review columns and advertising included.

Momentum, NCEA, Suite 350, One Dupont Circle, Washington, D.C. 20036.

Published quarterly. Contains articles of help to catechists and teachers in Catholic schools. Some book reviews are included.

National Bulletin on the Liturgy, Canadian Conference of Catholic Bishops, 90 Parent Ave., Ottawa, Ont. KIN 7BI.

Published five times a year. Usually devoted to themes so that each issue becomes a resource handbook for various committees in the parish. Excellent material and generous resource/review section. Basic for liturgy committees.

Network, 1029 Vermont Ave., N.W. Washington, D.C. 20005.

Quarterly journal and newsletter communicating what is happening in Congress on select areas of legislation. Network is a religious lobby working for social justice through legislation. Informative and helpful for social action committees.

Parish, 545 Island Road, Ramsey, N.J. 07446.

A bimonthly report of ideas and initiatives for parish staffs sponsored by the Catholic Bishops of the U.S. to encourage the kind of parish life envisioned by Vatican II.

Pastoral Music, National Association of Pastoral Musicians, 1029 Vermont Ave., N.W., Washington, D.C. 20005.

Published six times a year. Of great help to people involved in the music ministry. Includes articles, features, music, reviews and advertising.

Religion Teacher's Journal, P.O. Box 180, West Mystic, CT 06388.

Published eight times a year. Includes articles designed to help parish and school catechists teaching from early grades to adult level groups. Review columns cover books, audiovisuals, and catechetical aids. Advertising from other publishers included. This magazine is a mainstay support system for volunteer and professional religion teachers. Bulk discounts available.

Religious Education, 409 Prospect St., New Haven, CT 06510.

Published six times a year. Presents articles seeking to improve religious and moral education by authors from

Jewish, Catholic, Eastern Orthodox and Protestant traditions. A good guide for parish staff professionals.

Sojourners, 1309 L St., N.W. Washington, D.C. 20005.
Published monthly. Written for Christians who are breaking free from political conformity and spiritual lukewarmness. Gets to the heart of the biblical message and the core of the world's agenda. Excellent and inspiring articles and information for members of social action and community life committees.

Today's Parish, P.O. Box 180, West Mystic, CT 06388.
Published eight times a year. Contains parish staff section for parish administrators, parish council question and answer column, feature articles on success stories. current book reviews and advertising from other publishers. A basic "continuing education support system" for all council and committee members. Available in bulk rates.

Worship, The Liturgical Press, Collegeville, MN 56321.
Published six times a year and concerned with the problems of liturgical renewal. Includes book reviews and lists current workshops and liturgy training opportunities.

Audio-Visual

Parish Council Series, Parish Council Services, Archdiocese of Chicago, 155 East Superior Street, Chicago, IL 60611.
Created in cooperation with the Catholic Television Network of Chicago, this series of four half-hour *video cassettes* filmed on location in Chicago offers a helpful training program for parish council members. Program I: "Why Parish Councils?"; Program II: "So What's a Pastor?"; Program III: "Why Me, Lord?"; Program IV: "Organizing for Effectiveness." Available singly or packaged as a four-part unit. Study guide includes discussion leads and thoughts for group leaders.

(All other audio-visuals such as films, filmstrips, and teaching aids are available from publishers most of whom are listed in the key address list below.)

Key Addresses

The following list includes publishers of parish council materials, liturgical, catechetical, family life, social action, mission, evangelization, stewardship aids, etc. Each of these has brochures or catalogs available with their present and new listings. Not included here but not to be overlooked are the archdiocesan and diocesan publication offices where many valuable materials may be obtained. (Several addresses for these sources are listed following Chapter 14.)

Abbey Press
St. Meinrad, IN 47577

Abingdon Press
201 Eighth Ave., South,
Nashville, TN 37207

Alba House Communications
Canfield, OH 44406

Argus Communications
7440 Natchez Ave.,
Niles, IL 60648

Ave Maria Press
Notre Dame, IN 46556

Benziger, Bruce and Glencoe, Ind.
Ventura Blvd.,
Encino, CA 91316

Wm. C. Brown Co.,
2460 Kerper Blvd.,
Dubuque, IA 52001

Claretian Publications
221 W. Madison St.,
Chicago, IL 60606

Copyright Sharing Corporation
Box 3738 Olympic Station
Beverly Hills, CA 90210

Costello Publishing Co.
Box 9,
Northport, N.Y. 11768

Divine Word Publications
Techny, IL 60082

Wm. B. Eerdmans Pub. Co.
255 Jefferson Ave., S.E.
Grand Rapids, MI 49502

Epoch Universal Publications—
  NALR
2110 West Peoria Ave.
Phoenix, Arizona 85029

Franciscan Herald Press
1434 W. 51st St.,
Chicago, IL 60609

Fortress Press
2900 Queen Lane
Philadelphia, PA 19129

Hi-Time Publishers, Inc.
P.O. Box 7337,
Milwaukee, WI 53213

Ikonographics, Inc.
P.O. Box 4454,
Louisville, KY 40204

Thomas Klise Co.,
Box 3418,
Peoria, IL 61614

Liguori Publications
One Liguori Road,
Liguori, MO 63057

Liturgical Conference
810 Rhode Island Ave., N.E.
Washington, D.C. 20018

The Liturgical Press
St. John's Abbey
Collegeville, MN 56321

Modern Liturgy Bookstore
P.O. Box 444
Saratoga, CA 95070

National Assn. Church Business
Administrators
P.O. Box 7181
Kansas City, MO 64113

National Catholic Educational
Association
1 Dupont Circle-Suite 350
Washington, D.C. 20036

National Catholic Reporter
Cassettes
P.O. Box 281,
Kansas City, MO 64141

National Catholic Stewardship
Council
1234 Mass. Ave., N.W.
Washington, D.C. 20005

National Catholic News Service
1312 Mass. Ave., N.W.
Washington, D.C. 20005

Orbis Books
Maryknoll, N.Y. 10545

Our Sunday Visitor
Huntington, IN 46750

J.S. Paluch Co.,
1800 West Winnemac Ave.,
Chicago, IL 60640

Parish Evaluation Project
1307 S. Wabash Ave.,
Chicago, IL 60605

Pastoral Arts Associates of
North America
4744 West Country Gables Drive
Glendale, AZ 88306

Paulist Press
545 Island Road
Ramsey, N.J. 07446

Paulist Office for Evangelization
3031 4th St., N.W.,
Washington, D.C. 20017

Peter Li, Inc.
2451 E. River Road, Suite 200
Dayton, OH 45439

Publications Service
Canadian Catholic Conference
90 Parent Avenue
Ottawa, Ont. KIN 7BI

Publications Office, USCC
1312 Mass. Ave., N.W.
Washington, D.C. 20005

Pueblo Publishing Co.
1860 Broadway
New York, N.Y. 10023

ROA Films
1696 N. Astor St.
Milwaukee, WI 53202

W.H. Sadlier, Inc.
11 Park Place
New York, N.Y. 10007

St. Anthony Messenger Press
1615 Republic St.
Cincinnati, OH 45210

St. Mary's College Press
Winona, MN 55987

The Seabury Press, Inc.
815 Second Avenue
New York, N.Y. 10017

Servant Publications
237 N. Michigan St.
South Bend, IN 46601

Silver Burdett
250 James Street
Morristown, N.J. 07960

Teleketics
1229 South Santee St.
Los Angeles, CA 90015

Twenty-Third Publications
P.O. Box 180
West Mystic, CT 06388

Winston Press
430 Oak Grove
Minneapolis, MN 55403

World Library Publications, Ind.
5040 N. Ravenwood
Chicago, IL 60640

Worldwide Marriage Encounter
3711 Long Beach Blvd.
Long Beach, CA 90807

Chapter 9

Selection of Members

Once a year most parish councils elect new members. Sometimes they appoint a special elections or nominations committee to serve on an *ad hoc* basis. Other times one of the
standing committees, such as communications, is given this
added responsibility. Whatever system is adopted, elections
of new members is a serious and important event for the whole
parish. The word *election* has a heavy political connotation.
It brings with it visions of kissing babies, campaign speeches
and partisan debate between opposing candidates. While
election may be a good word to describe an important aspect
of democracy in action, it's hardly the best word to describe
that Spirit-inspired process whereby a Christian community
discerns who is gifted with the ministry of the leadership for
the parish council.

In the Christian community, it might be better to talk about
selection. When a Christian community chooses its leaders,
it is indeed involved in process of spiritual discernment. It's a
discernment which takes place, first of all, in a context of
prayer for light and guidance from the Spirit. It also takes
place in a context of certain spiritual criteria. In the first
selection process, in Acts 6:3, the apostles lay down the following criteria: ". . . pick out from among your own number seven
men of *good repute full of the Spirit and of wisdom . . .*" (Italics
mine). "To be of good repute" means that the community
respects them for their public Christian witness in their daily
life. Since ministry in the church is by its very nature a public
function, the public needs to have a high regard for the minister

even *before* he/she is selected. The phrase "full of the Spirit and of wisdom," clearly recalls Nb. 27:18: "Yahweh answered Moses, 'Take Joshua, son of Nun, a man in whom the spirit dwells . . . give him a share in your authority, so that the whole community of the sons of Israel may obey him."

The first requirement, then, is that those selected for the council be people of deep faith who are responsive to the Spirit and his wisdom. They will be people who are more concerned about God's will than their own. That is the quality that needs to be discerned in a spirit of prayer and reflection. In Acts 13:2 the Spirit selects Barnabas and Saul while the church of Antioch is "worshipping the Lord and fasting." Since service on the council is a true public ministry, the ministers need to meet certain criteria for ministering in and to the church. It's not enough that they are articulate spokespersons for a particular faction in the parish. Nor is it enough that they represent a particular point of view, i.e., liberal, conservative; for or against the pastor, etc. Nor yet, is it enough that they are persons of good will who are willing to run. The process of selection and discernment may mean that the elections or nominations committee *selects* some who are in fact *not* willing to run.

God called some men to be prophets even when they were unwilling. Jeremiah protested to God: "Ah, Lord Yahweh, look, I do not know how to speak; I am a child!" (Jer. 1:6). And Isaiah objected: "I am a man of unclean lips." And Jonah was so unwilling to serve that he "decided to run away from Yahweh" (Jon. 1:3). But God chose them all anyway. St. Augustine (430 a.d.) didn't want to be bishop. But after he got the approval of the people and the neighboring bishops, he gave his consent. St. Ambrose (397 a.d.) didn't want to be bishop, either. But the people of Milan shouted: "Let Ambrose be our bishop." Ambrose, feeling afraid and unworthy, fled the city by night. But eventually he agreed to serve as bishop. In view of the history of both prophets and saints, it's at least possible that those who are *un*willing to run may actually be the best candidates for the council. Of course, such candidates, through prayer and dialogue, would have to arrive at a point where they can accept their call to serve before actually running for election. A councilor who *remains unwilling* and then sits on the council because "Father asked him" will do more harm .than good.

The pastor, as a member of the elections or nominating committee, should not hesitate to actively recruit candidates for the council. After all, if God is going to call an unwilling parishioner to minister on the council, he may very well do so through the pastor's gift of discernment. If the pastor is practicing the pastoral principles explained in chapter 6, he will know who will and who will not make a good candidate for the council. Of course such candidates would still be submitted to a process of discernment in the elections or nominations committee.

The process of discernment asks if the prospective candidate is a person of faith and prayer. Is he/she in step with the changing church? Is he/she concerned about all the people? Is he/she more concerned about the demands of the gospel and the needs of the church than about a particular pressure group? The discernment which selects candidates for the council operates on two levels: first, in the elections committee which *screens* and *discerns* the prospective candidates; second, in the discerning vote by the people.

It may be helpful to outline the whole selection process. It has five basic steps: 1) *preparation of the people,* 2) *nominations,* 3) *getting to know the candidates,* 4) *selection by the people* and, 5) *installation of new members.* Let's take these five steps in order:

1)   Preparation of the people:
   a)   Plan a time table of three months
   b)   Use pulpit, bulletin, special inserts, and visual aids
   c)   Explain the role and purpose of the council in the parish
   d)   Publish and distribute copies of council constitution
   e)   Distribute copies of election procedures (from the constitution)
   f)   Hold public, parish forums, preferably in parishioners' homes on a regional basis. These meetings will find out how the people feel about the council and how it is dealing with parish problems.
   g)   Distribute a summary report on the council's past activities

h) Stagger elections on a two or three-year rotation basis so that not more than one-half or one-third of the council is elected each year.

2) Nominating Procedure:

Before discussing the actual process of nominations and elections, it may be helpful to discuss the relationship between the *representative* and the *functional* principles. People are concerned about the representative principle when they say: "We need a black nominee to represent the blacks, a youth to represent the youth, a senior citizen to represent the senior citizens." People are concerned about the functional principle when they say they need a teacher, to serve on the education committee, an accountant, to serve on the finance committee, a liturgist, to serve on the liturgy committee. Conditioned as they are by democracy, councils often place too much emphasis on the representative principle, to the detriment of the functional principle. A good mix of age, sex and color may seem very democratic and very representative. But it doesn't mean the council has enough skill, talent, knowledge and expertise to effectively carry out the *functions* of the parish. If the parish has a mission in education, the council needs members, of whatever sex, age or color, who have skill and knowledge in the area of education. If the parish has a mission to promote Christian family life, it needs members who have knowledge and experience in Christian family life.

In determining who will offer the *best* ministry on the council, the primary question is: can the members of the council do the job the council is called to do? Age, sex and color do not, by themselves, contribute to the council's skill, knowledge or competence in carrying out the mission of the church. It's worthy of note that Paul in his three lists of gifts and ministries which build up the body of Christ (1 Cor. 12, Eph. 4, Rms. 12), lists only functions, i.e., healers, helpers, teachers, administrators, etc. Nowhere does he mention age, sex or color. The assumption is that all the ministries listed are given by the Spirit according to the *measure of faith,* not according to age, sex or color. Paul's church gets built up by upbuilding *functions.* It doesn't get built up merely because representatives from various castes, classes, factions or pressure groups have come together.

Adequate representation, however, is still important in putting together a council. But representation in a Christian community is based not on any historical form of democracy, but on the Pauline principle that the manifestation of the spirit "is given to each" (1 Cor. 12:7). For this reason the council cannot discriminate against any groups in the parish. And, therefore, adequate representation of age, sex and color remains important, not to be democratic, but to witness to the biblical truth that the Spirit is given to all the baptized. In selecting members for the council, however, the functional principle is primary; representation, while still important, is secondary. Often the two principles can be combined in the same person, i.e., a black councilor can be an accountant, an Indian can be an educator, etc.

The elections committee itself should have broad representation. It should be composed of members who are thoroughly familiar with the workings of the council and with the people of the parish. On the other hand, it shouldn't be an inner circle or parish clique which invites candidates from it's own narrow circle of friends. It's especially important that the pastor be a member of the elections committee. He may have information of a confidential nature which may eliminate a particular candidate. If he's on the nominating committee, his input will be available at an early stage. It will save the committee the embarrassment of eliminating a candidate after he has agreed to run.

The elections committee, therefore, has two functions—*to screen* and *to select*. Both are functions of discernment. In exercising its screening function, the elections committee will do well to agree in advance on a list of qualifications. Since service on the council is a public ministry, the committee can indeed insist on certain minimum qualifications. As mentioned in an earlier chapter, doctors, pilots, bus drivers who are licensed to offer a service to the public, must have certain qualifications.

A list of qualifications will also help the elections committee to be more objective. It will keep the committee from playing favorites or being arbitrary in making its selections. The list of qualifications should, of course, be kept to a minimum. It should also allow for a very flexible interpretation. The council should definitely not become the exclusive preserve of an educated elite. The following list of qualifications may be some help to the elections committee's discernment process:

1) Age—16 or over

2) Believing, praying Christian

3) Active, registered member of the parish

4) Adequate knowledge about the parish and its tasks

5) Desire to serve the church

6) Desire to unify and reconcile the whole parish and the community

7) Commitment to attend a weekend workshop, or its equivalent, to prepare for ministry on the council

8) Willingness to devote considerable time and effort to meetings and committee work

9) Acceptance of the teachings of Vatican II

10) Good reputation and moral character.

The second function of the nominations committee is to select prospective candidates. The committee should consider the following steps:

a) Select some nominees from existing council committees to insure continuity. Ask council committees themselves to recommend names.
b) Select some nominees who have specific skills, i.e., accountants, educators, liturgists, musicians, etc.

c) Invite all parishioners, preferably in groups, to submit nominees in accordance with published elections procedures.

d) Encourage parishioners to nominate themselves.

e) Ask the pastor to review the list of nominees at an early date. He may have information about a nominee's reputation or moral character which will eliminate him/her before his/her name gets on the final list.

f) Obtain nominees' consent in writing.

g) Insist on nominees' commitment to attend a weekend workshop, or its equivalent, as preparation for service on the council. They might even be asked to sign a *commitment to service,* if elected.

h) Be sensitive to the need for adequate representation from both geographical areas and from different groups, such as women, youth, senior citizens, etc.

i) Avoid cliques both on the council and on the nominating committee.

j) Invite diocesan director of the parish council office, if there is one, to meet with the candidates to share his/her insights regarding diocesan structures and services.

k) Invite nominees to express their concerns and their reasons for offering their service to the council.

Some councils ask candidates to run for a specific committee. Then they print their ballots accordingly. (See appendix II) Other councils ask candidates simply to run for the council. Then, when elections are over, the executive committee or the full council, after dialoguing with the new councilors about their special gifts, talents and interests, appoints them to serve on a specific committee. Both systems seem to work. The main point to remember is that each new councilor should end up on the committee which will provide maximum opportunity for him/her to exercise his/her unique ministry. Even at-large councilors should be encouraged to serve on a specific committee; otherwise they will soon lose interest in the council.

3) Getting to know the Candidates:

In large parishes especially, it's important that people get to know the candidates. Since the people's vote will be a form of discernment, the parishioners need to know who is gifted with the most useful ministry to build up the parish community. It won't do to vote merely out of friendship or because the candidate has a familiar ethnic name. To help the parishioners to get to know the candidates the elections committee could consider the following:

a) Print special bulletin insert with resumes of all candidates. Resumes should be limited to 75 words or less and include name, address and phone number, areas of concern and interest, past activities in parish and community, recent picture, brief statement regarding the service the candidate expects to contribute to the parish as a council member.

b) Conduct meet-your-candidate sessions. These may be held before or after all the Masses, in parish hall, and/or in neighborhood meetings.

4) Selection:

At election time, the election committee could consider the following:

a) Celebrate special liturgy on the discernment of gifts and the call to service in the church.

b) Provide plenty of opportunity to vote.

c) With proper explanation, invite parishioners to vote before or after Sunday liturgy: "On one occasion, while they were engaged in the liturgy of the Lord and were fasting, the Holy Spirit spoke to them: 'Set apart Barnabas and Saul for me to do the work for which I have called them;" (Acts 13,2).

d) Print clear, simple ballots, listing candidates by committee, with different colors for different geographical areas. (For sample ballots, see Appendix II and III at end of this chapter).

e) Mail ballots to all registered parishioners. That way they will have more time to think about their selections.

f) Do not allow any nominees to count ballots.

After elections it may be necessary for the pastor, *after consulting the full council,* to appoint one or two members to the council. This can happen when the council is lacking in sufficient representation, (not enough women) or in expertise (no educator). More about that in chapter 14. In any case, *at least half* the council should be elected by the parishioners.

5) Installation Ceremony:
Since service on the council is a public ministry, it is fitting that there be a public installation ceremony. It is common practice to have a ceremony (sometimes with the bishop) to install lectors, C.C.D. teachers and ministers of the eucharist. Besides, every new mayor, no matter how small the city, goes through some kind of swearing-in ceremony. In the same way, some brief installation ceremony for newly elected council *ministers* is entirely appropriate. In preparing for the installation ceremony, the election committee could consider the following:

a) Discuss the reasons for an installation ceremony with the new members.
b) Invite their input in planning the ceremony.
c) Plan installation ceremony with the Sunday liturgy.
d) The ceremony itself could include the following elements:
   1) thanks and *certificate of appreciation* to all outgoing members
   2) thanks to all those who ran for election
   3) announcement of the winning candidates
   4) installation ceremony (See Appendix I at end of this chapter)
   5) conferral of certificate for ministry on new members (See Appendix V)
   6) reception with refreshments in the parish hall.

Once councilors have been selected and installed, it will probably be time to go to the first meeting. Naturally they will hope the meetings will be a successful and satisfying experience. But successful meetings don't just happen. They have to be planned. The next chapter, therefore, will offer some pointers on how to plan efficient and satisfying meetings.

Appendix I

Installation of New Parish Councilors

Since the parish council is a ministry of service for the entire parish, the installation of new councilors should take place at a Sunday Mass, with members of the parish present. The ceremony outlined below may serve as a help in planning such an installation. It assumes that each council will change and adapt it to reflect its own needs and circumstances. The ceremony should include an expression of appreciation for those members who are retiring. Space in the front pews could be reserved for committee members as well, for they, too, serve important functions. To help form community and bring new councilors into the group gracefully, plan a simple breakfast to follow the liturgy for councilors and committee personnel.

A Parish Council Commissioning Ceremony

Leader: May we now ask parish council members to come before the congregation to be commissioned (installed). (Each is called by name.)

Pastor: On behalf òf this parish community of _____ , whom you have been designated to serve, and in the name of the (Arch)bishop, I commission you as parish councilors. Your sharing in responsibility in the mission of the church and in the ministry of Jesus will be joined with the efforts of others throughout this (arch)diocese, to effectively build up the body of Christ. Service to the people of God takes many forms and requires a diversity of gifts and talents, as well as a total gift of self. Christ calls us to the challenge of discipleship, to be a sign of God's Kingdom in this time and place!

Do you understand and accept the responsibility of ministry on the parish council?

Members: We do.

Pastor: Will you do your best to work for the spiritual and material welfare of the parish, our archdiocese, and ultimately the world?

Members: *We will. With the help of God, we pledge our service on this parish council, offering the gifts and talents with which God has endowed us. We ask the support and prayers of all the parishioners so that we may continue to deepen our spiritual lives and open our hearts to the Spirit.*

Congregation's Response: We accept your commitment of ministry to our parish. We thank you for your willingness to serve; may we grow together in love, faith and joy.

Pastor: God, our Creator, Redeemer and Sanctifier, bless and strengthen today these our sisters and brothers who have committed themselves to this special ministry of leadership on our parish council. Help them to be formed in your Word, sensitive to the needs of others, and reconciling in their relationships. Give them vision and courage to seek the truth and to discern your will in all matters they will be asked to consider. We ask for them the grace to fulfill their unique roles in the priestly, prophetic and kingly mission of Jesus Christ. God, please accept our prayer in the name of that same Jesus, the Lord.

All: *Amen!*

NOTE: Symbolic gestures may also be used (with explanation to congregation): Retiring council members could, as a sign of blessing and support, lay hands on the heads of new members, or pass on to them a lighted candle, to show that they are to be light for one another. The pastor might anoint the hands of the new members with blessed oil to recall their baptismal anointing and to show that they are sharing in the priesthood of Jesus Christ. The gifts of bread and wine, as well as other symbolic gifts, can be brought up by the new members of the council, representing the congregation.

Suggested readings for the liturgy: Ephesians 4:1-16; Exodus 3:10-16; John 17:20-23; Matthew 20:20-28; Col. 1:9-14; Acts 2:41-47; Luke 5:1-11; 1 Peter 2:4-10; I Cor. 1:12-31; Mark 4:3-9.

Suggested songs for the liturgy: The Spirit of God (Lucien Deiss); *All That I Am* (Sebastian Temple); *We Are the Light of the World; Of My Hands I Give To You* (Ray Repp); *Be not Afraid* (St. Louis Jesuits); *Though the Mountains may Fall* (St. Louis Jesuits).

Note: This installation ceremony is adapted, with permission, from a form suggested by the Archdiocese of Milwaukee.

Appendix II

Sample Ballot

Councils vary considerably in their election procedures because they adapt to local needs and situations. The form of the ballot, therefore, depends on the constitution and local customs. Here is a sample ballot which can be adapted to local needs:

St. Bede Parish Council Election Ballot

NOTE: VOTE FOR JUST ONE CANDIDATE FOR EACH OFFICE.

All candidates will serve a three-year term.

Polls close at 2:30 p.m. Sunday, April 29, 1979.

1. Young Adult Representative on the Parish Council (At-Large)
   - ☐ David C. Kovac
   - ☐ Sheryl S. Mills

2. Senior Citizen Representative on the Parish Council (At-Large)
   - ☐ Patrick T. Collins
   - ☐ Dorothy Corbett

3. Area 4 Representative on the Parish Council
   - ☐ Edward B. Harrington
   - ☐ Frederick H. Herveat

4. Representative to the Parish Council on the Christian Education Committee
   - ☐ Roberta Kramer
   - ☐ Jane Maczei

6. Representative to the Parish Council on the Christian Service Committee
   - ☐ Mary C. Mulhern
   - ☐ Ronald Micetic

Appendix III

Sample Ballot

PARISH COUNCIL BALLOT
YOUR VOCATION—A CALL TO SERVE
GOD'S PEOPLE
CHRISTIAN LAY LEADERS

Dear Parishioner,

The parish needs Christian leadership to help make decisions about such things as:
(a) How to spend parish monies (Administration)
(b) How to pray well (Worship)
(c) How to educate parishioners of all ages in the Catholic faith (Education)
(d) How to serve individual and community needs (Christian Service).

Christian leaders have these characteristics:
1. Their faith is alive and active.
2. Their faith in the eucharist is most important to them.
3. They are creative and energetic.
4. They are willing to give about two years of their time.
5. Their family life is such that they are free to give some of their time.
6. They are willing to take some training in how to be effective leaders.
7. They relate with people. They are not so strong-minded that they do not listen.
8. They can work as members of a team and offer support to one another.

Granted, nobody meets all these qualifications. However, given the above, please name three (3) parishioners whose opinions you most respect. Add a brief note explaining your reasons.

THE THREE (3) PARISHIONERS WHOSE OPINIONS I MOST RESPECT ARE:

1. NAME _____

   Comment:

   _____

   _____

2. NAME _____

   Comment:

   _____

   _____

3. NAME _____

   Comment:

   _____

   _____

MY AGE IN GENERAL IS:

_____ 15-17	_____ 18-23	_____ 24-34
_____ 35-44	_____ 45-54	_____ 55-64
	_____ 65 and over	

Note: This ballot is suggested for use by the parishes in the diocese of Kansas City-St. Joseph, Mo.

Appendix IV

A Parish Council Model

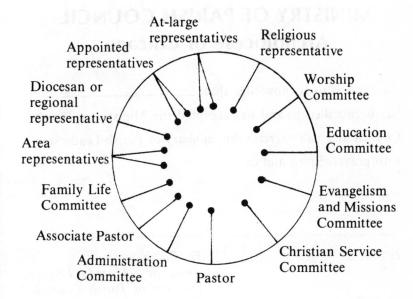

Note: This model was first published in *New Life for Parish Councils* by Twenty-Third Publications.

Appendix V

MINISTRY OF PARISH COUNCIL
Archdiocese of Chicago

This is to acknowledge that _____
has been called to and has accepted the Ministry of Parish
Council and will exercise this ministry of Parish Leadership
with prayer, Spirit and care.

_____

Pastor

_____

Date

_____

Fr. Ralph Starus
Associate to Vicar for Laity/
Director of Parish Council
Services of the Archdiocese
of Chicago

Chapter 10

Efficient and Satisfying Meetings

In this country, we like speed and efficiency. That's why McDonald's has sold over 25 billion. That's also why we pay attention to efficiency engineers and management experts. We like to "get things done." Efficiency is usually defined in terms of production. It means "the capacity to produce desired results with a minimum expenditure of energy, time, money or materials." As most people know, councils are rarely models of efficiency. They don't often get things done with a "minimum expenditure of time and energy."

Parish councils can hardly be blamed if efficiency is not their top priority. After all, Jesus wasn't all that big on efficiency. He chose poor fishermen as his first disciples. He invited conflict by choosing a tax collector (Matthew) who was working *for* Rome and a zealot (Simon) who was working *against* Rome. Besides that, he left them all to fend for themselves without by-laws, constitutions or *Robert's Rules of Order!*

Like the first disciples, councils have a different priority. They have to take time to pray, to discern the Spirit, to figure out what is God's will here and now. They have to take time to be human and more time to be Christian. And that may not get them a high rating on the efficiency scale. On the other hand, we are called to be good stewards of God's gifts (1 Cor. 4:1-2). We all have a vocation to get on with the work of the Lord. Time itself is a gift from God. We are accountable to him for its

use in his service. For these reasons I would like to offer some
pointers on how to plan and run effective council meetings.

When council meetings are over, the members sometimes
reconvene at the nearest bar. There they express their real feelings about the meeting just concluded: "What a drag!" "I
thought Carol would never shut up." "I had the feeling Father
wasn't telling the whole truth about our parish finances."
"What a waste of time." "The pits!" Councilors often feel something went wrong but they don't know what will make it go
right. They want to get something out of a meeting, but don't
know what they have to put in.

Meetings can indeed be boring. "A long-winded exchange of
mutual ignorance!" "The penance we do for our sins!" On the
other hand, they can be exciting, stimulating, productive.
Everything—well, almost everything—depends on planning
and preparation. While there is no sure-fire formula for success, meetings will be much more satisfying if both planners
and participants pay special attention to the following: 1)
motivation, 2) *preparation,* 3) *process and dynamics* and, 4)
leadership skills. Let's take them in order.

Motivation

Every council meeting, first of all, should be an experience of
faith. The council meeting is a communion of those who are
sharing and growing in their faith in the Lord. They have come
together to discern the will of God. They have gathered as disciples in their own "upper room" to make decisions in dialogue
with, and in prayerful obedience to, their Lord. They have
come to hear the call of the Lord--a call which will become concrete through prayer, dialogue and discussion.

Second, every meeting should be an experience in spiritual
growth and development. Contrary to the slogans of religious
Pelagianism and secular pragmatism, the Lord wants his disciples' love more than he wants their work. The meeting will
advance the kingdom of God only insofar as the Lord's disciples
become more effective servants. It's the Lord's holiness, working through the baptized members of his body, that will renew
the parish. It's not so much neatly designed programs as effective Christian witness which will change the face of the earth.

Every agenda needs to foster and nurture this growth in holiness; otherwise, the council meeting will be just another board meeting. (See chapter 12, "Growing in Holiness")

Third, council meetings should be a community building experience. They should be warm, pleasant, friendly. Members should know one another on a first name basis. An occasional party with wine and cheese or beer and pizza will help bring about a meeting of persons. Prayer for sick members, their wives, husbands and children, Get-well cards, visits to the hospital, celebrating the birth of a new baby or a job advancement,—all of these will go a long way in building a loving, human, Christian community. Motivation can never be taken for granted. It needs to be nurtured and recharged constantly. True commitment is always a process of recommitment. For this reason every council meeting has to pay special attention to the faith, the spiritual life and the community spirit of its members; otherwise, their motivation will wane.

Preparation

With due deference to the miraculous intervention of the Holy Spirit, meetings will succeed if they are well planned; they will fail if they are poorly planned. In general, planning a good meeting requires a careful preparation of an agenda, preparation of the physical arrangements and, of course, preparation by the committees and the individual councilors. Let's chat briefly about these four kinds of preparations.

The Agenda

The *first* step in getting ready for a meeting is the preparation of the agenda. Usually an agenda or executive committee, composed of the pastor and two or three officers of the council, prepares the agenda. Sometimes councils use the last few minutes of each meeting to prepare the agenda for the next meeting. It should never be prepared by one person alone, whether he/she be the pastor or the chairperson; otherwise, councilors will easily suspect the meeting is being manipulated through the agenda. To control the agenda is to control the meeting. It's true that committees can also control the agenda and therefore manipulate the meeting, but it's less likely. To make sure that the agenda preparation remains an open process, the chairperson could announce, now and then, that all members, indeed all parishioners, are welcome to suggest items for the agenda.

In preparing the agenda, the committee has to go through a sifting process. It has to make sure first, that only policy matters get on the agenda. There is a rather important distinction between policy and administration. A policy is a broad course of action which allows for a certain amount of personal interpretation. Thus a parish council could accept a policy to hire minority-owned businesses, whenever possible.

> This policy sets a context within which each individual decision can be made regarding the specific instance at hand. Policies cannot, and should not be written to cover every conceivable situation... Policies should be written to cover only those situations calling for major decisions. Minor decisions must be left to the discretion of the individual person responsible for that particular program.[1]

Administration, on the other hand, is concerned with technique and procedure. Often it requires the skill, training, and competence of full-time staff, such as the pastor, the director of religious education, the minister of music and maintenance personnel. It's up to them, not the council, to determine when a Mary Jones is ready for confirmation, when the parish hall needs to be painted, etc. Although it's not always easy to distinguish between policy and administration, the council needs to be aware of its proper role in the overall parish structure. It has neither the time nor, in most cases, the competence to oversee the details of administration. When it gets into administration, it is overstepping the boundaries of its authority. (The best way to lose a good janitor is to let the chairperson of the administration committee hover over his shoulder.)

Canon 1185 of the Code of Canon Law, for instance, establishes the principle that the pastor is responsible for hiring and firing the parish personnel. It's his responsibility, therefore, and not the council's to oversee and supervise their work.

That's part of his job as full-time administrator and executive of the parish. Fr. Orville Griese's comments are very much to the point:

> The basic distinction is that the parish council is a policy-making body; the administration and implementation of policies rests with the pastor and his administrative council... This is not saying that the help of the parish council cannot be enlisted in making major decisions in carrying out basic policies or in establishing important standards of procedure. Much misery will be avoided however, if the basic policy-making vs. administrative distinction is kept in mind.[2]

Second, getting back to preparation for the meeting, the agenda committee, in consultation with the full council, has to decide what should be discussed by the council and what by the individual committees. Thus, if the church roof leaks, it may be an agenda item for the administration committee, but not for the full council. If the school tuition needs to be raised, it may be an agenda item for the education committee, but not for the full council. If a prepared agenda contains picayune details, like a new carpet for the rectory, everybody will feel compelled to deliver themselves of an opinion regarding the kind and color of carpet to be purchased. Precious time, which could be devoted to serious policy matters, will be wasted. Council meetings aren't committee meetings. They should not discuss matters which are best handled either by one of the standing committees or by the full-time parish staff.

Third, the agenda should include fact sheets or an "Agenda Notebook" on the more complicated issues. (An "Agenda Notebook" contains background information on the items on the agenda.) Fact sheets should be prepared by the appropriate council committee or by the agenda committee. Thus a proposal for hiring a director of religious education, could include a brief history of the religious education program, the number of students enrolled, the number of teachers, type of training programs, the diocesan guidelines for the religious education programs, etc. Such fact sheets encourage members to prepare for the meetings and save precious time during the meetings.

Discussion will then begin with common knowledge of the pertinent facts.

Fourth, the agenda, along with the minutes of the last meeting, should be in the hands of the council at least 10 days before the meeting. Significant agenda items should also be published in the parish bulletin two weeks before the meeting, the better to engage the interest, reactions, and expertise of the whole parish. Such parish and council interaction will also increase the voter turnout at the next council elections.

The agenda should follow this general format:

1) Call to order
2) Opening prayer (Council members could take turns in preparing and leading a 10 minute prayer and scripture service.)
3) Roll call (The names of those present and absent should be listed in the minutes.)
4) Approval of minutes of previous meeting (A copy of these minutes should always be mailed with the agenda so everyone will have had ample time to read them.)
5) Comments from visitors (10 minutes)
6) Committee reports (These should be in writing so they can be filed with the council's records. They could well follow the form suggested by the diocese of Pittsburgh.[3])
7) Old business
8) New business
9) Closing hymn or prayer

It would be helpful, too, if the agenda included a brief statement of the purpose and objectives of the meeting. A clear purpose has power to motivate and generate interest. Agenda items under old and new business could have a notation indicating whether they are for:

a) Decision i.e., adopting a policy, approving a budget, etc.
b) Discussion i.e., sharing, reacting, proposing, etc.
c) Information/education i.e., reports from pastor, chairperson, etc.

Resolutions or recommendations proposed to the council could be prepared in the form suggested by the diocese of Pittsburgh.[4] Alternative recommendations should also be prepared and included with the agenda.

As soon as the council meets it's rather important that the whole council be invited to *own* its own agenda.[5] Councilors should feel free to set the priorities regarding the various items on the agenda. They should determine what topics should be taken up first, second, third, etc. They should also agree on what time the meeting is supposed to end. Just to make sure it has covered everything, the agenda committee might conclude its preparation by going over a check list like the following: Did we:

— 1.   determine purpose and definite objectives (why this meeting?)

— 2.   plan for who will report, preside or participate?

— 3.   plan what actions will be requested or what information will be given?

— 4.   set a time limit (when will meeting begin and end?)

— 5.   pre-plan in detail? (What information, material, equipment, will be needed?)

— 6.   plan what physical arrangements would be best?

— 7.   prepare for group participation by providing the necessary facts and information?

— 8.   honestly evaluate the last meeting? What changes are indicated?

— 9.   establish the responsibilities of the chairperson? Did we plan in advance who does what?

—10.   plan for adequate and effective follow-through?[6]

Physical Arrangements

When the agenda or executive committee has completed the preparation of the agenda, it may be time to check out the physical arrangements for the meeting. The physical setting should be such that it fosters and sustains a feeling of community. The room (and the chairs) should be comfortable for adults. It should create a climate for a conference meeting. If at all possible, classrooms and church halls should be avoided. Libraries and rectories should be chosen instead.

To promote better eye contact, councilors should be seated in an oblong, circular or horseshoe style (never rectangular). Only voting members should be in the circle. Visitors should have a comfortable place outside the circle. Beverages may be available before and during the meetings. Naturally, the meeting room should be well ventilated, for the health and comfort of all. The meeting room should also contain all the materials necessary for the meeting: paper, pencils, lectern, blackboard, chalk, newsprint, overhead projector, etc. It's a good idea to make a check list and go over it for every meeting. Other groups may have used the room and removed some of the equipment.

The Committees and the Councilors

If the meeting is going to be a success, all council committees will have to do their homework. They are the working arms of the council. They gather the facts. They do the necessary research. Then they discuss the issues in the light of the council's stated priorities. If the committees don't do their work or if they fail to meet, the council meetings will usually be a waste of time. Of course, the individual councilors have to do their homework too. They should prepare for the meeting by studying, consulting, and reflecting. At the minimum, they should read the fact sheets which come with the agenda. At the maximum, they should read pertinent articles in books and journals and study the resource materials available from the diocesan offices.

Next, members should consult with other parishioners, especially with those who have some expertise in the matters to be discussed. They could even go a step further and make some phone calls to get the feelings and opinions of the parishioners who have seen the agenda in the parish bulletin. Finally, the councilors should just sit and reflect. They should put together what they have read and what they have heard. Then they should reflect prayerfully on what demands the gospel is making on them and on the parish in regard to the topics on the agenda.

The Process and Dynamics

Once everybody and everything are prepared, it's time to devote some attention to the process and dynamics of the meeting. It's time to think about how the councilors relate to one another and how they actually go about getting through the business of the meeting. In spite of the best advance preparations, a meeting can still fall on its face. The style, method or atmosphere of the meeting can generate negative, hostile or passive-aggressive feelings. In other words, the meeting can go sour because the process and dynamics aren't right.

While the human and divine chemistry of any council meeting is, to some extent unpredictable, there are, nevertheless, certain principles which can be helpful in creating a healthy, wholesome satisfying climate for conducting the meeting. Let's talk about *five* of those principles, *viz., consensus decision-making, the discernment process, problem solving, conflict resolution* and *evaluation.*

Consensus Decision-making

Most councils are familiar with the parliamentary form of decision-making. In this system a simple majority rules. If a motion gets 51% of the votes, it passes. A few motions, such as unseating a member, require a two-thirds majority. The parliamentary system of voting is derived from the English Parliament. General Henry Robert incorporated that system into his famous *Robert's Rules of Order.* In use since 1915, the system is carefully explained in Article VIII of the *Revised Edition.*[7]

This system works well in minor decisions. It's probably the best way to keep some kind of order in the meetings of large assemblies. However, it's only *one* system. It may not be the best system, especially for major decisions, like closing a school. Often it divides the council into winners and losers. Even if it doesn't polarize the council, it often means the losers are not disposed to support the "other side's" decision. At best, they feel it isn't really their decision. At worst, they feel angry and frustrated. In either case, they won't jump with ecstatic enthusiasm when it's time to commit their time and energy to

implementing the decision. Many councils feel that the win-
lose syndrome, which is often a byproduct of the parliamentary
system, is inappropriate in a Christian community. Besides,
they say, there is nothing distinctively Christian about *Robert's
Rules of Order.*

In recent years, more and more councils have adopted the
consensus form of decision-making. It is a process of decision-
making in which a workable decision is reached through compromise and modification of the contribution of all council
members. Many councils feel this community way of making
decisions has a number of advantages: it puts more emphasis
on maintaining the unity of the Christian community in the
council; it gives a higher priority to persons and the growth of
the council as a community of persons; it's less rigid, less formal; it's another way of saying, contrary to tendencies in our
modern society, that people are more important than efficiency,
productivity or "getting things done;" it provides a better
forum for exercising the gift of discernment and for the emer-
gence of the prophetic voice. In 1 Cor. 12:10 it's clear that the
gifts of discernment and prophecy are given to every baptized
Christian. Decision-making systems need to be in the service of
the Spirit's gifts.

Consensus decision-making can be described in two phases:
the first deals with consensus on broad goals and objectives;
the second deals with the group process regarding specific
issues which are discussed during a particular meeting. Councils generally work toward a consensus on broad goals and
objectives during a weekend workshop. First, they arrive at a
common vision of the mission of the church both at the diocesan and at the parish levels. (This requires small group discussions and lots of blank newsprint.) They reach agreement
on the mission of the parish by working out a mission statement. Then they arrive at a common understanding about the
goals and objectives for their own parish. Goals are further
specified as long or short range. Next, the council members a-
gree on a list of parish needs and resources. Then they set objectives which respond to their needs and goals. Finally, they
agree on specific criteria and timetables for evaluating their
performance as a council in view of their stated objectives. (See
chapter 11)

The second phase of consensus decision-making concerns the process used in discussing specific issues during a council meeting. In this phase, the council should first decide whether it's going to use the consensus or the parliamentary system. In the consensus system there is no vote. Consensus is achieved when everyone can live with the decision. In actual fact no one has achieved exactly what he or she wanted. But everyone has offered input which has been taken seriously. In most cases the proposal under discussion has changed because of this input. Thus more people can identify with the final decision.

In most cases the chairperson gets a feel for consensus by listening to the discussion and by watching for signs of agreement. Sometimes he/she may have to ask a specific question: "Joe, do you feel you can go along with this decision?" Or again the chairperson, while looking at a silent member, may say: "We've agreed haven't we, that silence means consent?" If a council can't reach consensus, the chairperson is careful to define the exact area of disagreement. He/she then asks for a listing of all the reasons on the negative and all the reasons on the affirmative side. Finally he asks: "Do we have all the facts?" At this point the council may be quite willing to table the proposal to allow more time to gather additional data or to study the issues at greater length. This is especially true when a straw vote indicates the council is really divided on the issue. Generally, more facts and more time will move the council toward a compromise solution.[8]

A parish in Detroit has developed a technique for getting a feel for consensus by using a consensual value rating. It works like this: When the topic under discussion has been developed to the point of decision, all information having been surfaced and evaluated, the chairperson asks each member to indicate his/her position on the topic. Each member may choose a number from 0 to 5. This number is, in effect, their last word on the topic. *0* means "Totally not in favor of the topic." *1* means "Not in favor, but see some merit in it." *2* means "No, but I accept passage." *3* means "Yes, but I accept non-passage." *4* means "Favorable, but with some reservation." *5* means "Totally favorable toward the topic." The number-statements given by the members are added together and then divided by the total membership present. No abstentions are allowed. A total ranging from 4 to 5 (83%) is automatic passage. A total of 3 to 3.9 (43 - 83%) means an automatic tabling. A total of 0 to 2.9 (-43%) means an automatic rejection of the topic.

Granted that this process may seem a bit mechanical and far from the ideal of full and total discussion leading to final consensus, it does, nevertheless, carry with it a satisfaction and finality that is helpful to decison-making. Each councilor has said his/her word and said it both effectively and positively. All statements have a positive value, including *0* which is not a veto, but a firm statement of a differing opinion.[9]

The archdiocese of Denver has summarized the process of consensus decision-making in the following four principles:

1. *All* members of the decision-making body must contribute their ideas and feelings concerning the issues being discussed.
2. The basic condition of decision-making through consensus is the attitude of the decision-makers. When a group accepts this type of procedure they are accepting the responsibility of working in an optimistic, supportive, and informed atmosphere. Each member is expected to have done his or her homework in regard to any item which is up for a decision.
3. The objective of consensus decision-making is to work together to reach a *workable* decision which will carry the support of all those involved in that decision.
4. To enhance this process when one or several members of the group have difficulty living with a possible solution or decision, in the area where they disagree, they should be asked to give alternative solutions. The group must continually work through possible solutions and *engage in compromise to make the system work.*[10]

It would be naive to assume that the consensus system will work in every council. It's a fact that some councils simply are not *faith* communities. Others are polarized around strong personalities. Still others are being manipulated by pressure groups. In such cases, the council would do well to admit honestly where it's at and then set aside some meeting time to build up a faith community and to reflect on its internal dynamics. If the council is not at least trying to become a faith community, long discussions about decision-making techniques will be a waste of time.

The word, decison-*making,* carries with it a real danger of a misplaced emphasis. In actual practice councils spend most of their meeting time, not in decision-*making,* but in decison-*reaching.* They learn, discuss and share information. They may need four or five meetings of this kind of sharing before they reach the point of decision-*making.* The whole process of decision-*reaching* is, of course, more important than the moment of decision-*making.*

The Discernment Process

Since Vatican II we've added many new words to our Catholic vocabulary. Discernment is one of them. It's closely related to the consensus decision-making just described. Its use is indeed becoming more common in the meetings of parish councils across the country. The *diocesan guidelines* of Newark, N.J. and Columbus, Ohio, devote considerable space to an explanation of the discernment process. Both dioceses present it as an aspect of consensus decision-reaching.

Right off, let's explain what discernment is not. First, it's not a Catholic form of democracy. It's not merely a question of getting a majority vote on a difficult issue. It's not a new process for diagnosing the dominant feelings about a question being discussed. It's not a system designed to manipulate the consent of the council. Like so many of the "new" words, discernment comes right out of the New Testament. In 1 Cor. 12 Paul is talking about the spiritual gifts given by the spirit to *each* believing Christian. First, he mentions the gifts of healing, of working miracles and of prophecy; then, in verse 10, the gift of *discerning* of spirits.

The word *discernment (diacrisis)* in its literal Greek can also mean *appraisal, assessment, judgment, separation* or finally, *distinguishing,* especially between good and evil. The word, in its Old Testament sense of judgment, is used in the context of the process which reveals the will of Yahweh. In Paul's writings the use of the word is not separated from his firm belief in the omniscient God who is *the* judge and who sees man through and through. Nor, of course, is it separated from faith in the Spirit. Discernment needs to be understood in the context of the other spiritual gifts. These are all distinguished by their conformity to the Christian faith. Even though they are diverse in their operation and manifestation, all the gifts come from one divine source. They are all directed to the aim of building up the well-being of the church, i.e., The People of God. In fact, the value of the individual gifts is measured by their usefulness in building up the church. Such gifts are not always to be considered extraordinary. For Paul includes in his lists teaching, serving, helping, exhorting, administering and giving aid.

In Paul, the gift of discernment is one which enables certain members of the community to sift, as it were, the wheat from the chaff in any assessment of the mind of the church on matters pertaining to its spiritual welfare. Against the background of the unbridled religious enthusiasm of Corinth, Paul is saying that God wants his creatures to use the faculties he has given them. The use of common sense and intelligence should be ranked among such faculties. Paul is saying, further, that the gift of discernment may not be as striking as the gifts of oratory, prophecy, or speaking in tongues. But it is important, nevertheless. In the midst of all kinds of ecstatic outbursts, it's no small gift to the church when a member can disentangle his thoughts from his emotions and prejudices and *think straight*.

In its biblical meaning, therefore, the act of discernment is a participation in the process which reveals God's will on earth. It's a process in which God is the active agent, and Christians, who are humbly and prayerfully disposed, become the blessed receivers of some of the wisdom and knowledge of God. Now the tough question, of course, is: how does one recognize true discernment: The *guidelines* of the archdiocese of Newark and the diocese of Columbus tell us that there are three basic steps in the discernment process: 1) *Prayerful reflection;* 2) *Gathering data;* and 3) *Confirmation.*

During the first step, *prayful reflection,* the diocese of Columbus recommends: "The council and the entire parish community should be called upon to pray intensely for the grace of discernment. A discipline of preparation should characterize the initial stage. Times of quiet, fasting, scripture reading, setting aside personal ambitions and concerns, sacrament of penance, active listening to the truth of the Lord, should be incorporated into the parish life and the council's life."[11]

In the second step, *gathering data,* Newark suggests the following: "Careful observation of all concrete circumstances of the situation. communication with experts on the subject, and dialogue among the members of the community.

a) Communal dialogue stresses hearing each person out with respect to his/her opinion.
b) Discussion of negative factors and positive factors for the proposal would be in separate sessions. Negative and affirmative views presented at the same time could easily replace dialogue with debate and counter arguments.
c) It is necessary to examine all available data in order to achieve valid discernment.
d) The presentation of new data requires new discernment."[12]

In the third step, *confirmation,* the diocese of Columbus describes the process as follows: "When consensus seems to have emerged from the process and is characterized by an inner calm and peace among the members, that peace is identified as the gift of the Holy Spirit confirming and assuring that, indeed, God's truth has been found. At each step along the way as well as at the conclusion of the process, whoever is leading the process should seek to determine whether all members are indeed at peace with the results. If positive indication is given by the vast majority of all members, then the conclusion should be duly recorded in the council records as resulting from a discernment process of the council.

"If a consensus does not occur, then the decision will have to be arrived at in another way, or postponed until later because, for some reason, discernment was impossible. At a minimum, a communal discernment process would normally take at least a full evening to complete and could be carried on for a day or several days depending on the issues being dealt with. It should not be incorporated into an ordinary business meeting."[13]

One rather important criterion for recognizing the results of true discernment process is the feeling of peace. Paul writes in Gal. 5: 22-23: "But the spirit produces love, joy, peace, patience, kindness, goodness, faithfulness, humility and self-control." Another criterion might well be: Will the results be for the upbuilding of the church? Will the council's resolution be for the common good? "Let all things be done for upbuilding" (1 Cor. 14:26). And finally, is the resolution truly the fruit of faith, prayer and listening to the Word of the Lord?

It's not facetious to say that at times it may be necessary to have a process of discernment to find out if genuine discernment of the Spirit has occurred. After all, the conclusions of communal discernment may very well be repugnant to human nature and desire. They may challenge us to respond, even though we are unwilling, to the tough demands of the gospel. The peace of discernment is a truly *spiritual* peace which comes from a knowledge that the council is answering the call to self-sacrifice and is sharing in the difficult, prophetic mission of Christ.

Problem Solving

Councils often have to wrestle with some tough problems. Sometimes it's an internal problem growing out of the human chemistry of the council. Other times it's a parish problem, like closing the school. Still other times, the problem is that no one can figure out what the problem is. In any case, councils need to develop some skill in dealing with problems. Again, it's impossible to come up with a sure-fire system to solve all council problems. On the other hand, many experts in group dynamics have developed some common sense principles to help small groups deal with problems. Many of these principles can be used by parish councils.

The following *pointers for problem-solving* have been adapted from *T.E.T. Teacher Effectiveness Training.* They can be used by the chairperson or a special outside facilitator who has a special ministry for group dynamics and problem-solving. I have arranged them in five steps:

Step One: setting the stage

1. Make sure the time is acceptable to the council.
2. Have a pencil and paper or chalk and chalkboard.
3. Explain that the solution must be acceptable to both (or all) parties in the council.
4. Use active listening in all phases, e.g., when coming up with the proper time to discuss the problem.
5. Do not require the members to justify their ideas.
6. Begin with an "I" message. Councilors must *own* their feelings. ("I feel angry")
7. Don't let anyone introduce a *new* problem during the problem-solving process.

Step Two: defining the problem (Getting to the real needs)

1. State your need in a good "I" message.
2. Use active listening whenever feeling is expressed.
3. Don't buy "promises" that things will get better. "I'll try not to do that anymore."
4. Stand your ground that problem-solving has to be done.
5. Don't start off with *your* solution to the problem.
6. Don't start generating solutions until everyone agrees with the statement of the problem and some kind of understanding of everyone's needs. Check them out—"As I understand the problem, it is. . ."

Step Three: generating solutions

1. Try to get the councilors to offer their possible solutions first.
2. Do not judge or evaluate any solutions—even the "far out" ones.
3. Write down all the solutions offered.
4. Feel free to contribute your solutions. If they are judged immediately, say: "We'll settle that later. Right now we only want all possible solutions."
5. Offer feedback, i.e., lead the discussion.

152   The Practical Guide for Parish Councils

6. Restate the problem when things bog down.

Dealing with Conflict

After the meeting, council members often express the feelings they are afraid to express during the meeting. Such debriefing may take place at the corner bar or at the home of a member where they feel they are with friends *they can trust.* Such sessions often surface the conflicts and mistrust which are repressed during the actual meetings. Conflicts should, of course, be expected among free, thinking Christians. In the New Testament we see that the first Christian community experienced conflict. There is that famous case in Gal. 2:11 when Paul "opposed Cephas to his face" on the matter of circumcision. And Luke reports other conflicts in the early church: "This led to a disagreement and after Paul and Barnabas had had a long argument with these men it was arranged that Paul and Barnabas and others of the church should go up to Jerusalem and discuss the problem with the apostles and elders" (Acts 15:2). "Barnabas suggested taking John Mark, but Paul was not in favor of taking along the very man who had deserted them in Pamphylia and had refused to share in their work. After a violent quarrel they parted company and Barnabas sailed off with Mark to Cyprus" (Acts 15:38-39).

In A.D. 155, St. Polycarp, the bishop of Smyrna, had a disagreement with Pope Anicetus about the right date for celebrating Easter. Eusebius, an early church historian, describes the conflict:

> And when the blessed Polycarp was at Rome in the time of Anicetus, and they disagreed a little about certain other things, they immediately made peace with one another, not caring to quarrel over this matter. For neither could Anicetus persuade Polycarp. . . nor Polycarp, Anicetus. . . But though matters were in this shape, they communed together, and Anicetus conceded the adminstration of the Eucharist in the Church to Polycarp, manifestly as a mark of respect. And they parted from each other in peace.[15]

It's not unchristian, therefore, to experience conflict. Denial of conflict or refusal to deal with it, however can indeed become unchristian. Besides generating mistrust, bitterness and anger, such behavior shows a lack of faith in the Lord's reconciling power which is always at work where two or three are gathered in his name (Matt. 18:20). There can be at least five different responses to conflict:

1) We can just refuse to see it. "It's the neighbor's house that's dirty, not ours."
2) Even if we see it, we can refuse to see it as a *problem.* "After all, it's our dirt—and that makes it o.k."
3) We can see it, but refuse to take any personal responsibility. "It's *our* dirt, but not *mine.* After all, if those dumb people came around to my point of view, there wouldn't be any conflict."
4) We can see it, but decide (by doing nothing) not to deal with it, either because we don't have the nerve or because we're afraid. After all, we might get dirty in the process. We aren't ready. Our faith community is too fragile. We'll come apart at the seams. When conflict does raise its head, we take refuge in humor. (Crack a joke.) Or change the subject: "Nice weather we're having!" We feel more comfortable in clinging to the false assumption that all is lovey-dovey. "Let's give each other the handshake of peace and sing a song."
5) We can see it and honestly and courageously deal with it. We can overcome our fear and then trust in the Spirit and in one another. We can learn to disagree without becoming disagreeable. Together, we can take one giant step toward a more mature and more Christian council.

It's impossible, of course, to lay down a bunch of rules for dealing with conflict in the council. There are too many unknown and intangible factors. For instance, what is the trust level in the council? How comfortable are the members with one another? Do they often pray together? Do they share their spiritual life with one another at deep levels? Every council is a unique and mysterious chemistry of the human and the divine. The dynamics of the council, especially that of conflict, cannot be "guided" in advance by neat rules from a printed page. Nevertheless, some *general* guidelines may still be helpful. It's

up to the individual councils to use, adapt or reject them as they
see fit.

John Burns recommends the following ten principles for
dealing with conflict:

1) the parties involved must realize and indicate to themselves and to each other that a conflict is taking place
   between them.
2) each party must be brought to objectively see the nature,
   character, and implications of his position.
3) each party must be brought to objectively see the nature,
   character, and implications of the other party's position.
4) there must be a common language or set of meanings
   employed.
5) resolution must be defined by both parties as advan-
   tageous or at least acceptable.
6) the parties must interact in a mutually communicative
   way in which each can pick out clues that the other offers
   for resolving the conflict.
7) the duration and intensity of the conflict must be considered by the negotiator of a conflict if one is present.

The following points also should be considered when con-
sidering the resolution of intergroup conflicts:

8) awareness of the structure of thinking of each group relative to what each considers to be defeat and victory. On
   the personal level as well, there should be a consideration of what each party will accept in the resolution and
   still believe a sense of self-respect has been maintained.
9) there should be an understanding of the role and character of leaderhip within each group.
10) as much of a cultural understanding as possible should
    be encouraged between the parties. Differences in ways
    of viewing things or doing things by two different cul-
    tures can reenforce basic conflict situations.[16]

Naturally, no one should assume that all conflicts can be resolved. As mentioned earlier, tensions and conflict are part of
the normal life in a Christian community. Conflicts can, however, be utilized to clarify diverse points of view. They can also

deliver both the "conservatives" and the "liberals" from dogmatic absolutism in their positions. In the last analysis, councils need to learn to live with some conflict out of respect for the freedom and dignity of their fellow Christians.[17]

Evaluation

As a way of monitoring their own process and dynamics, councils should evaluate their meetings at least twice a year. This can be done by inviting an outside observer from a neighboring council to critique a typical meeting. Norman Lambert explains the role of this outside observer:

> The observer should sit outside the group, not taking part in the discussion but rather noting those things that seemed to affect the way that the group worked together at reaching (or not reaching) consensus. When the group reflects on this exercise, members can ask the observer for a complete report, or simply for his input regarding a specific issue that they might raise.
>
> The observer's role is to help the group understand its own processess of decision-making. He should be careful, therefore, to report only what he actually heard and saw, and not to interpret the behavior of any group member. Nor should he "punish" members who may have dominated the group or excluded certain other individuals from the discussion. His role is to facilitate the group's learning about itself; the members must decide what to do with the information he provides.[18]

A second way of evaluating the meeting is to use the Flow-chart Recorder. Lambert describes the system in this way:

> One member is selected to sit outside the group to record the flow of conversation. This is done by drawing a line on a chart to show the direction of the first statement each person makes—both to the group (a circle in the middle of the chart) and to another individual within the group. Remarks that follow are noted with a caret indicating the direction of the flow of conversation. A finished chart might look something like this:

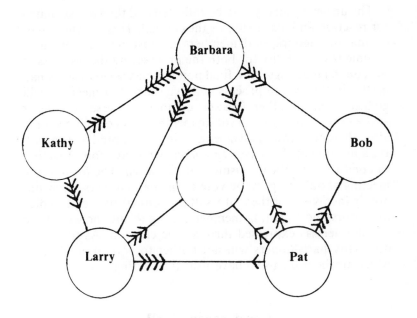

When this group has finished its task, the flowchart
recorder displays his diagram. The group immediately sees that Bob had not spoken a word during
the meeting, that Barbara seemed to dominate the
conversation, and that few members directed their
remarks to the total group. The members use this
concrete documentation of their discussion to determine possible changes in the way they operate.
Often, just seeing the lines and carets is enough to
bring about improved communication.[19]

A third way of evaluating a meeting is simply to distribute a
survey sheet to all the councilors after a typical meeting. Members should answer the following three questions:

1) What did you like best about this meeting?
2) What did you like least?
3) What suggestions do you have for improving future
   meetings?

The unsigned surveys can be collected and then redistributed for reaction and discussion by the council. This system of self-evaluation encourages all members, not just the chairperson, to assume responsibility for both the process and the progress of the council meetings. As a final point, it may seem to be a small matter in the overall process and dynamics, but meetings will go faster and smoother if visitors do not sit in the same circle or at the same table with the voting members. A council meeting, after all, is not a town hall meeting. Nor is it a grand free-for-all. It's a meeting of *duly elected members* who have come together to conduct the official business of the parish. The form of the meeting should respect the vote of the parishioners. They did not, in fact, vote for the visitors. If the council gives equal voice to visitors and to voting members, it's ignoring the will of the parishioners as expressed through the election. As time goes on, many parishioners will not bother to vote in an election which to them seems to have lost its meaning.

Leadership Skills

All council members are, of course, called to be leaders. Each councilor, however, will lead through his/her own unique gifts and skills. Each will develop a personal leadership style. While the different styles may not necessarily be right or wrong, some styles will be more effective than others. All styles can, to some extent, be improved and adapted to changing situations. But to do this, one must be aware of one's own leadership style. It may be helpful, therefore, to reflect on the leadership role of the chairperson of the council and then finally, on the possible leadership styles of the council members.

The Role of the Chairperson

The chairperson has a key role in creating a pleasant and positive atmosphere for council meetings. He/she fosters a climate of trust and openness. He shows genuine respect for the members' ideas and abilities. He is the yeast which enables the councilors to grow to their full potential as ministers in the church. To do his job well he should at least be striving for the following qualities:

1) *Spirituality*—the chairperson's relationship with Christ and appreciation of Gospel values is the keystone to his or her effectiveness in directing the activities of the parish council.
2) *Fairness*—A healthy detachment from vested interest instills trust and confidence.
3) *Ability to Unify*—the chairperson should work to bring all parish groups and factions together in harmony.
4) *Knowledge*—An understanding of the nature of church and an openness to learning are essential.
5) *Leadership*—The ability to motivate people to do their parish council tasks is vital.[20]

Much of the chairperson's work is done outside of the actual meeting. As part of his/her extra-meeting activity he/she should:

1) maintain regular contact with the pastor to insure open communications.
2) be in frequent communication with the pastoral team, committee chairpersons and other appropriate council members, encouraging them in their activities and obtaining feedback and status reports on programs and projects. Motivating committees between meetings is an important aspect of the chairperson's function.
3) see that council members make use of available resources and training programs.
4) insure that the Executive Committee meets and fulfills its functions.
5) communicate with the other officers and encourage them in the fulfillment of their tasks.
6) be personally available to parishioners to receive their input and feedback.[21]

As soon as the meeting begins, the chairperson becomes the main facilitator of the council's process. He/she has to resist the temptation to give speeches or to teach the council. He has to present proposals for discussion in an objective manner. He doesn't give his own opinion until all the other members, especially the timid, have been heard. L.H. Mouat gives the following advice to chairpersons: 1) Follow agenda; 2) Bring out pertinent matter; 3) Encourage participation; 4) Discourage disruption; 5) Try to resolve differences; 6) Bring out agreements; 7) Don't waste time; 8) Summarize from time to time.[22]

As the meeting progresses, the chairperson may find he/she is performing five distinct functions:

1) *Initiating*—Keeping the group action moving or getting it going. This may be done by reviewing progress to date, posing a problem, pointing out a goal, clarifying an issue, or proposing a procedure. The chairperson should avoid prematurely shutting off discussion.

2) *Moderating*—Influencing the tempo and flow of the group's work. This can be done by summarizing discussion, pointing out time limits, and restating goals. The chairperson walks a tightrope between controlling the group and allowing the meeting to become too loose and unorganized. In general, when a person is argumentative, off the subject, rambling, or too dominant, the discussion should be returned to the whole council.

3) *Informing*—Bringing information or authoritative opinion to the group. This should be done to be helpful, but not to prejudice the questions.

4) *Encouraging*—Creating a climate which holds the group together and makes it easier for members to contribute to work on the task. In attempting to harmonize group activities and relieve tensions, the chairperson should: *listen* with interest and show respect for all members and all opinions without judging them; *encourage* ideas and allow members to change their minds gracefully; *provide* breaks for prayer or refreshment to relieve tension or tiredness.

5) *Evaluating*—Helping the group to evaluate its decision, goals or procedures. The parish council chairperson should seek to become familiar and comfortable with the procedures of consensus making.[23]

Council meetings will, of course, bring together a wide variety of personalities. The chairperson will have to learn to deal with all of them—from the aggressive autocrat to the timid, nonassertive.[24] There are no magic formulas. The chairperson will learn and develop leadership skills in the crucible of experience during the council meetings. In dealing with the council's personalities, he/she needs to be aware that there is a distinction between a meeting which is called to conduct the official business of the parish and one which is called primarily for social purposes. Without becoming too rigid or formal, the chairperson needs to use the agenda to keep the meeting on the right track. Councilors who wish to socialize can, of course, do so after the meeting.

The chairperson also needs to be conscious of the time factor. Meetings generally should not last longer than two hours, including the time for prayer and reflection on the scriptures. If they go on longer than that, something is probably wrong with the council process, viz., no committee work, no individual preparation, lack of trust, (with consequent nitpicking), poor communication, poor group dynamics, etc. Needless to say, the chairperson will not be the actual leader at every moment of the council meeting. Leadership may, in varying degrees, pass from one councilor to another depending both on the topic being discussed and on the leadership skill of the individual councilor. For this reason, every member of the council will have an opportunity to exercise some kind of leadership. Naturally, that leadership will be more effective if the councilor is aware of his/her own leadership style.

The management experts have identified five of the most typical leadership styles. It may be helpful to describe each of them briefly:

1) *Authoritative*—The leader identifies a problem, considers alternative solutions, chooses one of them and then tells his/her followers what they are to do. He may or may not consider what he believes the group members will think or feel about the decision, but they clearly do not participate directly in the decision-making. Coercion may or may not be used or implied.

2) *Persuasive*—The leader, as before, makes the decision without consulting his/her group. Instead of simply announcing his decision, however, he tries to persuade the group members to accept it. He points out how he has considered organization goals and the interests of group members and states how the members will benefit from carrying out the decision.

3) *Evaluative*—The leader identifies a problem and proposes a tentative solution. Before finalizing it, however, he/she gets the reactions of those who will implement it. He says, in effect, "I'd like your frank reaction to this proposal, and I will then make the final decision."

4) *Participative*—The leader here gives the group members a chance to influence the decision from the beginning. He/she presents a problem and relevant background information, then asks the members for their ideas on how to solve it. In effect, the group is invited to increase the number of alternative actions to be considered. The leader then selects the solution he regards as most promising.

5) *Laissez-faire*—The leader here participates in the discussions as "just another member"—and agrees in advance to carry out whatever decision the group makes. The only limits placed on the group are those given to the leader by his/her superiors. (Many research and development teams make decisions this way).[25]

As parish councils gain more experience their meetings will surely become more efficient and satisfying. They will develop their own style, character and personalities. Each meeting will at least be another step "on the way" to becoming a unique experience of the life, love and truth, which is the heart of a genuine Christian community. While no printed page can guarantee the perfect meeting, maybe it can be a helping hand in that direction. Once councilors have learned to conduct satisfying meetings, they will be ready to tackle the larger issues. They will be ready to set the goals and policies of the parish. But that too requires skill and know-how. The next chapter, therefore, will discuss some of the essential steps in the goal-setting process.

Footnotes

1.   Norman Lambert, *Managing Church Groups* (Dayton, Ohio: Pflaum Publishing, 1975), p. 72.

2.   *The Priest*, Vol. 33 (February, 1977), p. 22.

3.   See Appendix I at end of this chapter.

4.   See Appendix II at end of this chapter.

5.   Thomas Gordon, *L.E.T. Leader Effectiveness Training* (New York: Wyden Books, 1977), p. 130.

6.   Adapted from *Leadership Conference*, NFPC (Chicago: unpublished paper).

7.   Henry Robert, *Robert's Rules of Order, Revised* (New York: William Morrow and Co., 1971), pp. 188-206.

8.   Wm. J. Rademacher, *Working with Parish Councils?* (Canfield, Ohio: Alba-books, 1976), pp. 123-24.

9.   James Trent, Unpublished Paper (July, 1978).

10.   Cyndi Thero, Unpublished Paper (1977).

11.   *Parish Council Guidelines* (Columbus, Ohio: Diocese of Columbus), p. 28.

12.   *Parish Council Guidelines*, (Newark, N.J.: Archdiocese of Newark), pp. 40-41.

13.   *Parish Council Guidelines*, (Columbus, O.) op. cit. p. 36.

14.   Thomas Gordon, T.E.T. Teacher Effectiveness Training (New York: Peter Wyden Publisher, 1974), pp. 228-233.

15.   F.J. Bacchus, *The Catholic Encyclopedia*, (New York: The Encyclopedia Press, 1913, Vol XII), p. 220.

16.   Unpublished paper, (February, 1973), p. 36.

17.   For another approach to conflict, see Appendix III.

18.   *Managing Church Groups*, op. cit. p. 22.

19.   Ibid, p. 23.

20.   *Parish Council Guidelines*, (Newark, N.J.), op. cit. p. 36.

21.   Ibid.

22.   *Planning and Running Meetings*, (San Jose, Cal.: The Sanford Publishing Co.,), p. 5.

23.   Adapted from *Parish Council Guidelines*, Newark, N.J. op. cit. p. 37.

24. See Appendix IV.

25. For more information on the various leadership styles see Douglas McGregor, *The Human Side of Enterprise,* New York: McGraw-Hill, 1960 or Norman Lambert, *Managing Church Groups.* Dayton, Ohio: Pflaum Press, 1975.

Resources

Allport, Gordon. *Becoming.* New Haven:Yale University Press, 1955.

Black, Robert and Mouton, Jane. *Group Dynamics-Key to Decision-making.* Houston, Texas: Gult Publishing Co., 1961.

Blumer, Herbert. *Human Nature and Collective Behavior.* Englewood Cliffs, N.J.: Prentice Hall, 1970.

Bradford, Leland. *Making Meetings Work.* La Jolla, California: University Associates, 1976.

Coleman, J. *Community Conflict.* New York: Free Press of Glencoe, 1956.

Fromm, Erich. *The Anatomy of Human Destructiveness.* New York: Holt, Rinehart and Winston, 1973.

Gordon, Thomas. *L.E.T. Leader Effectiveness Training.* New York: Wyden Books, 1977.

Gordon, Thomas. *T.E.T. Teacher Effectiveness Training.* New York: Peter Wyden Publisher, 1974.

Lambert, Norman. *Managing Church Groups.* Dayton, Ohio: Pflaum Publishing, 1975.

McEniry, Robert. "Parish Councils and Group Dynamics." *Pastoral life.* October, 1977.

McGregor, Douglas. *The Human Side of Enterprise.* New York: McGraw-Hill, 1960.

Maslow, Abraham. *Motivation and Personality.* New York: Harper and Row, 1970.

Mouat, L.H. *Planning and Running Meetings.* San Jose, California:Sanford Publishing Co., Inc.

Rademacher, Wm. J. *Working with Parish Councils?* Canfield, Ohio: Alba-books, 1976.

Robert, Henry. *Robert's Rules of Order, Revised.* New York: William Morrow and Company, 1971.

Schindler-Rainman, Eva and Lippitt, Ronald. *Taking Your Meetings out of the Doldrums.* La Jolla, California: University Associates, 1977.

Simmel, Georg. *Conflict.* Trs. by Kurt Wolff. New York: Free Press of Glencoe, 1955.

Appendix I

Suggested Committee Report Form
To Be Filed Regularly with the Parish Council

Committee..

Date ....

1. Programs and Policies

    (a) Under Study

    (b) Planned

    (c) Under Way

    (d) Completed

2. Problems and Needs

3. Remarks

_____

Signature of Committee Chairperson

Appendix II

Suggested Form for Resolutions

Coming from Committee to the Parish Council

Committee...................Date ....

Statement
Whereas,
Resolution
Be it resolved,

Background: statement of need or problem that gave rise to
               resolution.

Alternatives: list other alternatives considered and rejected.

Implementation: outline action plan for implementation of
                  resolution.

_____

Signature of Committee Chairperson

Parish Council Action

Rejected _____

Accepted_____

Amended _____Remarks:

Referred _____

Tabled_____

_____

Signature of Parish Council President

Appendix III

Resolving Conflict

Parish Council Office
Archdiocese of Denver

Conflict is inevitable and even valuable in human experience. The question is not to avoid conflict but to deal with it constructively. By understanding the following principles we can learn to recognize:

1) When a person needs help
2) What we do that is harmful
3) What we do that is helpful

I.   Our "success" as people is dependent upon our ability to resolve conflict.

   A.   Conflict means: to be at variance; two or more opposing viewpoints; to clash.
      1)   Conflict of perspective
      2)   Conflict of values
   B.   There are two kinds of conflicts:
      1)   Internal (Person against self)
      2)   External (Person against person)
   C.   Resolution of conflict produces growth.
      1)   Conflict is not bad and to be avoided, but rather good and to be resolved.
      2)   The success of all of us is dependent upon our ability to handle internal and external conflict.

II. We often resolve conflict in 3 ways that do us great harm.

   A.   Fighting (symptoms: physically fighting, gossiping, arguing, blaming, excusing, defending, bragging, lecturing, etc.)

B. Running (symptoms: physically running, crying, pity-ing, attacking oneself, becoming silent, etc.)

C. Ignoring (symptoms: "intellectualizing," remaining apathetic, acting unaffected)

III. These methods of resolving conflict do us great long-term damage.

A. We develop a lifestyle built around one of them.

B. We *concede control* of our lives.
   1) We fail to solve the real problem
   2) We fail to control our feelings
   3) We fail to grow

IV. Leaders, with helpful intentions, often perpetuate poor conflict resolution.

A. Fighting evokes *obedience* (so we give in); *resentment* (so we ignore); *anger* (so we fight)

B. Running evokes *guilt* (so we play up to); *resentment* (so we ignore); *pity* (so we moralize)

C. Ignoring evokes *envy* (so we pull back); *anger* (so we attack)

V. There is a constructive means of dealing with conflict: "leveling"

A. The key to leveling is developing an awareness of one's honest feelings.
   1) One must *recognize* his/her feelings: the hurt; the fear; the anger; the threat; the inferiority
   2) One must *admit* his/her feelings (verbally and physically): "I feel hurt" "I feel angry" "I feel threatened" "I feel unappreciated"
   3) One must *accept* his/her feelings as a part of him: "I feel hurt and yet I cherish myself" "I feel unloved and yet I like myself"
   4) One must concede the feelings of others
   5) We must concentrate on problem-solving behavior

    B.   That awareness grows into two personal concepts which are essential in order to resolve conflict constructively.

        1)   I am responsible for what I am and for what I become. "I can blame (run, ignore) but what will it accomplish?" "I have to take control and solve the problem if it is to be solved."

        2)   I am valuable. "I can defend (run, cry, ignore) but it won't change what I am. I love myself despite these conflicts."

VI.   Leaders can set the "leveling" climate so that councilors can resolve conflict constructively.

    A.   Recognize the methods being used by a councilor to resolve his/her conflict (fighting, running or ignoring)

    B.   Change the method to that of "leveling"

        1)   By communicating: You are responsible. You are worthwhile.

        2)   By communicating: You are valuable. (I trust you even if you make mistakes.)

Appendix IV

Parish Council Office
(Archdiocese of Denver
Denver, Colorado)

How to deal with the *autocrat:*
1. Maintain a strong personal emotional stability
2. Clarify and purify your own objectives and attitudes
3. Assume the responsibility of being the one that understands
4. Listen
5. Monitor your own verbal, non verbal and extra verbal behavior
6. Find a point of agreement
7. Tell how you feel, what you see—not what you think
8. Avoid "yes but" phrases
9. Avoid apologetic and whiney tones of voice—speak with strength
10. Stand erect
11. Ask for clarification of points
12. Consider detailed "jargon" if necessary
13. As an absolute *final* attempt—be equally direct and assertive
14. Remember—we are more emotional than rational
15. Clarify your objective
16. Develop a personal dominance
17. Keep "selling" tools sharp—help visualize
18. Be persistent
19. Accept reality—sometimes improbable if not impossible.

How to deal with the *nonassertive:*
1. Avoid being "hooked" into being the opposite (manipulative aggressive)
2. Recognize their sensitivity to directness
3. Realize their vulnerability to intimidation
4. Respect their ability to counterattack with passive aggressiveness

5. Listen—"with the third ear"
6. Tell them how you feel, what you see and not what you think
7. Monitor their feelings and responses continually
8. Strive to build their self-esteem
9. Be sincere in praise—praise often—be specific
10. Build a bank account of good will
11. Be patient
12. Believe in them
13. Be sensitive to their self-criticism
14. Understand their needs
15. Help them experience achievement
16. Avoid having your prejudices stimulated or activated.

Appendix V

Prayer to be a Better Listener

We do not really listen to each other, God, at least not all the time. Instead of true dialogue, we carry on two parallel monologues. I talk. My compainion talks. But what we are really concentrating on is how to sound good, how to make our points strongly, how to outshine the person with whom we are talking. Teach us to listen as your Son listened to everyone who spoke with him. Remind us that, somehow, you are trying to reach us through the conversation. Your truth, your love, your goodness are seeking us out in the truth, love and goodness being communicated. When our words are harsh, hostile, angry, we convey the very opposite of these qualities. Teach us to be still, Lord, that we may truly hear our brothers and sisters and in them, you. Amen.

The Christophers

N.Y., New York

Chapter 11

Goal-setting

"Where there is no vision, the people perish." That's right out of the Good Book (Prov. 29, 18). It's a bit of biblical wisdom parishes and their councils could well take to heart. The pilgrim church will come to a halt, or exhaust itself in aimless talk so long as the pilgrims don't know where they are going. Councils can show a lack of vision in at least three ways: first, by perpetuating a "churchy" parochialism, i.e., by concentrating all their energies on *their* own parish, *their* own needs, *their* own church world; second, by concentrating on buildings, i.e., *their* school, *their* church hall, *their* parking lot, etc.; third, by constantly focusing on *one* issue, however important, e.g., finances, abortion, a good education for their children, etc. A "one issue" council is actually *un*catholic. Besides, it's as boring as an uncle who never talks about anything but fishing. It's not that such councils have no feelings for the hungry masses of the third world. It's just that that other world never comes into the purview of their vision.

Chapter 6 discussed what I feel ought to be the broad vision or mission of the Christian community. Council committee systems need to reflect that broad vision. As mentioned in that chapter, a council's committee system needs to be evaluated periodically to see if it truly reflects a broad Christian vision. The present chapter is concerned about the means or the technique for implementing a broad Christian vision in a concrete way at the parish level. It assumes that each parish council, through its own process, has to internalize, concretize and implement a new Christian vision. Since both the membership of the council and the needs of the parish and society change constantly, goal-setting has to become a regular event in the parish council experience. Otherwise, the council will soon be off the track. It will run the risk of becoming an inward-turning, self-serving clique. It will be unstable and unaccountable, simply reacting to one crisis after another.

Now how does a council go about the business of goal-setting? By way of introduction, councils need to be convinced that it's possible, in a Christian community, to arrive at a consensus on certain goals which truly flow out of the Christian tradition. Naturally, councils may not canonize or absolutize these goals. Nevertheless, it's possible, by the grace of discernment, to chart a fairly clear direction for the Christian pilgrimage. To give just one example, in a related area, James Fenhagen has come up with the following seven signs of life in a Christian community:

1. Parish life is enhanced when a congregation takes seriously the communication of its biblical and theological tradition.

2. Parish life is enhanced when a congregation works at building and sustaining authentic community.

3. A critical sign of life for a congregation today would be the capacity to help people take upon themselves the discipline necessary for authentic personal and spiritual growth.

4. Parish life is enhanced when there is a clear and organized response to the redemptive activity of God in the world at large.

5. Parish life is enhanced when caring for persons is viewed and acted upon as the work of the congregation at large.

6. Parish life is enhanced when an educational environment is created which exhibits in practice what is said in word.

7. Parish life is enhanced when the experience of worship is able to gather up feelings of belonging, celebration, and awe and offer them to the glory of God.[1]

These seven signs of life could become the point of departure for an individual council's goal-setting process. At the same time, they could become the criteria against which the activities of the council and the parish could be evaluated.

Right off, it has to be said that goal-setting is not an easy task. Usually the process takes a full weekend or its equivalent. Naturally, a weekend experience, away from the parish (at a retreat house), is ideal. The goal-setting process can be described in seven steps:

1. Arriving at a consensus on a common vision of the parish community; writing a *mission statement.*

2. Discernment of needs, problems or deficiences.

3. Discernment of strengths and resources.

4. Consensus-decision on goals.

5. Consensus-decision on objectives.

6. Consensus-decision on strategies (in appropriate committees).

7. Determination of a system for evaluating the achievement or nonachievement of objectives.

Now before going any further, let's get our terms straight. A *vision* is expressed in a broad mission statement. Every parish is an organic member of the church universal which gets its mission from the Lord. Neither the church at large nor any of its parishes exist for themselves. No parish exists apart from its mission. Without repeating chapter 6, the mission of the church (and therefore its vision) includes the following five functions:

1. to proclaim the Good News of Jesus Christ.

2. to build up a community of love.

3.   to celebrate the liturgies of praise and thanksgiving.

4.   to serve others, in the name of Jesus Christ.[2]

5.   to enable all the members to grow in their relationship with God and with one another.

Each individual parish, however, needs to internalize and express its own mission in a concrete form. Since the parish council is a policy-making body, it's responsible for defining the mission of the parish. It does this by preparing a MISSION STATEMENT which is simply a *broad statement of the overall direction and purpose of the parish.* It states why the parish as a unique group exists. This mission statement "must be clear enough so that its intent is obvious, yet not so detailed that it becomes burdensome...Though the statement should be flexible enough to allow for interpretation according to current conditions and needs, it should not try to cover every conceivable situation that may arise. The mission statement must be short, clear, and understandable to all who are part of the organization."[3]

Every mission statement should answer the following four questions:

Who the parish is? For *what* (purpose)? *How* it will achieve that purpose? For *whom*?

These four questions can be used both in the actual writing of a mission statement and in testing its validity when it is completed.

Here are some examples of mission statements taken from the archdiocese of Detroit:

St. Stephen's Parish is a community of Christians under the guidance of the Holy Spirit, who, associated with other parishes of the Archdiocese and served by pastoral representative leadership, strive to provide mutual assistance in Christian life, witness, service, and worship and to promote the Kingdom of God as proclaimed in the scriptures.

St. Stephen's Parish Council
Port Huron, Michigan

St. Jude's Parish is a local group of baptized believers in the
Lordship of Christ, associated with the Bishop through his
pastoral representatives. Nourished by the sacraments, this
group proclaims Jesus and the Good News of salvation,
provides Christian education and serves the total community to bring about the Kingdom of God.

St. Jude's Parish Council
Detroit, Michigan

St. _____ Parish is a community of Christians responding to the call of Jesus under the guidance of the Holy
Spirit, who, associated with other parishes in the Archdio
cese and served by pastoral and representative leadership,
strive to serve the world by mutual assistance in Christian
life, witness, service and worship, and to prepare the Kingdom of God as proclaimed in the scriptures.

Bishop Thomas J. Gumbleton, D.D.
Archdiocese of Detroit[4]

After the full council has prepared a mission statement,
individual committees should also prepare their own mission
statements. These will, of course, flow from the broader mission
statement of the full council. Here is an example of a mission
statement of a parish maintenance committee:

The maintenance committee is responsible to the parish
council for maintaining parish grounds and buildings in a
functional and usable condition, paying particular attention
to safety requirements that minimize the possibility of in-
jury. It will set up and implement yearly inspections and
evaluations of all buildings and equipment, keep adequate
records, and make recommendations to the parish council
for repair, modification, or replacement, along with estimated costs and savings expected. It will implement and
keep adequate records of preventative maintenance programs
for all equipment and machinery being used by the parish.
The committee will submit a yearly budget that will include
regular, routine maintenance costs, estimates or major re-
placements, repairs or modifications that should be made

within that particular fiscal year, plus a recommended amount to be set aside for emergency repairs. It will base these recommendations on past records and a forecast drawn up from its regular inspection routine. Members are to utilize, wherever possible, the many resources and competencies of the parishioners in the maintenance function, and they are responsible as representatives of a Christian community to provide adequate living wages and full fringe benefits to any employees. When contracting with other organizations for services or goods, the maintenance committee will ascertain that those organizations follow fair employment practices and are equal opportunity employers. Whenever possible, they will hire and contract with minority-owned and operated businesses and service organizations.[5]

A *goal* is a clear statement of desired direction or activity in broad, general terms. It is the desired end result which is to be obtained when planning is complete. It can be a desired end state, a desired future condition or a desired norm. A goal can be defined as *long* term (5 years) or *short* term (1 or 2 years).

A goal statement has seven main characteristics:

1. It is a guide to action—stated as a desired outcome, a result, a desired condition or state of affairs.
2. It is general in its direction.
3. It is challenging, exciting, and inspiring to its participants.
4. It calls for investment and involvement by the participants.
5. It may provide a time target (2 or 5 years).
6. It is directly tied to the purposes and goals of higher units in the organization (example: diocese).
7. It can be attained through a series of objectives and strategies.[6]

Here are a few examples of *lead* words for writing goals: to discuss, to understand, to appreciate, to assure, to believe, to coordinate, to know, to improve. Here are some examples of goal statements: 1. To accept responsibility as unified Christian leaders. 2. To motivate parishioners to a new awareness of their spiritual relationship with God so they may better their own condition as well as that of their fellowmen. 3. To involve parishioners in all decision-making through varying media/ methods. 4. To establish and foster more effective means of communication among all facets of parish life.[7]

An *objective* is a specific, time-oriented, and realistic statement of *what* the council is going to do, *who* is going to do it, for *whom, when* and *how much*. Objectives are the main *intermediate results* needed to obtain a goal. A good objective has eight main characteristics:

1. It begins with the word "to" and is followed by an *action verb*.
2. It produces a *single key result* when accomplished.
3. It specifies *for* or *with whom* an action is done.
4. It has a *specific target date* for accomplishment (from three months to one year from planning date).
5. It is *quantifiable and measurable*—how much is to be done. It can be *evaluated*.
6. It is *clear and understandable* for all those participants in the action.
7. It is *realistic and attainable*—considers present and anticipated resources.
8. It helps the council achieve one or more of its stated goals.[8]

Here are a few examples of *lead* words for writing objectives: to advise, to compare, to eliminate, to write, to establish, to approve, to identify, to design. Here are some examples of objectives from the Archdiocese of Denver: 1. To establish an *ad hoc* committee to formulate a working constitution and by-laws, subject to approval by the parish council no later than December 31, 1979. 2. To sponsor for the parish a Lenten series one evening a week, two hours a night for four weeks during Lent. 3. To sponsor two general meetings a year for the parishioners in order to encourage more meaningful dialogue and accountability with the parish council. 4. To develop and administer a parish survey that defines parish needs more realistically by December 31, 1979, in order that the council will be able to meet parish needs more effectively.[9]

Here are a few more examples of objectives. These were developed by the parish council of the Church of the Resurrection, Memphis, Tennessee, on March 2, 1975:

A. *Long Range*:
   1. To have a demonstrative program, Dedication Week, reflecting the many and varied uses of our building.
       a. To have the committees submit a proposed building usage requirement by January 1, 1976.
       b. To have total community use of the building by January 1, 1976.
   2. To determine the estimated parish participation percentage at each annual workshop.
   3. To develop ecumenical relationships with two neighboring churches through a joint prayer service during the Week of Prayer for Christian Unity.

B. *Short Range*:
   1. To have each committee submit a job description prior to April 1, 1975.
   2. To have the membership committee submit a recommended Block Captain Program by the August, 1975, Parish Council meeting.
   3. To establish a sub committee of the Parish Council on the possible method of running a Time and Talent survey in 1975.
   4. To have the committee report returned with the methods available by the June, 1975 meeting.
   5. To charge the liturgical committee with submitting a one-year program for youth liturgy by the April, 1975 Parish Council meeting.
   6. To charge the youth committee to report back with their recommendations of a concrete program at the March, 1975 meeting.
   7. To charge the liturgy committee to evaluate the Youth Liturgy Program and present a one-year plan by May, 1975.

8. To establish an ecumenical committee whose first responsibility is to set up a Thanksgiving Ecumenical Service by November, 1975.
9. To discuss a Theme of the Month Program at the March, 1975 Parish Council meeting.
10. To establish a section in the Parish Bulletin for listing new members effective the first Sunday in April, 1975.
11. To have a reconciliation evening with the Parish Councils of Holy Rosary, St. John, and Holy Spirit by June, 1975.
12. To expand the Sacramental Parents Program to include Methodology by June, 1975.
13. To have a program of stewardship education initiated from the pulpit by September, 1975.

A *strategy* is one step or one specific action needed to attain an objective. A group of strategies is a plan of action spelling out how an objective will be reached. Strategies are usually planned in committees, not in the full council. It's in a strategy session that the individual members of the committees commit themselves to take one or more of the specific steps needed to achieve an objective. For example, if a council committee is planning a weekend retreat to develop deeper spirituality (objective) then someone has to commit him/herself to take care of transportation. Someone else has to make reservations at a retreat house (dates, meals, lodging, etc.). These are strategies to achieve an objective.

Now that we have defined our terms, let's get into the workshop itself. A typical schedule for a goal-setting workshop may go something like this:

First Session: consensus decision on a Mission Statement

This session may begin with some input regarding the broad mission of the Christian community. Chapter 7 might furnish the background material for a general talk on Mission. After the workshop facilitator has given a brief explanation about how to write a Mission Statement, the council breaks up into small groups (5-7 each). Then each group, supplied with news-print and felt pens, works on reaching a consensus on *one* Mission Statement. After the individual groups have each come up with a written Mission Statement, they return to the large group. After the statements of the individual groups have been displayed on the wall and the full council has studied and reflected on the similarities and dissimilarities, the full council puts the group statements together and comes to a unanimous consensus in formulating one final Mission Statement. This Mission Statement then guides the thrust and direction for the rest of the workshop. It remains in prominent display through the final session.

Second Session: discernment of needs, problems, deficiencies.

Sometimes the needs to be discerned are divided into inter-nal and external. The internal needs pertain to the human chemistry of the council itself. What internal factors, dynam-ics, hinder the council in achieving its goals and objectives? It may be mistrust, conflict, lack of unity, lack of sufficient education, spiritual formation, etc. External needs grow out of the unique situation of the parish itself, as it responds, or does not respond, to its mission in a specific time and place, in a specific community. For instance, the parish may have very poor liturgy, a poor religious education program, no ecumen-ical activities, etc.

In this assessment of needs, the council has to keep an eye on its Mission Statement. For discernment of needs, it's not sim-ply a question of counting up the *felt* needs of the councilors. For instance, the gospel, with all its tough demands, needs to be proclaimed, even if, and especially if, no one experiences that as a *felt* need. If members depart too far from their mission statement, the final list of needs will have a heavy emphasis on merely parochial, or maintenance, needs. It's not that these needs are not very real. They are and they need to be consid-ered. If the council focuses too much on these *felt* needs, however, it may lose contact with its mission statement and with the sometimes painful call of the gospel.

The discernment of needs can be a lot of fun. Everybody can "play." It's a good time to use the brainstorm system, which works best when the participants observe the following rules:

1. Everyone is encouraged to think up as wild ideas as possible. If wild ideas are not forthcoming in a brainstorm session, it's a sign that participants are censoring their own ideas. They are thinking twice before they express an idea for fear that they may come up with a silly one and sound foolish.
2. No evaluation of any kind is allowed. If members judge and evaluate ideas as they are thought up, people tend to become more concerned with defending their ideas than thinking up new and better ones. Ideas do not have to be justified.

3. Quantity of ideas must be encouraged. When a great number of ideas come pouring out in rapid succession, evaluation is generally impossible. The participants then feel free to give their imaginations wide range and then good ideas will result.
4. Everyone is encouraged to build upon, or to modify the ideas of others. Combining or modifying previously suggested ideas often leads to new ideas which are superior to those that sparked them.[10]

The brainstorm system works best in small groups. The silent and timid members become more active. When each small group has come up with its list of needs, it reduces its total number to five or ten. It does this by arranging the needs in an order of priority and retaining only the most important ones. Priorities can quickly be determined by dividing needs into: Got-to-dos; Ought-to-dos; Nice-to-dos.[11] Of course, some needs have to be eliminated entirely because the council doesn't have the time, the authority, or the competence to deal with them. For instance, the council can't abolish the infallibility of the pope. There's no sense in listing impossible needs and raising unrealistic expectations.

When the individual groups have reduced their lists of needs to five, they come back together in a large group to arrive at a consensus on a master list of needs, problems or deficiencies. Part of such a list might look like this:

1. No close feeling of community at Sunday Liturgy.
2. No one is visiting the sick at the local convalescent home.
3. No one is doing anything for those on welfare in the parish.
4. The parish school board is fighting with the religious education committee.
5. No programs for the senior citizens in the parish.

When a consensus has been reached, the master list of needs remains on display on newsprint next to the Mission Statement.

Third Session: discernment of strengths and resources

The first purpose of this session is to discover the gifts, charisms, and ministries which the Spirit has given to the parish. These gifts or resources will generally fall under the following headings: 1. the gospel; 2. the liturgy and the sacramental system; 3. gifted people; 4. time; 5. buildings; 6. relationships; 7. money. The second purpose of this session is to make the council aware of the fact that, in many cases, it has enough resources to respond to the needs discerned in the second session.

The process of this session is the same as the second, i.e., small group, then large group. A partial list of resources might look something like this:

1. an up-to-date census, with listing of talents and interests of all the parishioners
2. a social worker who is willing to offer free services
3. a competent public school teacher
4. an accountant
5. widows with cars to provide transportation for elderly

Fourth Session: consensus on goals

During this session councilors might first reflect on their relationship to the diocesan church. If the diocese, through its diocesan pastoral council, has achieved a consensus regarding diocesan goal statements, the parish council should consider these diocesan goals before it prepares its own goals. In this way, the parish council can reflect on how it will fulfill its responsibility in helping the diocesan church achieve its goals. Some of the parish goal statements may very well flow directly from diocesan goal statements.

Here are some examples of diocesan goal statements taken from the Archdiocese of Detroit:

1. Develop and implement affirmative action programs in all Catholic parishes and institutions in the archdiocese.

2. Develop more effective leadership in pastoral ministries (deacons, ministers of service, priests and religious).

3. The archdiocese will extend itself more directly to the needs of its senior citizens.

Here are two more examples of diocesan goals, written in a little different style. They were part of the conclusions of a discernment process undertaken by the diocesan pastoral council of Memphis, Tennessee:

1. Resolved, that the diocese of Memphis redefine and emphasize the importance of family life, its functions and responsibilities, and the reciprocal relationships between the church and families and the communities and families.

2. Resolved, that the diocese of Memphis, through its ecumenical commission, on which each parish is to have a representative, continue emphasizing the spirit of ecumenism as directed by Vatican II, and involve parish families in cooperating with other faiths in community and charitable endeavors, without compromising basic Catholic belief and traditions.

After reflecting on the diocesan goals, the councilors take another look at their own Mission Statement, their list of needs, and their list of resources. Then they go into small groups to write goal statements which flow from their Mission Statement and which at the same time, *match their resources to their needs.* After achieving a consensus on goal statements in their small groups, they assemble in a large group to reach a consensus on a master list of goals. Again, they may arrange these goals, like the list of needs, in an order of priority. They may also wish to label them as *long* or *short* range. This list of goals will then remain on display next to the list of resources.

Fifth Session: consensus decision on objectives

During this session each small group selects one goal and breaks it up into objectives. While remembering the definition of a good objective and using the consensus system, each small group formulates objectives which are designed to effect the accomplishment of its chosen goal.

When the small groups have completed their tasks, they reconvene in a large group to obtain a consensus on a master list drawn from lists of objectives which have been prepared for each goal. At this point it becomes rather important that whatever persons or committees are expected to accept responsibility for carrying out an objective actually agree that the objective is clear and understandable, realistic and attainable. They have to assume *ownership* of the objective. At the same time, they have to be sufficiently motivated and committed to invest their energies in working for the achievement of the objectives they accept.

Sixth Session: strategies

After objectives come strategies. As mentioned earlier, the decisions regarding the types of strategies needed to implement an objective should be left to the discretion of the various committees. When the council itself gets into strategies, it gets bogged down in endless details. It's the task of the council to give full responsibility to the committees and then hold them accountable. For this reason, strategies are not really a part of a goal-setting workshop.

Seventh Session: evaluation

During this session, the council draws up a schedule for receiving the reports of the various committees which will work on the objectives. It determines *who* will be accountable to *whom* for *what* by *what date*. It prepares a master list which will be duplicated and distributed to all the council members and their committees. This list also becomes part of the council's minutes. Reports from the committees will be on the council agenda according to dates listed on the schedule. If the objectives have been prepared correctly, this session will merely be a summation of the workshop. It is simply a way of building into the workshop a system whereby achievement of goals and objectives will be evaluated according to a mutually agreeable timetable.

Usually this kind of workshop concludes with the celebration of the liturgy. The readings and prayers are chosen for the occasion. The emphasis is on ministry and commitment. The council's liturgy committee is responsible for preparing this special liturgy.

When the workshop is over, the council faces its toughest job—getting the word out to the rest of the parish. The purpose of a goal-setting workshop is to chart a direction for the *whole* parish, not just for the council. For this reason the council will have to spend some time figuring out how to get the whole parish committed to work toward the attainment of the *parish* goals. Goals may look fine on paper. But they are useless unless the people of the parish bend their energies to make these goals a reality in the actual life of the parish and community. Councilors may be in for a real letdown when they return home to confront the hard facts of parish life. The rest of the parishioners will be slow to change. Apathy will continue. The parish at large will not commit itself to the "council's" goals and objectives just because they were all published in the bulletin. The chairperson's phone will not be rung off the hook by parishioners volunteering their services. Councilors need to be zealous, committed, enthusiastic. But they also need to be realistic. They might do well, especially after a goal-setting workshop, to reflect on the principles of change and group behavior. Dr. Charles Sheffieck has outlined both the degree of difficulty and the amount of time involved in bringing about a change in group behavior:

> Parish council members have been charged with the responsibility to work in a collegial mode to develop the local parish. In the few years that any one member might be on the parish council, the amount of change that will take place could be viewed as minimal. The task of bringing about desired change is not only complex, but it also requires time. The following diagram on the base, or horizontal axis, shows the amount of time needed for each type of change, and on the vertical axis, the amount of difficulty involved in achieving this change.

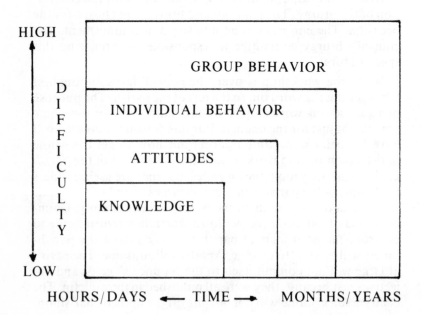

To bring about a change in *knowledge*, the difficulty is basically low, and the amount of time can be measured in hours or days. To change an *attitude* of an individual is more difficult and requires more time, maybe weeks or months. When it comes to changing individual *behavior*, again the amount of time increases and so does the difficulty. The most difficult change to bring about is that of a group behavior, and, accordingly, it requires the greatest amount of time, usually years. Parish councils, by their very nature, are groups that are responsible for bringing about changes in group behavior. The task of the parish council, therefore, requires considerable time and is extremely complex.[12]

Of course Dr. Sheffieck's chart doesn't include the prayer factor. No doubt the Spirit is always at work to bring about the conversion and inner renewal of his people. Through the power of his grace, even the poorest human efforts can and do bring about unexpected results. The Spirit, fortunately, is not limited to the laws of human behavior. At the same time, councilors need to remember that they themselves may not see the results of their work in their own lifetime. They will plant. Someone else will water. And God will give the growth in his own time (1 Cor. 3:6). Besides, it's often the case that the work of the prophet doesn't yield its fruit until after his death. When councilors have finished setting the goals of the parish, they may feel a bit overwhelmed by the task ahead. It's especially at this time that councilors sense the need for spiritual renewal. The next chapter, therefore, will show how the Lord's holiness, working in and through the councilors, will help the council achieve its goals.

Footnotes

1. Adapted from *Mutual Ministry* (New York: The Seabury Press, 1977), pp. 9-16.

2. *Parish Council Philosophy and Guidelines* (Denver, Colorado: Archdiocese of Denver, n.d.), pp. 7-8.

3. Norman Lambert, *Managing Church Groups* (Dayton, Ohio: Pflaum Publishing Co., 1975), p. 28.

4. Charles Sheffieck, *Planning for Parish Development in the Archdiocese of Detroit* (Detroit: Archdiocese of Detroit, 1974), p. 6.

5. *Managing Church Groups*, p. 30.

6. *Denver Guidelines*, p. 20.

7. Ibid.

8. Ibid., with some adaptation.

9. Ibid., with some adaptation.

10. Adapted from Simon, Howe and Kirschenbaum, *Values Clarification* (New York: Hart Publishing Co., Inc., 1972), pp. 204-205.

11. *Managing Church Groups*, p. 37.

12. *Planning for Parish Development*, p. 13.

Resources

Beckhard, Richard. *Organization Development: Strategies and Models.* Reading, Mass.: Addison-Wesley Publishing Co., 1969.

Lambert, Norman. *Managing Church Groups.* Dayton, Ohio: Pflaum Publishing Co., 1975.

Lindgren, Alvin and Shawchuck, Norman. *Management of Your Church.* Nashville: Abingdon Press, 1977. (This book is especially helpful in Mission Statement, Program-planning, and Problem Analysis).

Mager, Robert. *Goal Analysis.* Belmont, Cal.: Fearon Publishers, 1972.

Maslow, Abraham H. *Motivation and Personality.* New York: Harper and Row, 1954.

For information on Parish Planning write to:
    Church Management Program. (CARA, 3700 Oakville Terrace, N.E. Washington, D.C. 20017).

Appendix I

Instead of a Mission Statement, some parish councils compose a Covenant Statement. They do it first in a small, then in a larger group process as part of a three-hour Evening of Renewal. A *covenant*, in its biblical meaning, is a solemn agreement between God and His people. The parties to the agreement promise to be faithful to each other and bind themselves to keep their commitment. Similar to marriage, a covenant establishes a close and intimate relationship between God and His people. Below is a sample of such a Covenant Statement composed by the parish council of St. Mary, Kenosha, Wisconsin.

Covenant Statement

You shall be my people, and I will be your God. Ez. 36:28

We the people of St. Mary Parish, Kenosha, Wisconsin, by virtue of our baptism in Christ are called to be a faith community. As Church we are invited to spread the Word to our members and to the world around us and to be givers of life.

PREAMBLE

(WHO we are, WHAT we are about).

We believe that we are an *institutionalized servant community*

    a.   As a *community* of faith we grow together personally and as a body by the power of the Holy Spirit acting through our interpersonal relationships

What we BELIEVE AND PLEDGE ourselves to ACT UPON

IDENTITY as FAITH COMMUNITY

   b. As *servant*, we are a
       people who make a dif-
       ference in our parish
       and our society by reach-
       ing out in care and con-
       cern
   c. As *institution*, we are
       bound together in unity
       under the leadership of
       the Vicar of Christ and
       our local bishop. With
       Catholics throughout
       the world, we share the
       church's life-giving mis-
       sion of healing and re-
       conciliation.

We believe that
   we are touched by the pres-   **WORSHIP**
   ence of the risen Lord a-
   mong us most deeply at
   Eucharist; thus the Mass is
   the center of our parish life
   and the lives of our families
   and individuals.

   Therefore, we pledge ourselves to provide Eucharistic
   celebrations that will help us
   to hear and live the Gospel
   message of love, willing to
   offer ourselves, sacrifice
   ourselves, and share ourselves to care for others as
   Christ cares for us.

We believe that
   education is an ongoing pro-   **EDUCATION**
   cess freeing us from ignor-
   ance and enabling us in faith

to know God. Therefore, we commit ourselves to quality education on all levels and specifically to that education which enables us to respond in faith. To this end we direct the selection of staff and the planning of programs for our adults and youth, in our parish school and religious education department.

We believe that
each member of our parish community is God-gifted with skills and talents for the enrichment of human life. Our greatest wealth is our people. Therefore, we pledge ourselves to *treasure* PEOPLE and to use THINGS (funds and facilities) as trusted and concerned stewards.

PARISH RESOURCES
(Persons, funds, buildings)

We believe that
our caring and concern must extend to the total person, young or old, rich or poor, ill, handicapped or well, regardless of race or ethnic background. Therefore we pledge ourselves to weld through Christian love and community activity, a bond of harmony among us reflecting oneness of spirit and accord.

PASTORAL AREAS
(parish life)

We believe that
we do not exist by our-
selves, nor for ourselves, but
as a leaven, a light within a
city, a nation, a world.
Therefore, as our resources
both spiritual and physical
allow, we commit ourselves
and these resources to those
whose urgent human needs
lay claim on them.

SOCIAL
AWARENESS (Inter-
parish, city, state,
country, world)

Appendix II

A Covenant Statement
Archdiocese of Denver
Denver, Colorado

We, the parish family of Our
Lady of Nazareth, in the year of
our Lord, 1973, do hereby
covenant ourselves both individually and collectively to
God our Father by working to
accomplish the goals set forth
below:

Having been called by God our
Father, we are united by our
commitment of service to our
fellow men, as living witness to
the life, death, and resurrec—
tion of Christ as taught by the
Scriptures and His example. We
who are called to be
ministers,
missionaries, and
priests
covenant ourselves to the
following:

To develop authentic and meaningful
liturgical celebrations to praise God
and intensify our faith.

To advance the physical, social, and
emotional wellbeing of the parish family
and the community of man, by caring for
the needs of the aged, poor, lonely,
racially exploited, socially oppressed,
helpless and suffering people.

To provide ample social activities so that
we might develop as a parish family.

To provide continuous religious education
and formation for all parish members.

To provide adequate physical surround-
ings and financial resources and management to implement this covenant.

So help us, God!

Chapter 12

Growing in Holiness

"Put on then, as God's chosen ones, holy and beloved, compassion, kindness, lowliness, meekness, and patience, forbearing one another and if one has a complaint against another, forgiving each other" (Col. 3:12-13).

As newly elected members begin to serve on the council, they often become more aware of their need for a deeper spiritual life. And that's one of the most encouraging signs in the renewal of the postconciliar church. In the case of the parish council, it's an awareness which grows out of a deeper appreciation both of the problems and of the responsibilities connected with ministry in the church.

First, a word about the *problems*. New councilors soon begin to see the human side of the church at closer range. They see the warts on the face of holy "mother" church, i.e., the people of God. They see bias, conflict, apathy, selfishness, manipulation, narrow vision and power plays. They discover that some of their fellow ministers, including priests and sisters, can be rigid, insensitive, closed-minded and authoritarian—more inclined to deal in personalities than with issues. They experience in a new way, an aspect of the mystery of evil which is the common burden of the pilgrim church, "until he comes." Then, too, getting beyond the personal, they get a deeper appreciation of the complexity of many of the problems involved in change, renewal and pastoral leadership in the modern Roman Catholic church. They see that it's not easy to deal with pluralism, shared decision-making and the tensions between hierarchic and collegial styles of leadership. They see, finally, that there's more involved in serving on the council than merely taking care of the material things so "Father can take care of the spiritual."

Second, a word about the *responsibilities*. Some new councilors are a little overwhelmed when they are asked to make decisions about liturgy, about closing the school, about policies for religious education programs and about government spending on the arms race. They suddenly become aware that they are not really prepared to make these kinds of decisions. They also become more aware that prophetic leadership isn't easy; it's no fun to draw flak from the stand-pat parishioners. They understand now that they can't just pass the "buck" to Father, because now, they too, share responsibility for far-reaching pastoral decisions. And finally, they realize that if they are going to model holiness for the rest of the parish, they ought to be holy themselves.

Besides the unique problems which grow out of the parish council experience, there are others which are simply part of the growth toward maturity in the spiritual life of ministering Christians. Earnest Larsen mentions the following three obstacles to renewal: lack of courage, personal problems, and refusal to follow the Spirit.[1] Both the courage *to be* and the courage *to become* are often lacking in many of us. We are afraid to take any bold new steps in the spiritual life because we are afraid to venture out from our safe, familiar patterns of behavior. We don't know where the Spirit will lead us or to what frightening responsibilities he may call us. Besides, we feel so inadequate in the face of the tasks ahead. Better to do nothing than to fail.

Then, too, most of us have some personal problems. We often carry the burden of these problems alone because we can't muster the courage to share them with someone else. We are afraid of that kind of intimacy. We concentrate so much of our attention on these problems that we have little time or energy to pay attention to God, to prayer, and to the needs of others. These unshared, and therefore unresolved, problems give birth to anger, impatience, and frustration. We don't *own* our dependence on the Christian community. So we don't get help from it either. Also, we do find it hard, as Larsen reminds us, to listen to, and to obey, the *Spirit*. That's just too slippery for us. We are so used to getting our directions from the *law* that we look to the law to say it all—clearly, directly and finally. We just can't stand the freedom of living under the voice of the Spirit. We'd rather live a spiritual life in a neat framework of confessions, communions, novenas and simple obedience to law. The spiritual life is, of course, not reducible to a neat set of rules. It's not like buying a frozen food package, with clear directions guaranteeing a delightful dish. The Spirit, after all, continues to breathe where and how he wills. That's the difficulty. But that's also the challenge and the excitement.

We can, nevertheless, draw certain norms for the spiritual life from the treasury of scripture and tradition. Without pretending to be exhaustive, there are at least four norms or principles for growth in the spiritual life. The first norm is *the centrality of the Christ event in the church and in our personal lives*. In this norm Paul is our unfailing model. "...Christ will be honored in my body, whether by life or by death. For to me to live is Christ, and to die is gain" (Phil. 1:20-21). "And he died for all, that those who live, might live no longer for themselves but for him who for their sake died and was raised" (2 Cor. 5,15). "For while we live we are always being given up to death for Jesus sake, so that the life of Jesus may be manifested in our mortal flesh. So death is at work in us, but life in you" (2 Cor. 4:11-12).

There can be no growth in holiness, no ministry in the church, which does not get its life, its strength, its inspiration from Christ Jesus. Whatever is separated from him becomes mere activism, pragmatism or Pelagianism. Growth in the spiritual life will forever remain growth in the Lord. Anything else is nothing more than a grinding of wheels. We say it every Sunday in the third eucharistic prayer: "All life, all holiness, comes from you, through your Son, Jesus Christ our Lord, by the working of the Holy Spirit."

To take the Christ event seriously is to believe that he is ready to work in us to overcome evil, whatever its form. It is to believe wholeheartedly in his transforming power. It is to lean on him utterly. It is to offer ourselves as his servants and then to see with his eyes, to speak with his tongue and to serve with his hands. That may sound a little unreal, even mystical. But the scriptures tell us "that's where it's at" in this business of growing in holiness.

But before we can "put on Christ" we have to have a *metanoia,* a conversion, a change of heart. And that's the second norm of the spiritual life: *to be disposed to an ongoing conversion.* It's the law of the Gospel: "...The kingdom of God is at hand; repent..." i.e., change your mind, your heart, your attitude (Mark 1, 15). The first step in the spiritual life is not to set up a neat system of spiritual exercises, like a physical fitness program. The first step is an inner change of heart which opens the door to Christ and lets him take over. It's an honest-to-goodness admission of our own frailty and sinfulness and of our utter impoverishment without him. Again, Paul is our model: "...for three days he was without sight...And immediately something like scales fell from his eyes and he regained his sight" (Acts 9:9 and 18). Then he became the Lord's chosen instrument.

The third norm of the spiritual life is *vision*. It means to have the mind of Christ, to have a picture of the whole—the past, the present and the future. Especially, the future. It's this vision of the future which engenders hope. And hope is optimistic. It's contagious. It kindles energy in the hearts of all those who begin to share the Christian vision. Nobody has said it better than Paul: "...We rejoice in our hope of sharing the glory of God. More than that, we rejoice in our sufferings, knowing that suffering produces endurance, and endurance produces character, and character produces hope, and hope does not disappoint us, because God's love has been poured into our hearts through the Holy Spirit who has been given to us" (Rom. 5:2-5).

The Christian never forgets that it's by *His* great mercy that he has "been born anew to a living hope through the resurrection of Jesus Christ from the dead..." (1 Peter 1:3). It is because the Christian clings to a firm hope that the future belongs to God that he is able to "bring samples of the ultimate future into the pain of the present."[2] For this reason too, he can "proclaim and pioneer the future of the world within the horizon of faith in God's coming kingdom.[3]

The fourth norm is *prayer*. Husband and wife will not grow in love and knowledge unless they communicate with each other. So, too, the Christian will not grow in love of Christ without constant dialogue with him. It's a dialogue which speaks, listens and shares in a very intimate way. It's a dialogue which brings about change and growth. Since prayer is an expression of the mystery of the human person, it takes many forms. Now it will be a shout of praise and joy; then it will be tears of sorrow and repentance. Now it will be a song of love and thanksgiving; then it will be a cry of demand and petition.

In the Catholic church, of course, all prayer reaches its fulfillment and its earthly perfection in the celebration of the community liturgy. There is no Lone Ranger holiness. The Christian will grow in holiness only insofar as he/she is an organic part of a worshipping Christian community. He/she grows in a living partnership with a specific community or he will soon not grow at all. Vatican II restated the normativeness of the liturgy: "...the liturgy is the summit toward which the activity of the church is directed; it is also the fount from which all her power flows. For the goal of apostolic endeavor is that all who are made sons of God by faith and baptism should come together to praise God in the midst of his church, to take part in the sacrifice and to eat the Lord's Supper."[4]

Just as husband and wife discover their identity as husbands and wives in communion and conversation with each other, so we discover our identity as Christians in our communion and conversation with Christ and with our worshipping community. This worshipping community is a channel of the Lord's holiness to us. Even though holiness remains the Lord's holiness, the worshipping community is a vehicle or sacrament of that holiness. Participating in the liturgy is not the only way to holiness, but it is by far the most important one. We're used to instant rice and instant coffee. So we often expect *instant* holiness. However, growth in the spiritual life, just like growth in human and vegetable life, will be slow and gradual. It will take many years filled with new starts and half-starts, stumblings, failings, successes and half-successes. In fact, growth in holiness will not be complete until the coming of the Kingdom of God in fullness. Then, and only then, will there be a "new heaven and a new earth." "And night shall be no more; they need no light of lamp or sun, for the Lord God will be their light, and they shall reign for ever and ever" (Rev. 22:5).

Some Practical Steps

It stands to reason that spiritual renewal has to begin with the individual councilor. Earnest Larsen reminds us:

> ...Parish renewal, if it is to bear fruit, essentially demands that parish leaders formulate a *personal spirituality*. Then, in turn, this spirituality is amplified to become a *parish spirituality*, from which all programs originate. Without personal spirituality, there can be no parish spirituality... Therefore, without an open-ended, growth-oriented spirituality, there is no real renewal in progress.[5] (Italics mine)

Since spiritual renewal begins with where we are, the first step might well be the celebration of the sacrament of reconciliation. Besides celebrating the full sacrament, councilors could, now and then, celebrate a simple penitential service as part of their regular meeting. The following Penitential Service is recommended for councilors by the Archdiocese of Milwaukee:

1. *Opening Prayer*: God, our Father, we come together today to thank you for your mercy. We believe in you and we praise you, for you are our Father and we are your children. Help us to know our sins and to be sorry for them.

2. *Reading*: Matthew 7:1-5

3. *Response*: A clean heart create for me, O God, and a steadfast spirit renew within me!
   Cast me not out from your presence, and your holy spirit take not from me!

4. *Examination of Conscience*: (Pause for silent reflection after each question)

—Do we take the time to listen to one another and really hear?
—Do I talk too much and off the point?
—Do I like to control?
—Am I accountable for my ministry on the council? To whom?
—Have we talked about some of the human and social needs of our people?
—Have we led the way to model for the parish a caring and hoping community?

—Are we too parochial? Do we support some ministries in more needy parts of the Archdiocese?

—Do we have a "hidden agenda"?

—What are we doing for the sick, the elderly and youth in our parish?

—What do we do to support a positive vision of marriage and family life in our parish?

—Am I overextended with meetings and not spending time with my family?

—Have we ever reviewed the real purpose of the council?

—Are we candid with and supportive of the priests and the other parish staff?

—Do I delegate my authority and responsibility to others?

—Have I read a thoughtful book on church, family or theology lately?

—Are we planning or just reacting to crisis?

5.   *Prayer for Forgiveness* (all): By the power of the Spirit, we confess to Almighty God, to Jesus Christ, the Lord Redeemer, and to all of our sisters and brothers that we have sinned by unloving deeds, by leaving undone what we ought to have done; by doing what we ought to have left undone. We ask mercy and healing and forgiveness, and restoration to our place around God's holy table.

6.   *Common Penance*: The Lord's Prayer.

7.   *Sign of Peace and Reconciliation*

8.   *Closing Hymn* "Let There be Peace"

Twilight Retreat

In addition to an occasional penitential service, parish councils might schedule a three-hour twilight retreat twice a year or so. Such a retreat could be divided into three parts: experience-input, reflection, and sharing. Earnest Larsen suggests the following program for such a retreat:

First Hour:

7:30 - 8:00 p.m. *Input.* The theme: "What is the role of a parish council within the context of parish renewal?" An analogy that can be used is: A parish council is somewhat like management as related to workers. It is not a perfect

204   The Practical Guide for Parish Councils

analogy but it can serve as a jumping-off place. Management must: a) have a vision of the whole operation, b) be caring in the sense of taking responsibility for the whole. and c) be committed. As someone said: they must stick in there when it gets sticky.

Now relating this to parish councils as we see them: a) the purpose of the operation of the parish must be kept clearly in mind. We know that its purpose is to minister—not to function but to minister. Therefore the primary duty of every member of the management-parish council is to take responsibility for his/her own spiritual growth which is the beginning of ministry. We cannot lead or be led where we would not go. From each one's personal growth, we come together to collectively become a spiritual parish council. From the collective spirituality of the parish council we try, in turn, to invite and create the climate where each part of the parish becomes more spiritual. They lean on us and we on them.

b) Organization. Management has to know the complete organization. We, as parish council, must be aware of the danger of a "robber-baron mentality" and try to encompass the vision of the whole parish. We must know how the parts interrelate and need each other.

c) Futuring. Responsible leadership looks to the future. We must reach out beyond our present moment. Where are we going? As best we can figure now, how can we get where we want to go? What things help? What hinders?

8:00 - 8:10 p.m. Reflection on the specific question, "What do you see as the role of the parish council?"

8:10 - 8:30 p.m. Sharing.

Second Hour:

8:30 - 9:00 p.m. *Experience-input, building upon the first hour.* If the above is the role of the parish council, what is the atmosphere within which productive meetings happen? Or, what are the problems involved in achieving the role definition? Such things as the following should be considered: a) to what extent the meetings happen within the context of prayer. By this we mean more than just a Hail Mary at the start. The whole atmosphere should be one of prayer; b) what

it means to listen to one another. We should not presume
that we know what other people are going to say before they
speak. We should not confuse our liking or disliking someone with what they have to say; c) what does it mean to come
to meetings prepared both mentally and ready to handle the
business at hand? d) how we have to support one another
and encourage each other to feel free in expressing ourselves;
and e) how we can avoid the trap of mere functionalism,
do-ism.

9:00 - 9:10 p.m. Reflection on the question of, "What attitudes and atmosphere do you find most productive, most
creative?"

9:10 - 9:30 p.m. Sharing in groups.

Third Hour:

9:30 - 10:00 p.m. *Experience-input: the need to evaluate.*
Actually this input can be very short. Each member should
take the time to write out what he/she thinks are the strong/
weak points of the council.

10:00 p.m. to close—large group sharing on results.

Concrete suggestions based on the shared insights can be
formulated at this point. For example, the group might
come to realize that all too often prayer is thrown in as a routine preliminary to our meetings. Then we can "get down to
business." To correct this, an effort can be made to devote
the start of each meeting to genuine prayer of some kind. It is
hard to fight with people you pray with. And actually, so
much more gets done with so much less stress when everything is done "in prayer."[6]

Of course, every meeting should devote some time to shared
prayer and reflection on the scriptures. Councilors could take
turns in preparing such brief prayer services, perhaps with the
help of the liturgy committee. Councilors should also consider
regular spiritual direction. It's an old principle of the spiritual
life that we need someone to guide us along the path of spiritual
growth. Lay councilors should not hesitate to seek out a personal spiritual director. They have a claim on such direction
not only in virtue of their call to holiness, but especially in view
of their call to minister in the church.

Councilors should, now and then, celebrate the liturgy together. It's a time for healing whatever hurts and misunderstandings develop during the council discussions. But it's also a time to celebrate the real feeling of community which grows up among councilors because they work, share and minister together. The spirit of community and of the celebrations should spill over into the whole parish. In this way, the council's witness will be the spark that kindles renewal in the whole parish. Once councilors have made spiritual growth part of the council's ongoing program, it's time for the council to assume responsibility for its growth in all areas. And that means that the council will, as a matter of course, constantly evaluate itself. So the next chapter will offer some pointers to help the council sharpen its evaluative skills.

Footnotes

1. *The Renewed Parish in Today's Church* (Liguori, Mo.: Liguori Publications, 1976), pp. 17-19.

2. Carl E. Braaten, *The Future of God* (New York: Harper and Row, 1969), p. 119.

3. Ibid., p. 109.

4. *The Constitution on the Sacred Liturgy*, Austin Flannery, O.P., ed. (Northport, New York: Costello Publishing Co.), p. 6.

5. *Spiritual Renewal of the American Parish* (Liguori, Mo.: Liguori Publications, 1975), p. 52.

6. *The Renewed Parish in Today's Church*, op. cit. pp. 54-56.

Chapter 13

Accountability and Evaluation

"This is how one should regard us, as servants of Christ and stewards of the mysteries of God. Moreover, it is required of stewards that they be found trustworthy" (1 Cor. 4:1-2). If councilors are truly ministers (Chapter 4), then they are accountable for the quality of their ministry. The ministers must render an account of their stewardship. At election time politicians are held accountable by the public for their public service. At the end of the school year, teachers are evaluated for their teaching. Before the renewal of their contracts, civil service employees get rated by efficiency reports. The assumption is that the public has a right to receive quality service from its public servants.

In the church, when we assemble for the sacrament of reconciliation, we examine our conscience. When we gather together to celebrate the liturgy, we confess publicly "to almighty God and to our brothers and sisters that we have sinned...in what we have done and what we have failed to do." As Catholics, we are quite comfortable in admitting before the church and the world that our ministry isn't perfect, that it's still flawed by the mystery of evil. It should come as no surprise, then, that councilors should be held accountable for their ministry. Since parish councils serve within a system of relationships, it makes sense that they should be held accountable within that system. Councilors, therefore, are accountable to the Lord, to the diocesan church, to the parish, to the civic community and finally, to one another.

First, councilors are accountable to the Lord. They are first called to be faithful disciples of the Lord. In baptism they have vowed themselves to their Lord. If they are not faithful to that commitment to him, their service to the church will be just about useless.

Second, they are accountable to the diocesan church. The parish lives as one cell within the larger body that is the diocesan church. It lives in communion with that body through the life-giving bonds of faith, morals, liturgy and law. It expresses its union with the diocesan church by sharing the same Lord, the same word, the same bread, the same cup, the same baptism. It needs to nourish and foster that unity both for its own life and for that of the diocesan church. Unity is not automatic. The parish, as a smaller cell within the larger body, has a twofold responsibility to the diocesan church. It has to be open *to receive* from the diocesan church the guidance, the gifts of discernment, which are the fruit of its larger faith experience. The diocesan church, in the normal course of events, just has more to share. If it's really in touch with the *faith* of all its parishes, it has a *broader* faith experience to share with each individual parish. If it's really in touch with its own tradition, it has a *longer* experience to share. For its own good, the parish needs to *own* its own dependent relationship on the *life* of the larger diocesan church. And for some American parishes, that's not easy to do. Often they suffer from a parochial, Congregationalist attitude. Also, the parish needs to do its share *in building up* the diocesan church. It needs to share with the diocesan church the fruits of its preaching, the fruits of its sacramental life, the fruits of its own discernment. Therefore, the parish needs to be present at diocesan workshops, conferences and assemblies to witness to its own unique faith experience; it needs to report to the chancery office and to diocesan offices and departments by writing letters regarding the strengths and weaknesses of diocesan programs; it needs to share with the diocesan church the many gifts and ministries which the Spirit has given to it in response to its faith; it needs to take the pulse of the grassroots and report its findings to the diocesan church.

Councils are not showing accountability to the diocesan church when they take up a petition to keep their pastor when the diocesan church needs his unique ministry elsewhere. The priest is ordained for the diocese, not for the parish. No congregation acquires ownership over the ministering gifts given to it. They remain the Spirit's gifts to be used where they build up the church most. If Paul's first congregation (Seleucia) had taken up a petition to keep him, he would never have been able to evangelize the rest of the Gentile world. His congregations were, of course, founded on Jesus Christ, (1 Cor. 3,11) not on himself. The parish council builds up the diocesan church by offering responsible criticism, by reading the signs of the times and by discerning the changing pastoral needs. Councils will not always find it easy to offer feedback to the diocesan church. It's no secret that some dioceses are not disposed to receive up-building input "from below."

Third, councilors are accountable as servants to their fellow parishioners, the "brothers and sisters." The council does not exist for itself, but for the whole parish. It is called to touch, to engage, the faith of all the parishioners and then, to challenge them to become holier and more responsive to the Spirit. Councilors show themselves accountable to the parishioners when they serve as models for them, when they keep in touch with their opinions and when they report back to them. The relationship of council to parish is expressed rather well in the *Guidelines* for the Archdiocese of Detroit:

> As a group of Christian leaders, the parish council should be a witness to the parish that barriers can be broken and separation healed by men and women of patience and good will. As members become a warm, loving, caring group themselves, they are a model of what the parish might be. By their unity with one another, as well as by their decisions, they gradually influence the people of the parish to make worship and service to people a priority in their individual lives, as well as the goal of the entire community of faith...
>
> It is important that the council members know what the people are thinking and feeling on the issues of their lives and of their parish. The effort to remain informed and in touch with the people must be a

> continuous one, because in a fast-moving society, the opinions and feelings of parishioners are also changing quickly...
>
> ...The parish council as a leadership group cannot be limited in its action to the present views of parishioners. Neither, however, can they afford to become an elite group passing decisions down from on high, with little or no regard for the feelings and views of the parishioners. The basic characteristic of leadership in a Christian community is not power but service...Every effort must be made to involve parishioners in the decisions that affect their own growth.[1]

So long as the councilors make no effort to invite parishioners to internalize the decisions of the council, they run the risk of becoming an elite power group. They may be using the parishioners (especially their money) to achieve their own hidden agendas. They may engage in political maneuvering to gain their own ends, but they are no longer ministering to build up the faith of the community they are called to serve. They may pass numerous resolutions and fund all kinds of programs, but they have lost the parishioners. Also, councilors need to be accountable to the parish staff. They need to report to the religous education director, to the sisters, to the associate and to the pastor. If the councilors' ministry is going to advance the mission of the parish, it will have to be carried out in relationship with all the full-time ministries. Effective coordination of the parish ministries is everyone's responsibility.

Fourth, councilors are accountable to the civic community. The church exists *for* the world not for itself. Therefore, the world can demand that the church's actions conform to its words, especially *the* Word. In practice, the council becomes accountable to the world by being accountable to the civic community. If the council professes ecumenism, it needs to relate to the other churches in its community. If it professes to feed the hungry, to clothe the naked, etc., then it must do it in its own community. If it professes to minister to the civic community, then it must listen and respond to the city council, the United Way, the public school board, etc. The council does this by being present at their meetings, by receiving and responding to their minutes, by writing letters to the newspaper regarding current civic issues, etc. That's one of many ways the council renders an account of its stewardship under the gospel.

Finally, the council members are accountable to one another. They need to support one another in their mutual ministry. They (and not just the chairperson) need to hold one another accountable for commitments they have made to meetings, programs and committees. They need to be prompt at meetings and do their homework. They need to call absentees to offer help when they are sick, to offer rides when they need one, to visit them when they become discouraged. They need to agree never to do alone what can be done with another. By personal example, they have to encourage openness and honesty in all of the council's activities. They also need to be accountable to one another for growth in faith and holiness. If council members have no concern for the growth of all the council will soon become static, sterile, dead. To relate to a living cell in the body of Christ is to accept some responsibility for its growth. For this reason, council members need to ask the hard questions about both the process and the content of council meetings; otherwise the council will drift into stagnation.

Evaluation

If council members are going to render an account of their ministry, they have to get in the habit of *evaluating* their own services. They have to measure their behavior and their activities against certain criteria they have agreed to apply to themselves. Of course, the first criterion is the council's constitution with its statement of purpose. Councils could well review their constitutions and bylaws at least once a year. They could ask themselves: "How do we stand with regard to our published purpose and functions?" A second set of criteria for evaluation could come from any goal-setting workshop held by the council. These could be applied both to the council and to its committees.

After the council has reflected honestly on the above criteria, it might examine its conscience regarding some of the more common faults of parish councils, viz.:

—power seeking
—putting personal desires (school, C.C.D.) before parish
  needs and goals
—a loss of the personal
—a loss of accountability to the parishioners
—a loss of shared faith and shared prayer
—a lack of honesty and personal support among the members
—not doing the homework before doing the talking.

A parish council might evaluate itself during a celebration of
the sacrament of reconciliation (as suggested in the previous
chapter). It might also keep some time at the end of a meeting
to reflect on some of the following questions, either individually
or as a group:

—How do we relate to the neighboring Catholic parishes? to
the civic community? to the churches of other faiths? to the
diocesan church?
—What are we doing to build up unity between our parish and
our diocese?
—Do we foster and encourage a positive attitude toward the
diocesan church?
—Have we groused about the past rather than looking to and
planning for the future?
—In our reports, do we give credit to those who help in parish
council projects?
—Have we tried to become ministers with a broad vision?
—Are we content with treading water when we should be
swimming faster and farther and deeper every year?
—Are we a Pentecost people or are we only bookkeepers?
—Have we considered an open parish forum? Or are we satis-
fied with a comfortable isolation in which our fellow parish-
ioners almost never share?
—Do we take the initiative or do we simply sit back and
wait for marching orders?
—Are we really going about the business of pastoral planning?
If not, why not?[2]

A thorough self-evaluation will reveal both *strengths* and
deficiencies in various aspects of the council's life. A maturing

council will, of course, accept the challenge and deal with the deficiencies as part of its own ongoing program of renewal. It may even design and administer its own evaluative instruments.[3] Self-examination and fraternal correction have been part of the Catholic tradition for centuries. After completing an evaluation, a council may wish to go back to its constitution to see if it needs to be revised. If that is the case, it may wish to review some of the more common features contained in other constitutions. The next chapter should be helpful in making such a review.

Footnotes

1. *Directives and Guidelines for Parish Councils.* Archdiocese of Detroit, p. 9, 10.
2. The last six questions have been adapted from Robert G. Howes "Parish Councils: Do We Care?" *America* (November 27, 1976), pp. 371-72.
3. See Appendices I, II and III for samples of evaluation forms.

Appendix I

Evaluation of the Parish and its Council

(The following questionnaire may serve as a point of departure for councils who wish to develop their own evaluative instrument. It is adapted from a questionnaire designed by Rev. James Trent for the councils of the Archdiocese of Detroit.)

Have you participated in any educational programs designed to prepare you for your work on a parish council? (Check one. If Yes, please respond further.)

        No   Yes

1.   ( ) ( ). . If YES, please describe: _____
                                      _____

2.   ( ) ( ) If YES, how well did it prepare you for your work?
              (Circle one number)

      NOT AT ALL   SOMEWHAT   FULLY
         1   2   3   4   5

3.   ( ) ( ). . If YES, was it at the beginning of ( )
           or during ( ) your term of Membership?

Where would you place your pastor (or oldest co-pastor) along the following behavior line: (Circle one number)
    AUTHORITARIAN DEMOCRATIC LAISSEZ-FAIRE
4.   1 2 3 4 5 6 7 8 9 10

Where would you place your assistant (or youngest co-pastor) along the following behavior line: (Circle one number)
5.   1 2 3 4 5 6 7 8 9 10

Where would you place yourself along the following behavior
line? (Circle one number)
> AUTHORITARIAN DEMOCRATIC LAISSEZ-FAIRE

6.   1 2 3 4 5 6 7 8 9 10

Below are some statements regarding committee and / or group
(altar sodality, men's club, etc.) representation on the parish
council. People feel differently about these statements. Do you
strongly agree, agree, disagree, or strongly disagree with them?
(Check *one* box on *each* line)

	STRONGLY AGREE	AGREE	DIS-AGREE	STRONGLY DISAGREE
7. Members representing committees or groups tend to feel a greater allegiance to their committees or groups than to the Council	( )	( )	( )	( )
8. Members representing committees or groups tend to raise greater conflicts over moneys, equipment, goals, objectives and / or values than do other council members	( )	( )	( )	( )
9. Members representing committees or groups tend to be concerned more with their area of interest rather than the overall picture of the parish	( )	( )	( )	( )
10. The council should appoint representatives to the committees	( )	( )	( )	( )
11. The pastor should appoint the committee chairpersons	( )	( )	( )	( )
12. The pastor or his representative should have the final say at committee meetings	( )	( )	( )	( )

The work of the parish council is to: (Check the one with which you *most* agree)

13.   _____Assist the priest in serving the parish.
        _____Guide the priest in serving the parish.
        _____Advise the priest in serving parish.
        _____Motivate others to serve the parish.
        _____Lead in serving the parish.

In order of importance, I feel that . . . (List 1 for first, 2 for second, etc., in the box next to your choice.)

14. ( )   The pastor is accountable to the bishop's office.
     ( )   The council is accountable to the pastor.
     ( )   The pastor is accountable to the council.
     ( )   The council and the pastor are accountable to the parishioners.
     ( )   The council and the pastor are accountable to the bishop.

Some parish councils consider the following to be problems at one time or another. Do you think these are problems for you? If so, how much of a problem are these to you at the present time? (Check at least *one* box on *each* line.)

	A Problem		How Serious		
	No	Yes	Little	Great	
15. The pastor acts first on most parish decisions concerning purchasing, hiring and changes, and then seeks council's approval					( )
16. Established parish groups (Men's, Women's, Scouts, etc.) will not coordinate their activities with committees					( )
17. Council members participate only in those discussions which reflect their interests					( )

18. Committees representatives support their committees more than the council .... ( )

19. Conflict and hostility be-tween members is a "hidden agenda" at most council meetings .... ( )

20. The council has no choice in a pastor's appointment other than that given to them by the diocese ...... ( )

21. Comunication between committees, between com-mittees and council, coun-cil, committees and pastor are bad (no one knows what the other is doing or why) .... ( )

22. The council is not able to hire or fire parish staff members .... ( )

23. Now go back and look at those you checked as "GREAT." In the brackets next to them, rank *only* the *three* you feel are the greatest problems for you. 1 for first, 2 for second, and 3 for third.

24. Generally speaking, I feel that a parish council is *most* competent when dealing with matters concerning: (Check your answer in the *first* column)

Educational Activities	( )	( )
Coordinating Calendars	( )	( )
Evaluation of Staff Personnel	( )	( )
Parish Worship Programs	( )	( )
Establishment of Goals	( )	( )
Monies and Budgeting	( )	( )
Evaluation of Parish Priests	( )	( )
Establishment of Objectives	( )	( )

25.   Now go back up the list and check in the *second* column
      the matter with which you think a council is *least* com-
      petent to deal.

26.   How many times has your constitution been rewritten or
      revised? (Check one)
None (   ), Once (   ), Twice (   ), More (   ), No Idea (   )

27.   The decision to change or amend your constitu-
      tion was based upon: (Choose in order of motiva-
      tion: 1, 2, 3, etc. Leave blank if it does not
      apply.)
      The diocesan directives/workbook............... (   )
      A study program concerning the nature and pur-
      pose of parish councils........................ (   )
      A desire to correct difficulties and situations
      experienced by the council .... (   )
      A change in pastorate .... (   )
      Other:_____
      _____ (   )
      to next
      question

There are a variety of opinions about the following statements.
Do you strongly agree, agree, disagree, or strongly disagree
with them?
(Check *one* box on *each* line)

	STRONGLY AGREE	AGREE	DIS-AGREE	STRONGLY DISAGREE

In formulating a Constitution, a parish council ought
to :

28.   Set it up exactly as the
      bishop says it should be set
      up ....   (   ) (   ) (   ) (   )

29. Consolidate representation
    by committees rather than
    by organizations .... ( ) ( ) ( ) ( )

30. First agree upon the nature
    of the church and the pur-
    pose of the parish .... ( ) ( ) ( ) ( )

31. Study the nature and set up
    of Protestant or Orthodox
    Catholic Councils and
    Assemblies .... ( ) ( ) ( ) ( )

32. Establish a constitutional
    committee to work with the
    pastor in writing or rewrit-
    ing it .... ( ) ( ) ( ) ( )

33. First agree upon the purpose
    of the parish .... ( ) ( ) ( ) ( )

34. Have its acceptance voted
    upon by the total parish .. ( ) ( ) ( ) ( )

35. See that long-standing
    parish groups and organiza-
    tions have direct repre-
    sentation on the council
    rather than through com-
    mittees .... ( ) ( ) ( ) ( )

36. Make it reflect where the
    parish is today regarding
    thinking, way of life, etc... ( ) ( ) ( ) ( )

Where would you place your council in its attitude and behavior in the way it implements its decisions concerning parish policy and procedure (regarding schools, committees, monies, etc.) (Circle *one* number)

37. **VERY AUTHORITARIAN**
    1. You will do it this way.
    2. We want you to do it this way.
    3. We would like you to do it this way.

    VERY DEMOCRATIC
    4. How would you like to do it?
    5. How will you do it?
    6. Do it as you think best.

    LAISSEZ-FAIRE
    7. We really don't care what you do.

Our council has agreed upon a way to handle conflict in our meetings (check one)

38. YES ( )   NO ( )   DOES NOT APPLY ( )
    Explain the procedure:_____
    _____
    _____

39. People involved in activities often find their attitudes and behavior toward those activities tend to change over time. Has this happened to you with your parish council? (In the following questions, *circle* the number closest to where you were when you joined the council. Then *underline* the number closest to *where you are* right now.)

    Interest and activity centered around . . .

    THE OVERALL NEIGHBORHOOD ←————————————→ **THE PARISH COMMUNITY**

       1   2   3   4   5   6   7

    Most time, energy at meetings spent dealing with . . .

    INSTITUTIONAL MAINTENANCE ←————————————→ **HUMANITARIAN/ FAITH VALUES**

       1   2   3   4   5   6   7

Decision making during council meetings . . .

POLARIZATION ◄─────────────────────────► **CONSENSUS**

1   2   3   4   5   6   7

About the possibilities of our parish council working
effectively . . .

OPTIMISTIC ◄─────────────────────────► **PESSIMISTIC**

1   2   3   4   5   6   7

Appendix II

An Evaluation of Parish Life
(Designed by Russ Lowe, Diocese of Green Bay, Appleton, Wisconsin

(This evaluation form is based partly on *Mutual Ministry* by James Fenhagen and partly on *Models of the Church* by Avery Dulles, S.J. Whoever administers it would do well to give a brief explanation of Dulles' five models for the benefit of those who are not familiar with his book.)

On a scale of 1 (lowest) to 10 (highest) please rate the performance of: pastors, staffs, parish councils, people as you see it in parish life at the present time.

	Pastors	Staffs	Par. councils	People
VISION: the ability to formulate goals and directions.........				
MINISTRY: serving the needs of all people.................				
STRUCTURE: the ability to organize, define purpose, take action....................				
EXPERIENCES: the ability to relate daily life to the gospel message				

On a scale of 1 (lowest) to 10 (highest) rate the degree of implementation of the following you see in current parish life:

The conciliar process.............. 1 2 3 4 5 6 7 8 9 10
Shared responsibility.............. 1 2 3 4 5 6 7 8 9 10
Lay leadership 1 2 3 4 5 6 7 8 9 10
Subsidiarity...................... 1 2 3 4 5 6 7 8 9 10
Liturgical ministry (lay) 1 2 3 4 5 6 7 8 9 10
Service ministry (lay).............. 1 2 3 4 5 6 7 8 9 10
Faith community 1 2 3 4 5 6 7 8 9 10

Response to the poor 1 2 3 4 5 6 7 8 9 10
Response to the alienated 1 2 3 4 5 6 7 8 9 10
Response to the unchurched 1 2 3 4 5 6 7 8 9 10
Social justice 1 2 3 4 5 6 7 8 9 10
Pastoral planning 1 2 3 4 5 6 7 8 9 10
Trust 1 2 3 4 5 6 7 8 9 10

On a scale of 1 (lowest) to 10 (highest), rank the presence of the Dulles' "models" of the church as you see them operative in current parish life:

Institutional 1 2 3 4 5 6 7 8 9 10
Communion 1 2 3 4 5 6 7 8 9 10
Sacrament 1 2 3 4 5 6 7 8 9 10
Herald 1 2 3 4 5 6 7 8 9 10
Servant 1 2 3 4 5 6 7 8 9 10

On a scale of 1 (never) to 10 (always) please rate the following statements:

—The parish facilitates justice 1 2 3 4 5 6 7 8 9 10
—The parish enchances the value and dignity of human
  life 1 2 3 4 5 6 7 8 9 10
—The parish is an integrated partner with the surrounding
  community 1 2 3 4 5 6 7 8 9 10
—The parish is bridging the past to the present, to
  the future 1 2 3 4 5 6 7 8 9 10
—The parish is open to options 1 2 3 4 5 6 7 8 9 10

Appendix III

(The following *Evaluation Tool* was developed by Robert G. Howes, a consultant in pastoral participation and planning. It was first published in the May/June 1977 issue of *Today's Parish*. I am grateful to Fr. Howes and to Twenty-Third Publications for their permission to reprint it here.)

Annual Parish Council Evaluation

The Council as Spirit	Yes	No
1. Membership on this council has been for me a spiritual experience.	☐	☐
2. We really pray together. We are not satisfied with perfunctory invocations.	☐	☐
3. We are seriously and constructively concerned with promoting vocations to the priesthood and sisterhood from this parish.	☐	☐
4. At least once a year we testify to one another on what membership on this council has meant in our personal, familial and parochial lives.	☐	☐
5. This council recognizes and implements its responsibility to assist the pastor in determining when and what kind of mission or retreat is needed in the parish.	☐	☐
6. We schedule and most of us attend an annual council Day of Recollection or retreat.	☐	☐

The Council as Committees

1. Our committees are active. They
    prepare helpful material for our
    meetings, and they help implement
    our approved decisions.   □   □
2. We pass no resolution which
    demands action without assigning
    it for implementation by a speci-
    fied date to a particular com-
    mittee or person.   □   □
3. Our committees are aides to but
    not masters of the council.   □   □
4. We make reasonable demands of
    our committees. We neither have
    them with nothing to do nor over-
    load them with homework.   □   □
5. We rotate committee membership
    whenever possible so as to avoid,
    on the one hand, over-control by
    the same few, or, on the other
    hand, exclusion of other parish-
    ioners from participation.   □   □

The Council as Outreach

1. We recognize that, while we
    supposedly represent the parish as
    a whole, many parishioners don't
    know or care what we do or attend
    our meetings. We are really con-
    cerned about this.   □   □

2. We have seriously considered
    the desirability of an annual parish
    assembly or town meeting at which
    we can report, receive input, and
    involve many more parishioners in
    parish "mission" and "business."   □   □

3. We are seriously concerned about Catholics in our area who are separated from the parish by neglect, marital difficulties, etc.   □   □

4. When confronted with apparent lack of success in a parish program (e.g., the number of high school students regularly attending religious formation programs, we are seriously concerned to help remedy the situation.   □   □

5. Outreach to the poor and other disadvantaged in our area is a regular concern of the council.   □   □

6. We do all we can to be a good ecumenical neighbor in our area.   □   □

The Council as Pastoral Planning

1. We see our council and our parish as challenged to grow dynamically in Christ. Our task is to enable such growth rather than to preside over drift or to bless inertia.   □   □

2. We are part of a church region (e.g., deanery). We are seriously concerned to know how our council and our parish can best relate to this region as a benefiting and contributing member.   □   □

3. We recognize that we are not alone either as council or as parish. We are seriously concerned to learn all we can from the trials and errors of other councils and parishes.   □   □

4. There are parishes in which pas-
    toral plans have been already
    developed. In these, relatively
    long-range goals are recorded and
    then specified into one year timed,
    costed and assigned objectives.
    We need this in our parish, too.   ☐   ☐

5. Even in the absence of a formal
    plan, our council is concerned
    with more than just immediate
    crises and putting out brush fires.
    We want to be a source and re-
    source for all-around parish
    maturity and growth.   ☐   ☐

The Council as Renewal and Results

1. We recognize the need for contin-
    ual renewal and update of our
    methods and vision. This is a high
    priority item on our agenda.   ☐   ☐

2. When the Pope issues an encyclical
    or other major statement which
    pertains to us, we try to get copies
    and we discuss how it should
    affect us and our parish.   ☐   ☐

3. We are concerned with the letters
    from our bishop. We discuss how
    they should affect us and our
    parish.   ☐   ☐

4. We appreciate that church results
    are often slow and hard to
    measure. Still we need to see and
    we can point to changes in parish
    life which have resulted, signifi-
    cantly, from our work.   ☐   ☐

5. We receive much mail from diocesan offices. We recognize that we need to understand and to help implement diocesan policies but we recognize, too, our right and our obligation to react to them and to make a real input into the deliberations of all diocesan offices. We need them, but they also need to know how we feel at the grass roots.   ☐   ☐

Chapter 14

A Model Constitution

There is, of course, no such thing as a model constitution designed to fit all parishes with their diverse size, needs, culture and history. In fact, it might be good pastoral practice for councils to operate without a constitution for the first few years. They could merely draw up some general *guidelines* (borrowed from the diocese) or *articles of understanding* until they have gained some experience. That way they would not be bound by rigid, and sometimes, artificial constitutions which don't really serve their unique needs or situations. It would also mean that whatever constitution emerges would truly be the fruit of a unique discernment process and the actual pastoral experience of the council and parish.

Insofar as constitutions reflect a continuity with the overall mission of the church universal and insofar as they flow from the larger cultural experience, they will be the same. Insofar as they reflect a unique incarnation of a church in a specific place with its own particular needs, they will be different. It's quite important that councils be able to own and internalize their own consitiutions. It's even more important that they evaluate them regularly and that they feel free enough to amend them when they no longer serve the gospel and the changing needs of the parish. Constitutions are not ends unto themselves but only means to an end. Therefore, they should not hinder, but actively build up the parish community as it carries out the mission of the church.

In developing or evaluating their constitutions, councils should learn as much as they can from other councils. They can learn from their successes and their failures. At the same time, they can gain the enrichment which comes from belonging to the larger Roman Catholic Church. It is in the hope of sharing with individual councils at least part of the experience of the larger church that this chapter offers a "model" constitution. Of course, it's not a *real* constitution. Nor should it be adopted by any specific parish as is. It may, however, serve as a useful discussion-starter for councils which are in process of developing or evaluating their own constitutions.

In what follows, I have put together a "model" by taking various parts from the suggested constitutions of the archdioceses of Baltimore and Milwaukee. I have chosen these, first because they seem to incorporate many of the features which flow from the theory and practice of parish councils as outlined in this book. Second, they retain the very useful distinction between constitution and bylaws or commentary. Third, they offer numerous options and therefore show a flexibility which allows both the room and the freedom for parishes to develop their own constitutions. Of course, I have no intention of canonizing or even blessing a standard constitution. In fact, the patchwork effect of this "model" should very well discourage mere imitation. And neither Baltimore nor Milwaukee is in any way responsible for what I'm doing to their constitutions with my scissors and scotch tape.

On the other hand, I feel the features in these two constitutions are quite deserving of consideration by many councils. They offer a rich smorgasbord of options from which councils can pick according to their own needs and situation. In putting together my "model", I have retained the parallel column style of Baltimore with the constitution on the left and the commentary or bylaws (Milwaukee) on the right. The various parts will be credited to the proper archdiocese. At the same time, I will add my own commentary wherever and whenever I feel it's helpful and appropriate. This chapter, therefore, will be a *three-way dialogue* between Baltimore, Milwaukee and myself.

A Parish Council Constitution and Bylaws

Before we get into the constitution itself let's first hear Milwaukee on *The Essential Characteristics of a Parish Council:*

1.   The purpose of the council is to investigate and weigh matters which bear on pastoral activities appropriate to

the Church at the parish level and to formulate in behalf of the parish practical conclusions regarding them. The council decides what specific actions or programs the parish should adopt to perform its *spiritual* mission, and then determines what temporal means (people, facilities, money) it needs to carry out those actions or programs and how to provide such means.

2. The council is to participate effectively in the decision-making process for the parish. There are two principles to be observed in this connection.

    a) Decisions are to be consistent with faith and morals, civil law, church law, and archdiocesan policies;

    b) The pastor has the right to ask for reconsideration of any decision of the council, subject to the right of the council to appeal to the Milwaukee Archdiocesan Commission on parish councils for mediation and decision.

3. The council is to be as representative as possible of the members of the parish. Hence the priest and religious attached to the parish are to be appropriately represented on the council and a sufficient number of lay persons are to be members. Every member of the council is to have a vote as well as a voice.

    a) The pastor, the associate pastor or pastors (or one or two associate pastors elected by all of the associate pastors), and one or two religious attached to the parish, elected by all the religious attached to the parish (or by all of the members of the parish), are to be members.

    b) The two lay trustees of the parish are to be members *ex-officio.*

    c) There are to be additional lay members in numbers proportionate to the size of the parish. These lay members are to be chosen by the parish at large in a procedure designed to provide adequate representation of women and men, youth and substantial minority groups of any type.

d) There are to be reasonable eligibility requirements for council membership and for voting for council members. "Reasonable" includes restrictions as to minimum age (but not as to sex) and to church and parish membership and good reputation. It is recommended that appropriate eligibility rules are to be adopted for youth membership and youth voting.

e) Members who die, resign, or are removed are to be promptly replaced by the council. Members may be removed for good cause related to their qualifications as active, representative, and reputable council members.

4. The Council is to have standing committees, not limited to council members, to help the parish do its part in making the Gospel known and people holy. In order to accomplish its mission, four areas of committee work should be covered: Liturgy/Spiritual Life; Christian Education; Human Concerns/Community Life; and Administration. Other committees or subcommittees may be established as required.

5. The Council is to elect its own officers. It is to meet regularly, preferably once a month. Adequate two-way communication between the council and other members of the parish is indispensable.

Preamble

Text	Commentary

Milwaukee: We, the members of _____Parish, _, Wisconsin, affirming our union with the People of God through the grace of the Holy Spirit, recognizing ourselves as sharers in the role of Christ, the Priest, the Prophet, and the King, declaring ourselves willing to accept the mission of our Lord Jesus Christ to carry on his work of salvation, pledging our cooperation with the priest assigned to our parish in carrying out the apostolate of the Holy Catholic Church through shared responsibility with respect to its spiritual, educational, social and administrative matters, do hereby join together and form a Parish Council.

Baltimore: We, the People of God, in the parish of __ in union with each other, with our pastor, with the chief shepherd of our diocese, and in union, too, with all the members everywhere of the One, Holy, Catholic and Apostolic Church founded by Christ and governed by His Vicar, the Bis-

Baltimore: The "People of God" is made up of all the members of the parish - priests, religious and laity - coming together in a unity which is theirs through their common Baptism and Confirmation. The pastor (as also the Bishop) is mentioned separately from the others because although he, too, is

Text

hop of Rome and successor of St. Peter, do hereby unite to form a parish council.

We do so conscious of the fact that everyone of us is a member of the Body of Christ (1 Corinthians, 12:27) and that in this body "there are different gifts but the same Spirit (and) different ministries but the same Lord (ibid, vv. 4-5)." We acknowledge that each of us is called upon to offer his particular gift of ministry for the service of the whole body, "so that in everything God may receive the glory, through Jesus Christ (1 Peter, 4:11)."

We do so in response to the recommendations of the Fathers of the Second Vatican Council, who, after urging that councils be formed in dioceses "to assist the apostolic work of the Church either in the field of making the gospel known and men holy, or in the charitable, social or other spheres," added that so far as possible similar councils should be established in parishes also (Decree on the Apostolate of the Laity, V, #26).

Commentary

a member of this People, he is also called upon to preside over it in a special manner by virtue of his canonical office.

The opening paragraph of the preamble also seeks to emphasize that the People of God in a particular parish cannot be taken in isolation, but that by the same Baptism and Confirmation they are united with all the members of the Universal Church throughout the world.

The second paragraph of the preamble finds a basis in Scripture for parish councils, and the third locates it more immediately and practically in the deliberations of the Second Vatican Council.

Text   *Commentary*

Finally, aware that Christ
has told us that without Him
we can do nothing (John
15:5), we ask for the guidance
of His Holy Spirit so that all
our words may be spoken
and all our works done in
His charity and that they
may contribute to the establishment of His reign.

Article I. Name

Baltimore: The name of this
body shall be the_____
parish council, hereinafter
referred to as the "Council."

Article II:
Purpose and Objectives

Baltimore: Section 1. The
purposes of the Council
shall be:

*Baltimore: The purposes
of the Council are stated in a
very broad manner, with little in the way of specific directives for their practical
implementation. To some
degree these are indicated in
Section 2, but for the most
part it must be left to the discretion of each parish, dependent upon its needs and
its resources, as to how these
purposes may best be ful-
filled.*

Text	*Commentary*
(a) To accept responsibility with the pastor for the life and mission of the Church in the parish;	*This purpose does not mean that the Council will abrogate or take away any part of the legitimate canonical authority of the pastor, but rather that its members will willingly bear with him, his heavy responsibilities.*
(b) To act as an authentic representative voice of the People of God—lay, religious and clerical—to the pastor;	*This purpose sees the Council as a channel of information from the people of the parish to their pastor.*
(c) To provide an open and honest forum of communication and dialogue regarding parish affairs among the pastor, associate priests, religious, the parish staff and the laity;	*The purpose here is to make the Council an appropriate place for full communication among all those who make up the parish community.*
(d) To assist the pastor in the administration of the parish through recommendations and active cooperation;	*As is evident, the assistance referred to here is of two kinds: (1) recommendations arrived as by Council deliberation, and (2) specific practical help, wherein each member of the Council would take an active part in the work of the parish in the area of his own particular knowledge and competence.*

Text   *Commentary*

(e) To encourage by all available means a vigorous and effective lay apostolate;

Since lay people constitute by far the largest segment of the total parish community, this purpose seeks to provide for practical means that will awaken them to a sense both of their privileges and their responsibilities as members of the People of God and bring them to a more active participation in parish life.

(f) To collaborate with other religious bodies and with civic, business and professional organizations in working for the common good of the community;

The primary aim here, of course, is to relate the parish to the community in which it is located and of which it forms a part, and to involve it actively in the problems and concerns of the community. Nevertheless, "community" need not be taken in just this restricted sense; it can also have far wider connotations.

(g) To participate, by active cooperation with Area Councils and with the Archdiocesan Pastoral Council, in the total life and mission of the Church within the Archdiocese;

As in the preamble, so emphasis is laid here upon the fact that the People of God in a particular parish do not exist in isolation. They must relate to all the parishes of the diocese, especially those that are their near neighbors, and they must relate, too, to the diocese as a whole. By their cooperation with the

Text   *Commentary*

Area Councils and the Pastoral Council, they are enabled to share with the Ordinary the heavy responsibilities of his office and his pastoral concern for all the souls in his care.

(h)   To be a visible witness to all men of the message and service of Our Lord Jesus Christ.

This is a summary statement. It is put last because of its summary nature, though really it is first in order of importance.

Milwaukee:
(i)   To discern the needs, temporal and religious, of the parish, its people, and the wider community of which the parish is a part, and to find resources to meet those needs;
(j)   To encourage coordination and mutual assistance in the practical working out of the programs of the various parish organizations;
(k)   To create an open, prayerful atmosphere in which the council can work effectively.

Baltimore: Section 2. Pursuant to the purpose set forth in Section 1 of this article, the council shall perform the following functions:

Text

Commentary

(a)   It shall prepare annually a statement of the needs and goals of the parish and, in union with the pastor, determine priorities among such needs and goals with respect to the allotment of personal, physical and financial resources;

A statement of needs and goals, and of priorities among them, may be very general or quite specific - or both. Only in the light of such knowledge can the Council effectively set about its work.

(b)   It shall do all that may be necessary to provide for the dignified and reverent celebration of the Sacred Liturgy, is such manner and at such times as shall be for the spiritual welfare and the convenience of all the faithful of the parish;

It pertains to the pastor and his associates to preside at the liturgy, assisted by the laity in such functions (cantors, lectors, etc.) as are provided for in current liturgical norms. Therefore, it is at least highly desirable that one of the parish priests be a member of the Liturgy Committee, and he should have associated with him those who take an active part in its celebration - again the cantors and lectors, along with music directors, choir, ushers, etc., etc. Other members of the parish who have special knowledge, competence or interest in the liturgy should be invited to contribute their talents. The committee should be sensitive to the needs and wishes of all segments of the parish population and should make every effort to respond to them, always having in mind,

Text

Commentary

of course, norms laid down by the Holy See and the Archdiocesan Liturgical Commission.

(c)   It shall review and approve, with emendations at its discretion, the proposed budgets of all offices and operations subsidized by parish funds, and shall prepare therefrom an overall parish budget;

(d)   It shall determine ways and means of increasing parish income and reducing expenditures, and take all necessary steps to provide for their practical implementation;

(e)   It shall see to the maintenance and good upkeep of parish property and undertake any improvements or enlargements to the property which may be deemed necessary, except where the decision in such matters is reserved to the Ordinary.

(f)   It shall approve or disapprove membership of the parish in any secular community or professional organization;

The functions enumerated in paragraphs (b), (c), (d), and (e) would, of course, normally be carried out by specific committees of the Council - e.g. review and preparation of budgets by the Finance Committee, property upkeep by the Maintenance Committee, etc., etc. To the maximum degree possible, each of these committees should have the autonomy and authority to discharge the duties assigned to it. On matters of great moment such as the approval of parish budgets or major improvements to property, however, the appropriate committee would, after its own full study and documentation had been completed, submit its conclusions to the full Council for its deliberation.

This clause permits the Council to decide upon the nature, direction and extent of its participation in community-oriented groups and projects, or to withhold participation where in its judgment this seems advisable.

Text

Commentary

(g) It shall render to all parishioners from time to time, but not less often than annually, a full report on the spiritual, material and financial condition of the parish.

The parish council is meant to be and should be a body representing and speaking for all the People of God in the parish community. It thus has a serious obligation to render an account of its stewardship to its constituents. Normally this would be done in the form of an annual report, and it may be done more often, wholly or in part, if in the Council's judgment, special circumstances seem to make such a thing desirable.

(h) It shall take whatever other action it may deem appropriate to fulfill the purposes set forth in Section 1 of this article.

Article III: Competence

Milwaukee: (1) The Council shall, in the manner and to the extent set forth in this constitution, be the policy making body for all matters of the parish, including but not limited to the spiritual, educational, social and financial, except to the extent limited by Church law, faith and morals, archdiocesan policy and civil law.

Milwaukee: This Article is one of the most important provisions of a parish council constitution. Because its subject is quite technical, it is recommended that it be adopted as set forth above. Parish council authority applies primarily to priorities and policies, and not to day-to-day administration.

Text

(2)   In any case where the pastor interprets an action of the Council or any of its committees to be outside the limits set forth in Section 1, he shall promptly present such interpretations to the Council or Committee and ask for reconsideration. Pending reconsideration, the effect of the action shall be suspended.
NOTE: (The pastor actually acts in the capacity of diocesan representative if requesting reconsideration.)

(3)   In any case where reconsideration has failed to resolve the problem, the pastor and a delegate or delegates appointed by the Council shall take the matter for mediation and resolution to an appeal agency such as the Archdiocesan Pastoral Council, the Archdiocesan Commission on Parish Councils or the Archbishop, depending upon the policies then in effect with the Archdiocese, and any decision reached by the appeal agency shall be final. Meantime, the effect of the Council's or Committee's action shall remain suspended. If either party fails or refuses to join

Commentary

It cannot be repeated often enough that no authority or power exists in the Church except as a means for service. The model of authority is Jesus himself washing the feet of the disciples. Authority in the Church is, therefore, quite unlike its counterpart in business or civil government.

Text   *Commentary*

or participate in such appeal,
the other party may proceed
alone with the appeal.

Baltimore: Section 1. The
Council shall submit its
recommendations to the
pastor in the form of conclusions consisting of motions
duly made, seconded and
passed by a majority vote.
Section 2. If the pastor, for
grave reasons of fidelity to
the Gospel, obedience to
Church or civil law, or other
serious financial or administra-
trative considerations, feels
that he cannot in good conscience accept and carry out
the recommendations of the
Council, he shall fully and
frankly communicate his
reservations with regard to
them to the assembled Council. If the pastor does not
communicate such reserva-
tions by the second next
regularly scheduled meeting
of the Council following the
date on which the recom-
mendations were submitted
to him, the Council shall be
entitled to presume their
acceptance.

*Baltimore: Article III is
the very heart of the parish
council constitution, since it
regulates the relationship
between the pastor and the
Council. Its various clauses
seek to establish a balance
between the pastor's canonical authority and the ex-
pressed will of his people.
Recommendations should
be made to the pastor in
writing, and since they
would be in the form of motions duly made, seconded
and passed by majority vote,
they would doubtless normally consist of the minutes of
Council meetings. Officers
or other members of the
Council may wish to enlarge
orally upon this written format and should have the
opportunity to do so.
Where the pastor feels that
he cannot in good conscience
accept and carry out the recommendations of the Coun-*

Text   *Commentary*

cil, his obligation to state his
reservations with regard to
them is to be considered a
very grave one. The Council
has an equally grave obligation to listen to and weigh
seriously these reservations,
and to reconsider its own
position in the light of them.
Full and frank communica-
tion between the pastor and
the Council is highly essential here, and if done with
openness and charity it
should lead to a speedy
resolution of the issue.

The phrase "and no other
means offers itself at the parish level to resolve the situation" leaves open a variety of
possible procedures. One
such might be a "referen-
dum" to determine the wishes of the majority of parishioners, so far as this was in
accord with Church law or
particular diocesan legislation. It goes without saying
that a petition to the Ordinary should be used only as a
very last resort, and the proviso that either the pastor or
the Council may present
such a petition is intended,
of course, to safeguard the
rights of both.

Text   *Commentary*

Section 3. If, notwithstand-
ing the reservations expressed
by the pastor, the Council
shall by a two-thirds majority
vote to sustain its original
recommendations, and no
other means offers itself at
the parish level to resolve the
situation, either the pastor
or the Council through its
president may petition the
matter at issue to the Ordinary for such action as he may
deem fitting.

*Rademacher: The role of the pastor is discussed at some length
in Chapter 6 of this book. Suffice it to say here that the pastor
performs two roles on the council. First, he is a voting, participating member equal to all the other members of the council.
Second, as delegated and "missioned" by his bishop, he repre-
sents the diocesan church. It is in this second capacity that he
ratifies or does not ratify the council's recommendations.
Naturally, if the council does its homework and uses consensus
decision-making, withholding ratification should be rare.
Some constitutions ask the pastor to give his reasons in writing
when he withholds ratification.*

Article IV: Membership

Milwaukee: There are three
general categories of council membership:
1) *ex-officio:* a person who
attains council membership
by virtue of another office
already held and not by e-
lection—for example, a
pastor.

Text   *Commentary*

2) *special elective:* certain parish groups might have their own elective process, and the person elected is seated on the council (example: youth group, Christian women society);
3) *members at large:* persons elected by the parish as a whole. All are voting members and are equal when functioning as a council. It is highly recommended that the number of *at-large* members always exceed the total number of ex-officio and special elective members combined.

Section 1. The Council shall be comprised of the following members, each having one vote:

a) *Ex-officio* members: all priests assigned to the parish; the two lay trustees of the parish.

b) One (or two) sisters serving in the parish, to be elected annually by the sisters serving in the parish;

c) One (or two) youth members who shall have attained age *16* but shall not have attained age *18* and who shall be registered members of the

Milwaukee: (Bylaws)
1. Pastors: The pastor should always be a member of the council. The pastor (and associates) are called to generously share responsibility with the council and to be models for consensus building. They are also called to be unifiers, building unity between the parish and the larger Church in the district and the archdiocese. In a parish served by a pastoral team, the priest designated as vice president of the parish corporation should be a member of the council.

Text

Commentary

parish, to be elected annually by the youths of the parish who shall have attained age *14* but shall not have attained age *18*;

e)   Eighteen (or any number divisible by three up to 30) at-large members who shall be registered members of the parish and who shall have attained age *18*.

2. Associate Pastors: In parishes which have two or more associate pastors, parishioners may feel that if all the associate pastors were council members, the council would be "top-heavy." These parishes may wish to provide for membership of only one associate pastor on the council. Other parishes, however, believe all of them should be council members, and to avoid "top-heaviness" they enlarge the number of religious and lay members.

3. Religious: The question of whether particular religious (sisters or brothers) are "attached to" a given parish so as to be eligible for membership on that parish's council, sometimes presents difficulties. A parish has the choice of several eligibility rules for the religious. The one chosen should apply to both membership eligibility and voting eligibility. The most obvious choices are: (1) the religious serving in the parish in the school, religious education programs or other work; (2) the religious who reside in the parish; or (3) both those serving the parish and residing in the parish.

Section 2. All elected members shall take office at the first regular meeting of the Council following their election and shall serve until their successors are elected and take office.

Text   *Commentary*

Rademacher: Some constitutions do not allow the pastor to have a vote. Two reasons are often given: first, that the pastor retains veto power and that that is equivalent to a vote; second, that the council is advisory to the pastor and therefore the pastor should not vote on the advice he gives himself.

In view of the theology of the first six chapters of this book, it should come as no surprise that I don't find the above reasons very convincing. The first reason makes too much of a fuss over the veto power. If the council is truly an organism of shared responsibility, refusal to ratify should be a rare occurrence. This is especially true if the council uses consensus decision-making. Why should the pastor sit through council meetings for five years or so before he gets to have a real voting voice in the council's decisions? Besides, it's not conducive to building community of gifts when the council identifies the pastor's role with only one of his functions, i.e., representing the diocese in ratifying a decision. Associate pastors should also have a vote. As baptized members of the community and as spiritual leaders in that community, they have their own gifts and insights. They should be able to vote their opinion the same as the other baptized members of the council. In the diversity and pluralism of today's church, constitutions should not assume there is such a thing as a "rectory" or staff vote.

The second reason, viz. that the council is advisory to the pastor, is not convincing either. As explained in Chapter 6, the council is not merely advisory to the pastor. It should not be set up as if it were apart from, or against, the pastor. It is a microcosm of the larger christian community, i.e., the parish. The council is the policy-making body of the parish and the pastor and the associate pastors bring their own unique charisms to that policy-making body. Of course, if councils use the consensus method of decision-making (chapter 10), the "vote" of the pastor and associate pastors is no longer a problem.

Text

Baltimore: (OPTION A) Permanent deacons of the parish shall be automatic members of the Council. They shall have full voice in its deliberations and each shall have a vote.

(OPTION B) Permanent deacons of the parish shall be automatic members of the Council. They shall have full voice in its deliberations, but among them shall have only one vote. The deacons shall decide for themselves, by whatever means they wish, on who their voting representative shall be.

Parish Organizations

Baltimore: Each of the following organizations shall be entitled to designate one of its members as its representative to the Council, and each such designated representative shall be an automatic member with full voice and vote:

_____

_____

or

Commentary

Baltimore: With the increasing importance of the permanent diaconate in today's Church and the active role that they will be playing in parish life, it seems well to make some provision for them on the Council. The two options permit the Council to decide on how it will handle this matter.

No attempt can be made here to list all of the organizations which may be potentially eligible for representation on a parish council, since the number of them and their size and importance will obviously vary from parish to parish. Each council will have to use its own judgment here, and its own knowledge of local circumstances should serve as a good guide. What is important is that the organization be an active and viable one,

Text	*Commentary*
No member of the Council shall represent more than one organization, and no elected or appointed member shall be designated by any organization as its representative.	*and not something simply existing "on paper." Size is one criterion, but it is certainly not the only one; the nature, importance and, necessity of the particular apostolic work in which the group engages must be taken into consideration too.*

or

The Council shall have the right, by a two-thirds vote, to add or to delete from the list of organizations above, at such times as it may see fit.

Rademacher: Since the council is the top policy-making body in the parish, it will have to deal with the parish organizations in one way or another. First, it needs to determine which organizations are apostolic and which are merely social. Then secondly, it will have to figure out which are "active and viable" and which are merely "on paper."

When both the council and parish organizations just go along "doing their own thing" they get tangled in a lot of competing and overlapping activity, with consequent tension and wasted energy. For this reason it would be helpful, especially after a goal-setting workshop (Chapter 11), if both council and parish organizations would do a self-evaluation regarding their respective roles in the mission of the parish. Parish organizations could evaluate themselves in the light of the parish goals, by reviewing their history, their bylaws and their actual programs. After such evaluation is complete, the council and parish organizations could meet together to determine which organizations should be dissolved in favor of an existing council committee. Often the members of such organizations can slip into a council committee very easily. No doubt some organizations could simply relate to the council through repre-

Text

Commentary

sentation on a council committee. For instance, the Home School Association could have a representative on the council's education committee.

On the other hand, the council might decide that a particular parish organization is so important in terms of the mission of the parish that it should have representation on the council itself. In some parishes it might be the Holy Name Society, the Altar Society, the St. Vincent de Paul Society, etc. When these organizations have a large and active membership devoted to a particular mission in the parish, their cooperation is often essential to the success of various programs. "Their representation on the council not only permits the solicitation of their support for these programs, but opens up channels of communication in both directions since matters decided by the council may affect the organization and its members."[1]

Resignation and Removal (Bylaws)

Milwaukee: Any member of the Council may resign by filing a written resignation with the Secretary. At any meeting of the Council, one or more elected members may be removed for just cause by vote of two-thirds of all members. Just cause shall include missing three consecutive meetings without excuse, physical or mental incapacity, moving from the parish, conviction of a felony, losing good reputation in the parish community. Any member whose removal has been proposed shall be given an opportun-

Text   *Commentary*

*ity to be heard at the meeting.
Vacancies among at-large
elected members shall be filled
for the unexpired term by the
presently eligible person who
received the next highest
number of votes at the previous election; vacancies a-
mong representatives of special groups shall be filled by
the group which has lost its
representation.*

Rademacher: Robert's Rules of Order *lays down the principle
that every deliberative assembly has "the right to purify its own
body" and therefore can expel one of its members for discipli-
nary reasons. One would hope that in a Christian community
such cases would be rare. On the other hand, we have to be realistic. Councilors are not exempt from the effects of original sin.
If a councilor promotes factionalism, divides the council, or
otherwise obstructs its purpose, the council may have to consider removal.*

*St. Joseph Parish Council of Huntsville, Alabama, has the
following provision in its constitution: "Removal from Office—
Any action by a member of the council which is considered detrimental to the best interest of the parish, or contrary to the
established objectives of the parish shall be considered just
cause for removal. The member involved in any such action
shall have the opportunity to meet with the pastor and the council in a closed session prior to removal from office. A two-thirds
vote of the total council membership shall be required for removal."*

*It may, at times, be a delicate matter, but the council needs to
be aware of absenteeism. The absent member, by his absence, is
saying something to the council. It's important that the full
council feel some responsibility regarding absent members. It
may show its concern by a phone call or by a visit. But continued*

| *Text* | *Commentary* |

absence should not pass unnoticed. It can be very demoralizing for a council if it begins to carry a lot of "dead weight."

(Bylaws)

Milwaukee: No member e-lected at large shall be eligible for election to consecutive terms, except that a member appointed to fill a vacancy in the Council shall be eligible for election to succeed himself/herself. Members elected annually by special groups (such as religious, youth, parish societies) shall be eligible for three consecutive one-year terms.

Rademacher: Councils do run the risk of becoming a clique. Therefore, councilors need a certain detachment from office lest they begin to see it as a power or status position for themselves. As soon as councilors are elected, they should prepare others to replace themselves. The true minister, the true leader, is always recruiting and training new ministers and leaders. Besides, if a council is to remain healthy it constantly needs new blood and new ideas. It's for these reasons that many constitutions don't permit councilors to succeed themselves. As always, councils should feel free to make exceptions in particular cases. But the general principle is sound.

Baltimore: The Council shall have three categories of membership; priestly, religious and lay; and three types: elective, automatic and appointive.

Baltimore: An effort should be made to achieve a proper balance among elected, automatic and appointed members. While a parish council is not a democratic body in

Text   *Commentary*

the same sense that our civil legislative bodies are, it should be as democratically constituted as possible and therefore, all other things being equal, the number of elective seats should be at least equal to and perhaps greater than the number of those that are automatic and appointive.

(OPTION A) The elected and automatic members of the Council shall, in consultation and agreement with the pastor, name not more than _____ lay persons to be appointive members, and such appointive members shall serve for the same term of office as the elected members of the Council to which they are appointed. Such appointments shall endeavor, so far as is practical, to achieve a proper balance among sexes, races, age groups, and areas of knowledge and competence desired on the Council.

OR

(OPTION B). The pastor, by and with the advice and consent of the Council, shall

Generally speaking, the number of appointive seats on the council should be held to a minimum-probably not more than five. The purpose of such a thing is to correct any imbalance that seems to result from the elected and automatic membership. If, for example, in a parish that was just about evenly mixed racially, one race was in a distinct minority on the council, some of the appointments could help to even this out. Again, if the elections and the automatic memberships resulted in the presence of all mature adults, some of the appointments could serve to assure that the voice of the young people was being heard. The two options do not greatly differ, except that Option B places a greater emphasis on the role of the pastor in making the appointments.

Text   *Commentary*

name not more than _____
lay persons to be appointive
members, and such appoin-
tive members shall serve for
the same term of office as the
elected members of the Council to which they are appointed. Such appointments shall
endeavor, so far as is practical, to achieve a proper balance among sexes, races, age
groups, and areas of knowledge and competence de-
sired on the Council.

Rademacher: Some councilors, including pastors, resist the idea, even as an option, that the pastor should ever appoint anyone to the council. There seem to be four types of resistance: some councilors just don't trust pastors. They are afraid that an authoritarian pastor may use this option in an arbitrary way to stack the council with his kind of people. Others, conditioned by democracy with its dual principle of election and representation, feel appointments are undemocratic. Still others, emphasizing the institutional and organizational aspect of the church allow no room or freedom for the prophetic principle. Finally, there are others who retain a sanctuary understanding of ministry and therefore have not internalized the truth that service on the council is a true ministry. Regarding the possible arbitrary use of the option, trust is so essential to the council that without it no constitution will be able to save it. No constitution can make up for the absence of trust by legislating for every possible misuse of freedom.

In response to the second objection, the council does not need to apologize for the fact that it isn't a democracy. The council is called to be "a seed and beginning...of the Kingdom of God."[3] If it is true to that vocation, it will be better than any of this world's democracies. While the council may indeed

Text   *Commentary*

*adopt democratic forms, its Christian witness to the kingdom
may also be a judgment on the deficiencies of democracy. While
election remains one important form of discernment, it's not an
absolute handed down from Mt. Sinai.*

*Third, the church, including the council, needs to allow free-
dom for the prophetic dimension in the church. In virtue of his
prophetic ministry, the pastor should be free to lead with a prophetic gesture by appointing a black, a Mexican or an Indian to
the council. Such an appointment because of its symbolic power, could stir the conscience of the rest of the parishioners regarding their neglect of the minorities in their parish and in
their community.*

*Regarding the fourth type of resistance, Chapter 4 tried to
make the case that service on the council is a real ministry. If
that's true then the Bible is a witness to the truth that God can
and does call ministers in other ways than through an election
by the people. God called Paul through the word of a disciple,
Ananias (Acts 9). He called Timothy through an appointment
by Paul (Acts 16:1-3). He still calls priests through the ordination of the bishop. So there's no reason why God can't call a
black or a Mexican through the prophetic discernment of his/
her pastor. Of course, the pastor should not appoint anyone
without first consulting the full council. He can then clearly explain his reasons. Councilors do not usually object when, in
special cases, the pastor appoints someone to serve as minister
of the eucharist or as minister of the word (lector). Once councilors understand ministry on the council as equal to sanctuary
ministries they will be more accepting of an occasional appointment by the pastor.*

*Councils are generally rather receptive to an appointment
which is designed to correct an imbalance in the representation.
(In this matter, they are often more concerned about being
democratic than about being a sign of the kingdom of God.)
Thus, they will be favorably disposed to accept the appointment of blacks, women, Mexicans, youth, senior citizen, etc.
They may not be so receptive to an appointment which is designed to provide the council with the necessary knowledge and*

Text   *Commentary*

expertise. This would be an appointment on the basis of function rather than representation. Thus it doesn't do much good if, after elections, the council has a full complement of blacks, Mexicans, women, senior citizens, etc., if no one on the council knows anything about education, liturgy, finance, etc. The council, after all, has a task, a mission, to accomplish. It needs the skill, the competence, the knowledge to do its job, i.e., to achieve the goals and objectives of the parish.

For this reason, the Baltimore Recommendations *wisely suggest that appointments could be made to fill up "whatever seems lacking in any particular field of knowledge or expertise." "If, for example,"* The Recommendations *continue, "neither the automatic nor the elective memberships resulted in the presence on the council of someone especially qualified in a field like accounting and finance, and it was considered desirable to have someone with this knowledge, an appointment might very well provide it."*[4]

Article V

Nominations and Elections

Baltimore: Section 1. Any lay person who (a) has attained to the age of _____ years by the date of elections, and who (b) is a registered member of the parish, shall be eligible for election to the Council, and all persons meeting these same qualifications shall likewise be eligible to vote in such elections.

Baltimore: The Archdiocesan Recommendations *recommends that the minimum age be set at 16 in order to allow for the presence of some young people on the council, but it leaves the decision in this matter to the discretion of the individual parish.*

In addition to the two qualifications mentioned here, a third should be added, viz.: willingness to devote to the work of the council the time and effort that is required. This has not been written into the constitution because there is simply no specific way that it can be assured in advance

Text   *Commentary*

but the Nominating Committee would of course wish to assure that any candidate had a clear understanding of what was involved and a willingness to meet this requirement.

Section 2. The Council, at the general meeting held in the month of _____, shall appoint a Nominating Committee and designate the chairman thereof and it shall be the duty of the Nominating Committee to consider qualified parishioners and to obtain their consent to run as candidates for the Council. The number of candidates shall be at least equal to twice the number of elective seats on the Council.

It is recommended that the Nominating Committee be formed and begin its work at least two months before elections are to be held, and preferably even sooner: e.g., if they are to be held in November with the new council taking over at the first of the year, the committee should have its work well under way in September.

The Nominating Committee should have complete freedom in its choices. Robert's Rules of Order, *Newly Revised (1970 ed., p. 380), the standard authority on parliamentary procedure, states that while the president of any organization is usually an* ex officio *member of all committees, s/he should never under any circumstances be a member of the Nominating Committee.*

Text

Commentary

Section 3. (OPTION A). Elections shall be held on _____. They shall be by secret ballot, which shall be mailed to all registered parishioners, and the _____ persons (in each tract) receiving the highest number of votes on the returned qualified ballots shall be declared elected. In the event of a tie, the members of the incumbant Council shall vote among themselves for one or other of the tied candidates.

OR

Section 3. (OPTION B). Elections shall be held on _____. They shall be by secret ballot, which ballots shall be distributed to all persons attending the Masses on the _____ Sunday of _____. The _____ persons receiving the highest number of votes on the returned qualified ballots shall be declared elected. In the event of a tie, the members of the incumbent Council shall vote among themselves for one or other of the tied candidates.

The Council may wish to insert a specific date, or—more likely—a certain day of the month: e.g., "the third Sunday in May." The two options provide some flexibility in electoral procedures, but the first at least assures that all registered members of the parish have an opportunity to cast their vote, even if they do not avail themselves of the privilege. The second carries no such assurance, and also allows for the possibility of votes being cast by unqualified persons.

Text

Section 4. (OPTION A).
Elected members shall serve
for a term of one year, or until their successors are duly
elected and qualified. No
parishioner shall be eligible
to serve more than two consecutive full terms.

OR

Section 4. (OPTION C).
In the first election held following the ratification and
adoption of this Constitution, the _____ person(s)
(in each tract) receiving the
highest number of votes shall
serve for a period of one year.
Thereafter all elections shall
be for a term of two years.
No parishioner shall be eligible to succeed himself for a
second consecutive full term.

Commentary

*The three options of Section
4 provide for various terms
of office, and the council (or
parish, or steering committee) may adopt whichever
one seems to serve its purpose best. Option A makes
the usual provision for two
successive one-year terms.
The disadvantage here, however, is that it does at least
raise the possibility, every
second year, of an entirely
new and inexperienced council coming on the scene. Option B provides for a partial
turnover each year, with the
assurances that half of its
membership would at all times
have had some prior experience. On the other hand, this
option also makes it possible
for one person to serve as
much as four years, and it
may be felt that this is too
long and limits too greatly
the opportunity of other parishioners to make a contribution to the council's work.
If this is the case, then Option
C prevents such a thing by
providing that nobody shall
serve more than one full two-
year term. The council or
parish will have to use its own
judgment in this matter.*

Text   *Commentary*

Section 5. The new Council
shall take office on _____.
In the event that a vacancy
occurs among the elected
membership during the Council year, the person who had
received the next highest
number of votes (in the tract
in which the vacancy occurs)
shall be asked to fill out the
remaining term of the vacat-
ing member and in the event
that he or she declines, the
remaining candidates shall
be similarly asked to fill it
out, in the order of the number of votes which each received.

*Milwaukee: The functions of
a nominating committee and
an election committee may
be handled by the same group
of people. Proper orientation
of parish council candidates
should also be a responsibility of this group. The spiritual mission of the council, the
concept of shared responsibility, and the role of the parish
councilor should be integral
to this orientation.*

Text   *Commentary*

Rademacher: Chapter 9 of this book is devoted to elections, or, as I have called it, selection. Suffice it to emphasize here that new councilors should indeed get a special orientation as Milwaukee suggests. Such orientation could include time for input, questions and recommendation of appropriate reading materials as preparation for ministry on the council. A hospitality hour would also be helpful. Many councils stagger their elections on a two or three-year basis so that never more than half or a third of the councilors will be new in any given year. This is especially important when new councilors have not come up through the council's committee system.

Article VI: Officers

Baltimore: Section 1. The officers of the Council shall be a President, Vice President, Recording Secretary, and Corresponding Secretary.

Section 2. The members of the incoming Council shall, at the Annual Meeting, vote among themselves for the four offices specified in Section 1 above. Following nominations, voting shall be by secret ballot, and in the event of a tie balloting shall be continued until a candidate receives a majority. Each office shall be taken individually, thus permitting candidates not elected to be nominated for the next subsequent office.

Baltimore: The terms "President" and "Vice President" have been chosen simply to prevent a confusion in nomenclature between the chief officers of the council and the chairmen of the various committees.

Text   *Commentary*

Section 3. The President shall preside at all meetings of the Council, and shall have the authority to call such special meetings as in his judgment may be necessary. In consultation with the other members of the Council, he shall appoint the membership of all standing and special committees, and shall himself be an *ex officio* member of all such committees except the Nominating Committee. He shall render periodic reports to the pastor and the parishioners on the completed and projected work of the Council, and shall perform all other duties that customarily devolve upon the office of President, not specifically mentioned herein.

Section 4. The Vice President in the absence of the President or in the event of the latter's inability for any reason to carry out the functions of his office, shall assume, during such absence or disability, the duties of the President. He shall coordinate the work of all committees and, where necessary, shall report to the Council on the meetings and activities of such committees. He

Text   *Commentary*

shall perform such other duties as may be delegated to him by the President.

Section 5. The Recording Secretary shall take minutes of all regular and special meetings of the Council, reduce such minutes to writing, preserve them in a permanent record, and send copies of such minutes to all members of the Council at least one week prior to the next regularly scheduled meeting, along with the agenda for that meeting.

Section 6. The Corresponding Secretary shall prepare and send out all correspondence necessitated by the work of the Council and shall maintain permanent files of such correspondence. He (she) shall also prepare notices to appear in the parish bulletin pertaining to the work of the Council, as well as any other publicity material which it is desired to use in various news media.

Section 7. In addition to the officers above-named, one person, who need not be a member of the Council, shall be designated by the President as representative. He shall act as liaison between

Text   *Commentary*

the Parish Council and the
Area Council, shall attend
all meetings of the latter, and
shall render regular reports
to the Parish Council on all
matters which may be of interest or concern to it.

Section 8. In the event of a
vacancy in any office except
that of the President, the
Council shall elect someone
from among its own mem-
bership to fill the office until
the next regularly scheduled
election. In the event of a
vacancy in the office of President, the Vice President shall
automatically succeed and
fill out the unexpired portion of the term.

Section 9. Each officer shall,
at the expiration of his term
of office, turn over to his
successor all books, papers,
and other records and property pertaining to his office
not later than ten days after
said expiration.

Article VII:

Executive Committee

Section 1. The Executive
Committee shall be com-
posed of the officers of the
Council and the chairmen of

Text   *Commentary*

the several standing committees, acting with such powers
as may be delegated to it by
the full Council.

Section 2. It shall be the responsibility of the Executive
Committee to coordinate
and prepare the agenda for
all regular meetings of the
Council, and to make such
agenda available to the Recording Secretary for mailing prior to the meeting.

Article VIII: Committees

Section 1.   The Standing
Committees of the Council
shall be _____

_____

each acting in such areas and
with such powers as may be
delegated to it by the full
Council.

*No attempt is made here to
specify the standing committees that a parish council
should have. The 1968 Guidelines for Parish Councils created five: Finance, Maintenance, Liturgy, Education,
and Parish and Community
Relations and these seem to
cover pretty fully the various
areas of parish activity. The
individual parish may wish
to retain this arrangement,
or to vary it in one way or
another. For example, it might
be thought more effective to
combine finance and main-
tenance under a single body
which could be called the
"Administration Commit-
tee." Again, a parish might*

Text

Commentary

wish to have committees covering such areas as Family Life, Ecumenism, Youth, etc., etc. Each parish or council will have to decide this for itself, but after its decision is made and the committees are created, the specific responsibilities and scope of authority of each should be very carefully spelled out in the standing rules or the minutes of the council.

Section 2. Each member of the Council except the officers shall serve on one Standing Committee, but not on more than one. The President, by and with the advice and consent of the other members of the Council at the Annual Meeting, shall designate the membership of each committee, having regard to the professional knowledge and competence desired in each case.

(In what follows, Milwaukee is commenting, not on the Baltimore text, but on the committee system in general.) Milwaukee: Chairpersons and members of committees need not be members of the Council, but if the chairperson of a committee is not a Council member, the president shall appoint a Council member to that committee for liaison purposes.

Baltimore: Section 3. The chairman of each Standing Committee, in consultation with the President, shall be free to name to his committee parishioners who are not members of the Council in order to provide the breadth and depth which the work of the committee requires.

Text

Such committee members shall have the right to attend all regular and special meetings of the Council and to have full voice therein, but they shall have no vote.

Section 4. The chairman shall have the authority to call meetings of his committee as often and at such times as in his judgment may be necessary, and he shall be prepared to render a report on the work of the committee at all regular meetings of the Council.

Section 5. The President, in consultation with the Executive Committee, shall have the authority to create any special or temporary committees which may from time to time be deemed necessary, and to designate the members thereof.

Aritcle IX: Meetings

Balitmore: Section 1. The regular meetings of the council shall be held on the ___ of each month, excepting the months of _____.

Section 2. The meeting held in the month of_____

Commentary

All committees shall function in an advisory capacity to the Council. However, the principle of subsidiarity shall prevail—decisions are to be made on the lowest possible level. Committees shall also carry out activities and implement programs, together with parish staff, within their respective fields, as may be authorized, directed or approved by the Council.

All committees shall make such investigations and hold such meetings and hearings, open or otherwise as may be necessary to handle their assigned responsibilities and shall make a full report of their current activities at each regular meeting of the Council, if possible, in written form (unless otherwise specified herein).

Baltimore: The Annual Meeting should be the first one immediately following the date on which the new council formally takes office. It is strongly recommended, however, that between the actual elections and the taking of office there be a sufficient in-

Text

shall be known as the Annual
Meeting, and shall be for the
purpose of electing officers,
designating the membership
of the standing committees,
receiving reports, and for
any other business that may
arise. Any such matters left
unfinished at the adjourn-
ment of the Annual Meeting
shall constitute the first order of business at the next
regular meeting.

Section 3. Special meet-
ings may be called by the
President, or by the Executive committee, or at the
written request of any ____
members of the Council. The
purpose of any special meeting shall be stated in the call.
Except in cases of emer-
gency, at least three days'
notice shall be given.

Section 4. Regular meet-
ings of the Council shall be
open to all parishioners as
observers. It shall be left to
the discretion of the Executive Committee as to whether
any special meetings shall be
open.

Section 5. A majority of
the voting members of the
Council shall constitute a
quorum.

Commentary

*terval of time to allow for a
smooth transition from the
outgoing to the incoming
council, for the naming of
appointed members, and for
the members of the new council to become acquainted with
one another. This might very
well be done in the form of
a day-long "retreat"-type
meeting where, in a prayerful atmosphere, the members
could consider the responsibilities they have accepted
and make plans for meeting
them. If this important ground-
work is laid, the council will
have the advantage of not
going into the Annual Meeting "cold" or virtual strangers
to one another.*

Text   *Commentary*

*Milwaukee: The agenda shall
be decided upon in advance
by the agenda (executive)
committee, based on written
committee reports received
from each standing committee and on a vision of the ongoing needs and concerns of
the parish. The agenda should
be submitted to council members no less than one week in
advance.*

*Prayer shall be an integral
part of every meeting and
shall not be excluded to save
time.*

*Advance notice of the time
and place of regular meetings
of the Council shall be published in the parish bulletin,
and all members of the parish
shall be entitled and welcome
to attend as observers. The
Council may open any meeting to discussion by parish
members on such subjects
and under such rules as the
Council may announce.*

*Rademacher: To show accountability to the parishioners and,
at the same time, to engage their interest, councils could well
conduct an open public forum on topics of parish interest at
least twice a year. During the actual meetings, however, councils need to keep a clear distinction between time which is open
to any and all parishioners and time which is devoted to the
councilors' official business of determining parish policy. These
matters are discussed in greater detail in Chapter 10.*

Text   *Commentary*

Article X
Parliamentary Authority

Baltimore: Section 1. The rules contained in the current edition of *Robert's Rules of Order Newly Revised* shall govern the Council in all cases to which they are applicable and in which they are not inconsistent with this constitution and any special rules of order the Council may adopt.

Section 2.   The President may at his discretion appoint a parliamentarian, who need not be a member of the Council, to assist and advise him in presiding at all meetings.

Article XI
Ratification and Amendments

Section 1.   The draft of this constitution shall be made available to all parishioners, together with a ballot enabling them to signify approval or disapproval, on____ , and upon its approval by two-thirds of the qualified ballots returned by_____ ,it shall be declared ratified and made immediately operable.

Baltimore: All parishioners should have an opportunity to pass upon the proposed constitution, since it is quite literally the charter which enables them, through their representatives on the Council, to exercise their voice in parish affairs. Its ratification should therefore be handled in somewhat the same manner as a council election, except that in view of the length of the document it may be thought

Text   *Commentary*

Section 2. This constitu-   *inadvisable to send it in the*
tion may be amended at any   *mail to all registered parish-*
regular meeting of the Coun-   *ioners. In such a case it may*
cil by a two-thirds vote, pro-   *be given out to those attend-*
vided that there shall have   *ing the Masses on one or two*
been appended to the call for   *designated Sundays, with*
such a meeting a copy of the   *the proviso that ballots, in*
proposed amendment.   *order to be counted, must be*
                                     returned by a given date - say
                                     two weeks. The importance
                                     of the matter may be empha-
                                     sized in the homilies on those
                                     Sundays and in the parish
                                     bulletin.

*Rademacher: It's a good idea to submit the constitution to all
the parishioners, both to educate them and to build up a two-
way relationship of responsibility with them. Rather than simply voting on the constitution, it might be quite worthwhile to
have an open parish meeting to offer the people ample opportunity to discuss and to react to the constitution. Approval
might take a little longer that way, but because of better parish
understanding and cooperation, it would be worth it in the
long run.*

Footnotes

1. *Recommendations for Parish Councils,* Archdiocese of Baltimore, p. 10.

2. *Robert's Rules of Order, Newly Revised* (New York: William Morrow and Co., 1971), p. 302.

3. "The Constitution on the Church," in *Vatican Council II,* Austin. Flannery O.P., ed. (New York: Costello Publishing Co.), p. 353.

4. *Recommendations for Parish Councils,* p. 11.

Diocesan and Archdiocesan Resource Materials Consulted

Baltimore, Archdiocese of. *Recommendations for Parish Councils*, 1973.
  Pastoral Planning and Management
  Archdiocesan Central Services
  320 Cathedral Street
  Baltimore, Maryland 21201

Birmingham, Alabama, Diocese of. *Guidelines for a Parish Council*, 1976.
  Department for Lay Organizations
  Diocese of Birmingham in Alabama
  P.O. Box 2086
  Birmingham, Alabama 35201

Columbus, Diocese of. *Parish Council Guidelines*, 1977.
  Planning Office
  Diocese of Columbus
  197 East Gay Street
  Columbus, Ohio 43215

Denver, Archdiocese of. *Parish Council Philosophy and Guidelines*, 1975.
  Parish Council Services Office
  Archdiocese of Denver
  938 Bannock Street
  Denver, Colorado 80204

Detroit, Archdiocese of. *Directives and Guidelines for Parish Councils,* rev. ed., 1976
>   Catholic Information Center
>   1232 Washington Boulevard
>   Detroit, Michigan 48226

Duluth, Diocese of. *Guidelines for Parish Councils,* 1978.
>   Diocesan Pastoral Council Office
>   2215 East Second Street
>   Duluth, Minnesota 55812

Evansville, Diocese of. *What is the Parish Council Anyway?*
>   Diocesan Councils Office
>   219 N.W. Third Street
>   Evansville, Indiana 47708

Fort Worth, Diocese of. *Your Parish Council.*
>   Diocese of Fort Worth
>   1206 Throckmorton Street
>   Fort Worth, Texas 76102

Galveston-Houston, Diocese of. *The Parish Council . . . Ministry of Service,* 1977.
>   Diocesan Pastoral Council
>   1700 San Jacinto Boulevard
>   P.O. Box 907
>   Houston, Texas 77001

Green Bay, Diocese of. *Parish Planning.*
>   Office of Pastoral Planning and Development
>   P.O. Box 66
>   Green Bay, Wisconsin 54305

Kalamazoo, Diocese of. *Parish Council Guidelines,* 1975.
>   Office of Pastoral Programs
>   Diocese of Kalamazoo
>   215 N. Westnedge Avenue
>   P.O. Box 949
>   Kalamazoo, Michigan 49005

Lansing, Diocese of. *Parish Council Guidelines,* rev. ed., 1976.
Diocese of Lansing
300 W. Ottawa Street
Lansing, Michigan 48933

Louisville, Archdiocese of. *Your Parish Council,* 1975.
Archdiocese of Louisville
Commission on Councils
Saint Thomas Center
2000 Norris Place
Louisville, Kentucky 40205

Milwaukee, Archdiocese of. *Documents of the Milwaukee Archdiocesan Commission on Parish Councils,* 1972.
Office for the Laity
345 N. 95th Street
P.O. Box 2018
Milwaukee, Wisconsin 53201

Newark, Archdiocese of. *Parish Council Guidelines.*
Office of Pastoral Renewal
300 Broadway
Newark, New Jersey 07104

New York, Archdiocese of. *Guidelines for Parish Councils.*
Archdiocesan Office for Parish Councils
1011 First Avenue
New York, New York 10022

Pittsburgh, Diocese of. *Parish Council: Diocesan Guidelines,* 1972.
Parish Council: Spiritual Renewal Through Structural Reform.
Office of Parish Councils
Diocese of Pittsburgh
125 North Craig Street
Pittsburgh, Pennsylvania 15213

Portland, Oregon, Archdiocese of. *Guidelines for Parish Councils,* 1969.
>Archdiocese of Portland in Oregon
>P.O. Box 351
>Portland, Oregon 97207

Richmond, Diocese of. *Called to Serve,* 1977.
>Diocese of Richmond
>P.O. Box 2G
>Richmond, Virginia 23203

Rochester, New York, Diocese of. *Parish Ministry: Guidelines for Parish Councils,* rev. ed., 1975.
>Office of Pastoral Planning
>1150 Buffalo Road
>Rochester, New York 14624

San Diego, Diocese of. *Guidelines for Parish Councils,* 1970.
>Diocese of San Diego
>Office for Apostolic Ministry
>P.O. Box 80428
>San Diego, California 92138

Wheeling-Charleston, Diocese of. *Parish Council Manual,* 1976. $2.75.
>Diocesan Pastoral Council
>Diocese of Wheeling-Charleston
>1300 Byron Street
>P.O. Box 230
>Wheeling, West Virginia 26003

Worcester, Massachusetts, Diocese of. *Informational Handbook for Parish Council Members,* 1971.
>The Diocesan Council
>Lay Apostolate Department
>49 Elm Street
>Worcester, Massachusetts 01609

Editor's Note: Write these offices directly from year to year for their announcements of revisions and new materials.

BIBLIOGRAPHY

I *BOOKS*

Anderson, James D. *To Come Alive! New Proposal for Revitalizing the Local Church*. New York: Harper & Row, 1973.

Bartlett, Chester J. *The Tenure of Parochial Property in the United States of America*. Washington, D.C.: Catholic University of America, 1926.

Bausch, William J., with Watkin, Edward. *What's a Parish For?* Chicago: Claretian, 1973.

Berning, Loretta, and Hosch, Margaret. *New Look in Parish Life*. Notre Dame: Fides, 1967.

Blochlinger, Alexander. *The Modern Parish Community*. Geoffrey Stevens, trans. New York: P.J. Kenedy & Sons, 1965.

Bordelon, Marvin. *The Parish in a Time of Change*. Notre Dame: Fides, 1967.

Brewer, Helen B. and Tewey, Thomas J., eds. *Understanding Coresponsibility*. Washington, D.C.: National Council of Catholic Laity, 1974.

Broderick, Robert C. *Parish Council Handbook*. Chicago, Franciscan Herald Press, 1968.

_____ . *Your Parish Comes Alive*. Chicago: Franciscan Herald Press, 1974.

Caputo, Mario V. *The Parish Church*. Boston: Mario V. Caputo, 1967.

Clark, Stephen B. *Building Christian Communities: Strategy for Renewing the Church*. Notre Dame: Ave Maria Press, 1972.

Clebsch, William A., and Jaekle, Charles R. *Pastoral Care in Historical Perspective*. New York: J. Aronson, 1975.

Connolly, Joseph M. "The Parish-The Church's Incarnation," in *Sunday Morning Crisis*. ed. Robert W. Hovda. Baltimore: Helicon Press, 1963, pp. 98-109.

Connolly, Michael P. *The Canonical Erection of Parishes: An Historical Synopsis and Commentary*. Washington, D.C.: Catholic University of America, 1938.

Curran, Charles E. and Dyer, George J., eds. *Shared Responsibililty in the Local Church.* A project of the Catholic Theological Society of America, sponsored by the National Federation of Priests' Councils in conjunction with *Chicago Studies,* 1970.

Currier, Richard. *The Future Parish.* Huntington, Ind.: Our Sunday Visitor, 1971.

——————. *Restructuring the Parish.* Chicago: Argus Press, 1967.

Davis, Charles, et al. *The Parish in the Modern World.* London: Sheed and Ward, 1965.

Diocesan Pastoral Council. Proceedings, Bergamo Conference, March 15-17, 1970. Washington, D.C.: National Council of Catholic Men, 1970.

Ernsberger, David J. *Reviving the Local Church.* Philadelphia: Fortress Press, 1969.

Fecher, Charles A. *Parish Council Committee Guide.* Washington, D.C.: National Council of Catholic Men, 1970.

Flanagan, Donal, ed. *The Meaning of the Church.* Dublin: Gil & Son, 1966.

Floristan, Casiani. *The Parish—Eucharistic Community.* trans. by John F. Byrne. Notre Dame: Fides, 1964.

Glasse, James D. *Putting It Together in the Parish.* Nashville: Abingdon Press, 1972.

Gratsch, Edward J. *Where Peter Is: A Survey of Ecclesiology.* New York: Alba, 1975.

Grichtig, Wolfgang L. *Parish Structure and Climate in an Era of Change: A Sociologist's Inquiry.* Washington, D.C.: Center for Applied Research in the Apostolate, 1969.

Group 2000, ed. *The Church Today: Commentaries on the Pastoral Constitution on the Church in the Modern World.* Westminister, Md.: Newman Press, 1968.

Hahn, Celia A., ed. *Patterns for Parish Development.* New York: Seabury, 1974.

Haldane, Jean M. et al. *Prescriptions for Parishes.* New York: Seabury, 1973.

Hamer, Jerome, O.P. "A Basis for a Pastoral Theology of a Parish." In *Apostolic Renewal in the Seminary in the Light of Vatican II.* ed. J. Keller and R. Armstrong. New York: Christophers, 1967, pp. 327-48.

——————. *The Church is a Communion.* Geoffrey Chapman, Ltd., (Ronald Matthews, trans.) New York: Sheed and Ward, 1964.

Hellman, Hugo. *Parliamentary Procedures for Parish Councils.* Chicago: Franciscan Herald Press, 1974.

Hillman, Eugene. *The Church as a Mission.* New York: Herder & Herder, 1965.

Hinnebusch, Paul, OP. *Community in the Lord.* Notre Dame: Ave Maria Press, 1965.

Hollings, Michael. *Living Priesthood.* London: Mayhew-McCrimmon, 1977.

Howes, Robert G. *Steeples in Metropolis.* Dayton: Pflaum Press, 1969.

Keating, Charles J. *Community.* W. Mystic: Twenty-Third Publications, 1977.

Kelly, George A. *The Parish.* New York: St. Johns University Press, 1973.

Kilian, Sabbas J., OFM. *Theological Models for the Parish.* New York: Alba, 1977.

Larsen, Earnest. *Spiritual Renewal of the American Parish.* Liguori, Mo.: Liguori Publications, 1975.

Lyons, Bernard. *Leaders for Parish Councils: A Handbook of Training Techniques.* Techny, Ill.: Divine Word Publications, 1971.

_____ . *Parish Councils: Renewing the Christian Community.* Techny, Ill.: Divine Word Publications, 1967.

_____. *Programs for Parish Councils: An Action Manual.* Techny, Ill.: Divine Word Publications, 1969.

McCaslin, Edward P. *The Division of Parishes: A Historical Synopsis and a Commentary.* Washington, D.C.: Catholic University of America, 1951.

McCudden, John, ed. *The Parish in Crisis.* Techny, Ill.: Divine Word Publications, 1967.

Mead, Loren B. *New Hope for Congregations.* New York: Seabury, 1972.

Mickells, Anthony B. *The Constitutive Elements of Parishes: A Historical Synopsis and a Commentary.* Washington, D.C.: Catholic University of America, 1950.

Mundy, Thomas M. *The Union of Parishes: An Historical Synopsis and Commentary.* Washington, D.C.: Catholic University of America, 1945.

Neill, Stephen C. and Weber, Hans-Ruedi, eds. *The Layman in Christian History.* Philadelphia: Westminster Press, 1963.

Nuesse, Celestine J. and Harte, Thomas J., eds. *The Sociology of the Parish* (symposium). Milwaukee: Bruce Publishing Co., 1951.

O'Donoghue, Joseph. *Elections in the Church.* Baltimore: Helicon Press, 1967.

O'Gara, James. ed. *The Postconciliar Parish.* New York: P.J. Kenedy & Sons, 1967.

O'Neill, David P. *The Sharing Community: Parish Councils and Their Meaning.* Dayton: Pflaum Press, 1968.

Pagé, Roch. *The Diocesan Pastoral Council.* Trans. by Bernard A. Prince. New York: Newman Press, 1970.

Parish Councils: A Report on Principles, Purposes, Structures and Goals. Washington, D.C.: National Council of Catholic Men, 1967.

"Parish Councils," Report by the Priests' Committee on Parish Councils. Chicago: Association of Chicago Priests, 1968.

The Pastoral Mission of the Church. (Concilium: Theology in the Age of Renewal, vol. 3). New York: Paulist Press, 1965.

Pastoral Reform in Church Government. (Concilium: Theology in the Age of Renewal, vol. 8). New York: Paulist Press, 1965.

Rademacher, William J. *Answers for Parish Councils.* West Mystic, Conn.: Twenty-Third Publications, 1974.

_____. *Working with Parish Councils?* Canfield, Ohio: Alba Books, 1977.

Rahner, Hugh, SJ, ed. *The Parish: From Theology to Practice.* Robert Kress, trans. Westminster, Md.: Newman Press, 1958.

Rahner, Karl, S.J. *The Dynamic Element in the Church.* New York: Herder & Herder, 1964.

_____. *The Shape of the Church to Come.* New York: Seabury, 1972.

_____, and Morrissey, Daniel, OP., eds. *Theology of Pastoral Action.* Vol. I: *Studies in Pastoral Theology.* New York: Herder & Herder, 1968.

Ryan, E.E., CMF. *Lay Participation in Parish Administration: A Step by Step Program for Setting Up Parish Councils.* Thesis. Baton Rouge, La.: Louisiana State University, 1967.

Sample Parish Council Constitutions. Washington, D.C.: National Council of Catholic Men, 1967.

Schaller, Lyle E. *Parish Planning.* Nashville: Abingdon, 1971.

Sheffieck, Charles F. *Planning for Parish Development in the Archdiocese of Detroit.* Detroit: Archdiocese of Detroit, 1974.

Tewey, Thomas J. *Recycling the Parish.* Washington, D.C.: National Council of Catholic Laity, 1972.

von Allmen, J.J. *Worship: Its Theology and Practice.* New York: Oxford University Press, 1965.

Your Parish Council. Detroit: Archdiocese of Detroit, 1969.

II *ARTICLES*

Abeyasingha, N. "Faith and the Pastorate after Vatican II." *Homiletic and Pastoral Review* 72 (December, 1971), 25-30ff.

"Accountability: the Listening Church." (symposium). *Chicago Studies* 12 (Summer, 1973), 115-223.

Albino, Joseph. "Where Laymen Run the Parish." *Catholic Layman* 79 (June, 1965), 32-39.

Arquett, Robert J. "Is the Parish Council Worthwhile?" *Homiletic and Pastoral Review* 67 (May, 1967), 645-49.

Barr, Browne, "Bury the Parish." *Christian Century* 84 (February 15, 1967), 199-202.

Bausch, William J. "What's a Parish for?" *U.S. Catholic* 38 (August, 1973), 6-13.

Bayldon, Michael. "The Cash-and-Carry Syndrome: Thoughts from a Parish on In-Service Training." *Clergy Review* 60 (October, 1975), 618-23.

Bishop, Jordan, O.P. "Priest and Parish in Renewal." *Listening* 3 (Spring 1968), 129-36.

Bligh, Bernard. "Parish Consultative Councils." *Clergy Review* 55 (April 1970), 258-64.

Boyle, John P. "Presbyters, Pastors, Laity: Decision-Making in the Church." *American Ecclesiastical Review* 169 (November, 1975), 592-609.

Broderick, Robert C. "Pastoral Guidebook: Organizing a Parish Council." *Pastoral Life* 26 (June, 1968), 366-68.

Brothers, Joan. "Two Views of the Parish." *Furrow* 16 (August, 1965), 471-78.

Buckley, Joseph C. "The Parish and the Future." *Clergy Review* 50 (December, 1965), 931-40.

_____. "Parish Councils." *Clergy Review* 53 (April, 1968), 264-74.

Carlson, Gerald E. "How Parish Executive Board Develops Lay Leadership." *Catholic School Journal* 62 (June, 1962), 63-64.

Chirico, Peter, S.S. "The Theology of the Parish: The Problem." *Chicago Studies* 7 (Spring, 1968), 89-100.

Coleman, William V. "Developing Programs for Parishioners' Needs." *Today's Parish* 9 (May-June, 1977), 27.

_____. "What is a Parish?" *Today's Parish* 9 (October, 1977), 42-43.

"Collegiality on Parish Level: Parish Committees." *Ave Maria* 102 (October, 1965), 17.

Corrigan, John E. "A Model for Parishes." *Furrow* 14 (July, 1963), 439-45.

Crichton, James D. "The Parish." *Liturgy* 29 (1960), 1-4, 28-32, 53-60.

_____. "The Parish: the Local Manifestation of the People of God." *Liturgy* 34 (July, 1965), 57-64.

Cunneen, Joseph E. "Realities of Parish Life: Laymen and the Council." *Commonweal* 76 (June 15, 1962), 298-300.

Davis, Charles. "The Parish and Theology." *Clergy Review* 49 (May, 1964), 265-90.

Day, Edward, CSSR. "Parish Council: Pastor and People Sharing Christ's Priesthood." *Liguorian* 64 (February, 1976), 20-25.

DeAmato, Norbert, OFM. "Evaluating Your Parish." *Priest* 30 (November, 1974), 21-23.

Dee, John C. "The Parish Apostolate: Does It Work?" *American Ecclesiastical Review* 158 (April, 1968), 217-27.

Deedy, John G. "Democracy Pierces the Church." *Columbia* 46 (May, 1966), 16-19.

DeWitt, John. "Making a Community out of a Parish." *Cross Currents* 16 (Spring, 1966), 197-211.

Downes, Tony. "An Approach to Parish Councils." *Furrow* 20 (May, 1969), 249-56.

DuBay, William H. "Democratic Structures in the Church." *Chicago Studies* 3 (Fall, 1964), 133-52.

"Evaluating Your Parish." *New Catholic World* 216 (September-October, 1973), 223-25.

Everett, James. "Do-It-Yourself Parish." *Catholic Digest* 34 (April, 1970), 109-13.

Fichter, Joseph H., SJ. "The Open Parish in the Open Society." *Catholic World* 201 (April, 1965), 16-21.

Fitzgerald, Patrick. "Overhauling a Parish Council." *Clergy Review* 60 (November, 1975), 684-91.

Fitzpatrick, Joseph P. "Parish of the Future." *America* 113 (November 6, 1965), 521-23.

Griese, Orville. "Pastor-Parish Council Collaboration." *Priest* 33 (February, 1977), 19-22ff.

Guerette, Richard H. "Experiments in Parish Community." *Homiletic and Pastoral Review* 68 (September, 1968), 1029-36.

Hamer, Jerome, OP. "The Universal Vocation of the Parish and Its Mission in the Church." *American Ecclesiastical Review* 150 (February, 1964), 136-46.

Harmon, John J. "The Parish: When Is It Alive, When Should It Die?" *Cross Currents* 15 (Fall, 1965), 386-92.

Howes, Robert G. "Annual Parish Council Evaluation." *Today's Parish* 9 (May-June, 1977), 6-7.

_____ . "Guide for Parish Council Members." *Liguorian* 63 (May, 1975), 49-53.

____. "Parish Councils: Do We Care?" *America* 135 (November 17, 1976), 371-72.

____. "So You're a Pastoral Planner." *Liguorian* 65 (March, 1977), 50-53.

Hathcock, C. Stephen. "Who's in Charge Here?" *Triumph* 10 (February, 1975), 11-14.

Hatt, Vincent. "The Team Approach to Service and Leadership." *Living Light* 12 (Spring, 1975), 42-55.

____. "Turning the Parish into a Christian Community." *Living Light* 10 (Winter, 1973), 503-21.

Hunt, Thomas A., OSA. "A Parish Survey." *Furrow* 20 (April, 1969), 198-203.

Kilian, Sabbas J., OFM. "Dialogue in Ecclesiology." *Theological Studies* 30 (March, 1969), 61-78.

Kipply, John F. "Parish Councils: Democratic Process or New Absolutism?" *America* 123 (August 22, 1970), 94-97.

Kung, Hans. "Participation of the Laity in Church Leadership and Church Elections." *Journal of Ecumenical Studies* 6 (Fall, 1969). 511-33.

LaDue, William J. "Structural Arrangements of the Parish." *Jurist* 30 (July, 1970), 314-27.

Lambert, Norman M. "How to Motivate a Parish Council." *Today's Parish* 9 (May-June, 1977), 28.

Legrand, Francis X. "The Parish Councils: Reflections on their Principal Purpose." *Christ to the World* 14 (Nov. 2, 1969), 118-20.

Losoncy, Lawrence. "How One Parish Established Its Priorities." *Liguorian* 68 (September, 1975), 18-21.

McCrea, Arlene. "A Proposal for the Parish of the 70s." *Homiletic and Pastoral Review* 74 (August-September, 1974), 33ff.

McNierney, Stephen. "The Parish of the Future." *Ave Maria* 103 (April 9, 1966), 21-23.

Menges, Richard A. "The Grass Roots Renewal: A Parish Senate." *Extension* 60 (February, 1966), 4-5ff.

Michael, Paul. "Everyone Responsible, No One in Charge." *U.S. Catholic* 40 (April, 1975), 28-32.

Mollard, George. "A Parish Priest." *Cross Currents* 12 (Spring, 1962), 156-57.

Moran, Robert E. "Theology of the Parish." *Worship* 38 (June-July, 1964), 421-26.

Mueller, Franz J. "Reflections on the Parish of our Time." *Social Justice Review* 59 (November, 1966), 236-52.

Murphy-O'Conner, Cormac. "Community and the Parish." *Clergy Review* 49 (May, 1964), 296-301.

Mussio, Anthony, J.K.. "Parish for Tomorrow." *Ave Maria* 99 (March 7, 1964), 5-8.

Neiman, Joseph C. "Is our Parish a Faith Community?" *Today's Parish* 9 (October, 1977), 39-41.

Novak, Francis A., CSSR. "Where Parish Councils Are Shaping Up." *Liguorian* 61 (March, 1973), 15-18.

Odou, John E., SJ. "The Emerging Parish: The Layman's Role." *Priest* 21 (September, 1965), 727-31.

O'Driscoll, P.D. "On the Parish: Where Leadership is Needed." *Clergy Review* 61 (September, 1976), 364-68.

Osborne, Charles. "A Blueprint for Parish Reform." *Clergy Review* 54 (May, 1969), 337-51.

Ottenweller, Albert H. "A Call to Restructure the Parish." *Catholic Mind* 74 (March, 1976), 5-7.

Palms, Charles L., CSP. "Is the Parish Fulfilling Its Role?" *Catholic World* 202 (December, 1965), 132-33.

"A Pattern for Parish Upkeep: Volunteers." *Catholic Property Administration* 28 (January, 1964), 16-17ff.

Rademacher, William J. "The Parish Council." *Priest* 27 (January, 1972), 19-26.
_____. "Parish Councils—a Direction for the Future." *Priest* 31 (September, 1975), 30-33ff.

Ralph, Sister, OSB. "Educated Women as Parish Leaders." *Catholic School Journal* 63 (December, 1963), 34.

"Reforming the Parish," (Symposium). *Commonweal* 84 (March 25, 1966), 3-31.

Riga, Peter J. "Parish of the Future." *Priest* 25 (December, 1969), 662-68.

Rodimer, Frank. "Are Parish Councils on the Right Track?" *Origins* 6 (May 5, 1977), 725ff.

Salamone, Anthony. "Training Parishioners for Leadership Roles." *Catholic School Journal* 62 (June, 1962), 62-63.

"San Diego Guidelines for Parish Councils." *Origins* 7 (June 9, 1977), 36-39.

Schaefer, Gerald M., et al. "Guide for Parish Council Elections." *Today's Parish* 9 (September, 1977), 36-39.

Smith, Virginia B., et al. "The Problem of the Parish." *Ave Maria* 100 (September 26, 1964), 12-15.

Stack, Tom. "Parish Councils." *Furrow* 20 (February, 1969), 90-93.

Stevens, Anthony M., CP. "Tomorrow's Parish, Culture and the Church Today." *Ave Maria* 106 (August 19, 1967), 16-17.

Sweetser, Thomas P., SJ. "Getting to Know the Parish." *New Catholic World* 216 (September-October, 1973), 204-6.

_____. "Parish Accountability: Where the People are at." *Chicago Studies* 12 (Summer, 1973), 115-28.

_____. "Parish Research and Planning: Parish Evaluation Project." *Today's Parish* 9 (May-June, 1977), 40-42.

Thomas, David M. "Recreating the Catholic Parish." *Homiletic and Pastoral Review* 74 (May, 1974), 20-26.

Thorman, Donald J., "Renewing Parish Life." *Marriage* 45 (September, 1963), 38-45.

____. "Report on the Underground Church." *Catholic Mind* 65 (October, 1967), 6-9.

"Tomorrow's Parish." *America* 117 (July 15, 1967), 50.

Vanucci, Anthony, O.S.S.T. "The Living Parish." *Homiletic and Pastoral Review* 64 (March, 1964), 506-10.

"What is a Parish?" (symposium). *St. Anthony Messenger* 75 (March, 1968), 13-43.

Whelan, T. "Thoughts on Setting Up a Council of Parishioners." *Clergy Review* 52 (July, 1967), 546-55.

Wood, Geoffrey E. "The Church as a Ministering Community: A Report on the Process." *Liturgy* 22 (November, 1977), 11-14.

Woodward, Kenneth. "Spotlight on the Parish." *Ave Maria* 103 (April 2, 1966), 22-26.

Zizioulas, John D. "The Eucharistic Community and the Catholicity of the Church." *One in Christ* 6 (September, 1970), 314-37.

Index

The Author

Rev. William J. Rademacher, Ph.D.

Ordained for the Diocese of Lansing in 1954, Father Rademacher served as associate and then as pastor. He formed a parish council in his own parish and developed Parish Council Guidelines for the Diocese of Lansing.

He earned a Doctorate in Theology at Aquinas Institute, Dubuque, Iowa and wrote his dissertation on Vatican II's *Constitution on the Church*. Besides serving as pastor, chaplain, and director of pastoral formation, he has been Professor of Systematic Theology at St. John's Seminary, Plymouth, Michigan and Instructor in Religious Studies at the University of Michigan, Ann Arbor. A theological consultant for the National Steering Committee for Diocesan Parish Council Personnel, Fr. Rademacher presently holds The Flannery Chair of Roman Catholic Theology at Gonzaga University, Spokane, Washington.

Popular for his workshops and lectures which have him criss-crossing the continent, he has also devoted much time to publishing books and articles. He has written *Answers for Parish Councils* and *New Life for Parish Councils* as well as *Working with Parish Councils?* His practical column in *Today's Parish Magazine* draws questions from interested readers all over the continent.

In Chapter 2 of this present work, Father Rademacher notes: "The Parish Council is a unique form of collegiality which brings the parishioners into the decision-reaching process of the church at an adult, responsible level. It is one of the fruits of Pope John XXIII's New Pentecost. It is an idea whose time has come."

REACTION SHEET

1.   What did you like most about this **Guide?**

_____

_____

_____

2.   What did you like least?

_____

_____

_____

3.   What suggestions do you have for improving this **Guide**
     when it is revised?

_____

_____

_____

_____

_____

_____

*(If you need more space, please use the other side of this sheet
or add your own.)*

Please mail your completed form to:
Rev. Wm. J. Rademacher
c/o Twenty-Third Publications
P.O. Box 180
West Mystic, CT 06388

**Here's your best
way to keep
'in-the-know' about
helpful ideas and aids
for church staff
and parish council
members:**

Call 1-203-536-2611
or write:
Twenty-Third Publications
Post Office Box 180
West Mystic, Ct. 06388

Ask for:
**Current catalog or materials
for your specific needs or
programs.**